ZOOS AND A... WITHDRAWN

Zoos and animal rights seem opposed to each other, but Stephen Bostock argues that this need not and should not be so. Examining the diverse ethical and technical issues involved, including human cruelty, human domination over animals, well-being of wild animals outside their natural habitat, and the nature of wild and domestic animals, Bostock clearly analyses areas in which misconceptions abound.

A controversial and timely book, it explores the long history of zoos, as well as current philosophical debates, to argue for a conservational view of their role in the modern world. Anyone concerned with humanity's relationship with other animals and the natural world will find this a thought-provoking and rewarding book.

Stephen Bostock is the Education Officer for Glasgow Zoo. He read English at Queens' College, Cambridge, philosophy and zoology at Hull University, and has a doctorate in philosophy from Glasgow University.

CPD

imp

ZOOS AND ANIMAL RIGHTS

The ethics of keeping animals

Stephen St C. Bostock

London and New York

First published 1993
by Routledge
11 New Fetter Lane, London EC4P 4EE

Simultaneously published in the USA and Canada
by Routledge, Inc.
29 West 35th Street, New York, NY 10001

© 1993 Stephen St C. Bostock

Typeset in 10 on 12 point Baskerville by
Computerset, Harmondsworth, Middlesex
Printed in Great Britain by T.J. Press (Padstow) Ltd, Cornwall

British Library Cataloguing in Publication Data
Bostock, Stephen St C.
Zoos and Animal Rights
I. Title
179

Library of Congress Cataloging in Publication Data
Bostock, Stephen St C.
Zoos and animal rights / Stephen St C. Bostock.
p. cm.
Includes bibliographical references.
1. Zoo animals. 2. Zoos–Philosophy. 3. Animal welfare. 4. Animal
rights.
I. Title.
QL77.5.B67   1993
179'.3–dc20
92–35167

ISBN 0-415-05057-X   0-415-05058-8 (pbk)

To the memory of my mother
and of my sister Ruth

CONTENTS

PREFACE

Zoos and philosophy probably seem the oddest combination, but this book is an attempt to examine some of the ethical issues raised by the never-ending debate over zoos. Having some acquaintance with both philosophy and zoology, and some experience of zoos, I am hoping that my contribution to that debate will be found useful by quite a range of people: those interested in the ethical aspects of zoos as students of philosophy or public affairs or veterinary medicine, or as professionals in those fields; those involved or interested in zoos as such, or animal keeping in any of its infinite varieties; and finally those genuinely concerned, whether as 'pros' or 'antis', with the arguments over zoos and animal rights – even if they think there's little to argue about, and that we should just get on as quickly as possible with sending all the animals back where they came from.

I have had enormous help and support from many who are, of course, in no way responsible for any of the views or information here presented: Professor Stephen Clark, who was a most stimulating supervisor of the Glasgow University thesis which has now been fully metamorphosed, I hope, into a book of wider appeal; my examiners, Mary Midgley and Elizabeth Telfer; and many other past and present members of the Philosophy Department at Glasgow. Without Janet Sisson's help, I'd never even have got my word processor to number the pages! Among other philosophers, I thank also the reader for Routledge for some critical but constructive comments.

For long-standing support and help, I thank Richard O'Grady, Director/Secretary of the Zoological Society of Glasgow and West of Scotland, the Society's President, William MacKenzie, and its Council; among colleagues at the zoo, I thank particularly Roger

Edwards, to whom I owe innumerable helpful suggestions; Graham Law, Leslie Brown, and many other keepers past and present, for information only they could provide; David Hughes for directing my way an endless stream of relevant books and articles; and far from least, Katie Jackson, Maria Park, and many education staff at the zoo for all sorts of help, most of which they will have long forgotten, but I haven't.

I must thank also the Librarian of the Zoological Society of London, and his staff; Dr Angus Dunn of the Glasgow University Veterinary School; and Dr C.B.F. Walker of the British Museum for assisting my enquiries about ancient Assyrian correspondence on animals. There are many others, especially in zoo education, I am very grateful to. I appreciate the interest of Frank Pignatelli, Director of Education for Strathclyde. I thank particularly Mary and Lionel Jackson, my sister and brother-in-law, and also John Myhill, for reading and commenting on portions of the book. Finally I owe a special debt to my wife Una for her support and patience with two pieces of work which sometimes seemed to grow, like Marvell's vegetable love, vaster than empires and more slow.

1

INTRODUCTION

These days zoos receive a lot of criticism, and some people think they would be best closed down. This is not a particularly new idea. Indeed, had you been around in Versailles two hundred years ago, you might have seen – and heard – a determined band of citizens, a group of local Jacobin sympathisers, marching across their park, drum beating, tricolour at their head, intent on liberating the animals from the former royal menagerie (Loisel 1912: II, 159–60). The Revolution was three years old, France had been declared a republic, and the menagerie, which had been founded by Louis XIV, was now the republic's property. Met by the menagerie's director, the group's leader addressed him in stirring words. They had come in the name of the people and of Nature, to demand the liberty of beings intended by their Creator for freedom but detained by the pride and pomp of tyrants. The director couldn't refuse, but just in case certain liberated beasts proceeded to devour their liberators, he declined to free the dangerous animals himself, instead offering the Jacobins the keys. Revolutionary fervour was tempered by reflection, and a decision made to leave the fierce beasts provisionally where they were. Sadly, most of the harmless animals ended up at the knacker's (understandably, as many people were starving). But some animals were liberated, including several pairs of Java rats, whose descendants were to wreak havoc with the structure of the château. Others, including deer and birds, acclimatised in neigh-bouring woods, according to an interesting report of fifty years later (Loisel 1912: II, 158–61).

One of the interesting things about this account is how close the animal liberators come to speaking of the animals' rights. This of course was the age of rights, with a vengeance. The American

1

Declaration of Independence of 1776 had held 'these truths to be self-evident, that all men are created equal, that they are endowed by their Creator with certain unalienable Rights, that among these are Life, Liberty and the pursuit of Happiness' (Kamenka 1978: 2). Thomas Paine had written the first part of his *Rights of Man* in 1791, in reply to Edmund Burke's *Reflections on the Revolution in France* of 1790, which had spelt out the dangers of the wholesale social reconstruction going on in France. While the French liberators don't actually mention animal rights, their appeal to nature and to the intentions of the animals' Creator recalls the language of the American Declaration, and that of the French Declaration of the Rights of Man and of Citizens of 1789 (Kamenka 1978: 2–4).

The sentiments of those animal liberators of 1792 are very similar to those of many today in 1992. When London Zoo was facing serious financial problems and probable closure in 1991, some people were almost delighted, including philosophers (Cooper 1991), politicians (Hattersley 1991) and (surprisingly) at least one zoo director (Hancocks 1991a; 1991b; 1991c).

Of course there are particularly pressing practical problems with closing a zoo, whether it is the danger posed to human liberators by large carnivores – if the liberation is a literal one – or the sad fate of any zoo animals who cannot be found new homes. Some seem to think the latter problem of lasting importance, but of course, as David Cooper (1991) wrote in a letter to the *Guardian*, it is not. The major question is whether the zoo, or any zoos, should be keeping animals at all, and if they should not be, we won't need to keep the zoos in existence indefinitely because of our responsibilities to their immediate animal residents, important though the interests of those particular individual animals are. (Their deaths might even 'be the price for saving tens of thousands of creatures from a life behind bars in the future' (Cooper 1991).)

My aim in this book is to examine the rights and wrongs of zoos – whether they can be morally justified. I shall try to make out a good case for them, and, having some involvement in them myself, obviously am not wholly disinterested. But I sympathise with those would-be French liberators. No doubt the animals in many menageries and zoos down the ages have been unhappy prisoners. And why should we not recognise them as having a right to freedom like humans? At any rate, I shall take seriously and discuss these kinds of objection to zoos. At the same time, many zoos have changed and are changing enormously, and these facts make it a good deal easier to argue the case for today's zoos than for many of the past.

However, it is important to realise that zoos – using that word in a rather wide sense – have a very long history (about 4500 years) and have occurred all over the world (China and ancient Egypt and pre-Columbian America for example as well as Europe), so they are by no means a minor or merely recent aspect of human activity. I shall start, therefore, with a quite extensive account of this human/animal history. Those in a hurry to get on to the main argument are of course welcome to skip the next chapter, but I hope most readers won't, or if they do, will come back to it later. For it not only recounts a fascinating – sometimes even entertaining – aspect of human history, but also provides very useful background for assessing the ethics of zoos, and underlines the extent to which modern zookeeping has changed.

Now, history apart, where to start? A good place is something agreed by people of every nationality and political persuasion, simply the conviction that keeping innocent humans captive is wrong.

Why is keeping innocent non-humans captive not wrong also? The American philosopher Dale Jamieson (1985: 109) has commented that there is a moral presumption against keeping wild animals in captivity. There are three main ways of defending animal captivity:

1 We can deny that animals are comparable enough to humans to make the moral comparison appropriate.
2 We can explain that the animals we are keeping captive are actually in a state of well-being, perhaps better off than they would be in the wild.
3 We can spell out the advantages to humans – and in some degree to non-humans too – that follow from keeping animals: notably assistance towards conservation, science and education, plus recreation or entertainment.

Significantly, we object to human captivity (except as a legal punishment or of enemies in wartime) for one reason only, that humans have a right to freedom, or just ought to be free. Whether the conditions of captivity are good, or whether the captors gain important advantages from keeping their prisoners, is, interestingly, beside the point. Why shouldn't this be the case with non-humans too? The similarities of at least some non-human animals to humans is much more obvious to us now than to our ancestors in the days, long before Darwin, when zoos (including London Zoo) started. This thorny problem of animal rights, including the obvious challenge to zoos posed by their animals' possible right to freedom, I shall examine in Chapter 3.

Having endeavoured to surmount the rights hurdle, I will go on in Chapter 4 to consider the confusing concept of 'wildness' itself, and then the possibly surprising question of whether zoos actually keep wild animals. In the same chapter I will face the direct charge against zoos of cruelty. Of course animals can be kept cruelly, and millions are today – most outrageously in factory farms (Serpell 1986: 5–11; Johnson 1991). Is zoo-keeping also cruel? Certainly it is important to be aware of a cruel streak in human nature. I will also look in Chapter 4 at something else zoos are often accused of: demonstrating domination or being institutions of power.

In the next three chapters, I will consider whether zoos do or can provide the right conditions for their animals. I will compare wild living with zoo living in Chapter 5, in regard to length of life, health, the quality of life, and animals' adaptations to their environment. Then, in Chapter 6, I will face up to the objection that we cannot tell what conditions are good for animals, or whether they are in a state of well-being, because they cannot tell us. I consider that they can in effect tell us, most importantly by how much of their natural behaviour they show, but in several other ways also. And then in Chapter 7, I shall show how there are in fact several different approaches, all of which may be acceptable, to keeping animals, and say more about ways in which natural behaviour can be encouraged. Then I will consider the aesthetics and purpose of displaying animals, and will also take a look at the very concept of captivity – as the term is used both of humans and of animals – and show how good animal captivity has very little in common with human captivity.

Then, from Chapter 8, I will examine three important functions which zoos are normally seen as serving – those of assisting conservation, science and education.

Chapter 8 will examine the moral nature of conservation, and how it involves a respect for animals as fine 'objects' which ought to be conserved. This is a respect both for the species and for the individuals who corporately make up the species, and parallels the respect we should have for a sentient animal in its own right (and which is well expressed by regarding it as a bearer of various rights).

Whether zoos really can help and are helping conservation will be the subject of Chapter 9. Zoos' conservational work has become far more sophisticated in recent years; which is just as well, for it is also becoming ever more important as a supplement to the conservation of animals in their natural habitats. It is also much more diverse than is often supposed. It is a striking fact, for example, that zoos are visited annually by millions of people who (even if they could afford it) could never, in comparable numbers, visit 'the wild' without damaging it irreparably.

Zoos' scientific and educational roles, both of which are to a great extent related to zoos' conservational role, are examined in Chapters 10 and 11. There is still a great deal that can most conveniently, and sometimes only, be learnt from animals studied at close quarters as in a zoo, as emphasised by Jane Goodall (1986: 13–14). The science possible is not limited to behaviour studies, or even to behaviour, anatomy and pathology as Jamieson (1985: 112–14) has suggested.

Zoo education may be important as education of attitudes and of the spirit as much as the acquisition of information or even understanding. In Chapter 11 I will reply to the comments of some critics of zoo education, and try to indicate both the range of approaches now taken in zoo education, and also its growing importance on a world scale.

In Chapter 12 I will examine what is perhaps zoos' most important recreational role, that of being a place for meeting real animals, and argue that this is far from being outdated, that zoos are not attempts to 'package' the wild for public consumption in a way absurdly out of tune with our 1990s environmental consciousness.

The weakest point of zoos is perhaps how the animals get there. Much capture in the wild, and much trade in and transport of animals, can be extremely cruel. Even where the collecting and transport are professional and humane, the capture of wild animals seems a particularly blatant trespassing upon their rights. I look at this problem in Chapter 13, almost at the end of the book, just because of its seriousness. We can hardly hope to justify taking animals from the wild unless we have thoroughly digested the richness of the gains to humans from doing so, and, still more important, the extent to which it is possible to keep animals – once they are in zoos – satisfactorily. When animals have to be taken from the wild today, government agencies or zoos or their authorised and qualified agents should be doing the collecting and the transporting. Trading and dealing in wild caught animals should be outlawed – though this is an over-simplification and, for a variety of reasons, a great deal more easily said than done.

There may be no final, knock-down argument for zoos, though the very diversity of arguments against zoos rather suggests that, while the critics have many good points, they haven't a knock-down argument either. Anyway, I shall try to show that the various zoo justifications, taken together, make an impressive case. But first let us get our historical bearings, the subject of the next chapter.

2

4,500 YEARS OF ZOOS AND ANIMAL KEEPING

EGYPT

Animals were probably more thoroughly involved in the culture of ancient Egypt than in any other. Egyptian civilisation dates from about 3000 BC.

Lining the tomb of a wealthy nobleman called Ti in Saqqara (5th Dynasty, 2495–2345 BC) are probably the earliest known illustrations of animal keeping (Lauer 1976: 50–3). Similar wall sculptures in a neighbouring tomb, that of Mereruka, son-in-law of Pharaoh Teti of the 6th Dynasty (2345–2181 BC) are the earliest known illustrations of a kind of zoo. Antelopes (oryx, addax, and gazelle) are shown tethered next to their mangers, and some are being fed by their attendants, others led by men holding their horns. Some unfortunate geese and a hyena are being force-fed (Lauer 1976: 57–61). The representations are stylised yet extremely detailed (the antelopes, for example, can be identified by their horns), probably because they had a religious or magical role, as scenes for a returning *ka* – or spiritual double of somebody whose body had been mummified – to gaze upon (Lauer 1976: 13–15). The hyena may have been bred in captivity and was probably being fattened for eating (Zeuner 1963: 422). The antelopes too were clearly in some degree domesticated.

The earliest wild animal keeping may have occurred for religious reasons (Loisel 1912: I, 9–17; Mullan and Marvin 1987: 89–91). An extraordinary range of animals was regarded as sacred at different places in Egypt and often kept in or near temples. Bulls and snakes were pre-eminent, symbolising respectively the sun and the primordial creative force (Loisel 1912: I, 12–13; Smith 1969: 308, 310). Hippopotamuses, owls, crocodiles and scarab beetles are other examples of sacred animals (Loisel 1912: I, 13–

14), the killing of which in some cases carried the death penalty (Herodotus 1954: 127–8).

The actual animals kept were divine representatives and had the best of food – sometimes live prey in the case of a lion in the temple of Ammon Ra at Heliopolis. Sacred crocodiles wore collars and were called to be fed. Hawks would seize their meat in flight (Loisel 1912: I, 14–15; Herodotus 1954: 129). The poor physical condition (bone deformities, overgrown hoofs and so on) of animals actually kept in temples has been shown by study of excavated animal mummies. But it seems most sacred animals were kept outside in 'semi-liberty' (Loisel 1912: I, 16–17). All kinds of animals – bulls, antelopes, cats, shrew-mice, ibises, crocodiles, fish – were embalmed (Loisel 1912: I, 17–20).

Hunting was also a long-standing Egyptian concern, at least of the rich and the royal. Leopards, cheetahs and lions were trained for hunting; small cats retrieved birds killed in the marshes with boomerangs.

Tame lions were often kept by pharaohs. Many monuments show a king's favourite lion at the side of his throne. Rameses II's lion, Antam-nekt, was normally chained in front of the king's tent, but when Rameses rode in his chariot, Antam-nekt walked a little in front beside the horses. He fought alongside his master, repelling any who approached with a blow of his paw. Anyone rich enough could own lions, at least in the Roman period, and a Roman visitor describes one which was led by a simple cord, followed his master into the inside of temples and houses, and appeared very sweet-tempered, caressing whoever approached (Loisel 1912: I, 22).

The emphasis on attempting to domesticate indigenous wild species was later replaced by a taste for animals from abroad. Queen Hatshepsut, of the 18th Dynasty, sent five vessels to Somalia to collect ebony, ivory and gold, and also animals (Cary and Warmington 1963: 75–6). They returned with monkeys, leopards, a giraffe, cattle and numerous birds, as well as whole trees transported with their roots surrounded by soil (Loisel 1912: I, 26; Mullan and Marvin: 91). The animals were kept (about 1400 BC) in what Loisel regards as the first acclimatisation garden – that is, a place where animals brought from abroad could adjust, prior to their being domesticated or released as additions to the local fauna. This one was called the Garden of Ammon. The trees were planted in long terraces outside a temple at Thebes, today know as Deir el-Bahri (Loisel 1912: I, 25–6). Hatshepsut's successor, Thutmes III, brought birds and mammals from Syria, depicted in the great temple at Karnak. In his reign the first elephants came to Egypt (Loisel 1912: 26–7).

New animals came into Egypt with the Ptolemies – trained African elephants, pheasants and parrots – together with a renewed religious involvement with animals through the cults of Osiris (which required sacred bulls) and of his spouse Isis (whose cult required bears, monkeys and especially owls, which were kept at liberty in gardens around temples) (Loisel 1912: I, 29). The cult of Dionysus (or Bacchus) involved religious processions with hosts of animals: for example elephants, buffalos, leopards, lynxes, a great white bear and an Ethiopian rhinoceros (Loisel 1912: I, 30–4). But about the supposedly most famous ancient zoo, at Alexandria, very little information seems to be available, except that it was founded by Ptolemy Philadelphus (Scullard 1974: 133). It may have been attached to the museum, and have been an acclimatisation garden (Loisel 1912: 30–1).

MESOPOTAMIA

The earliest zoo with large carnivores such as lions was probably in Sumer (Whitehouse 1975: 70–1), and was King Shulgi's (2094–2047 BC) of the 3rd Dynasty of Ur. The workings of Shulgi's bureaucratic system are recorded upon tens of thousands of 'book-keeping' clay tablets found in several Sumerian cities (Oates 1979: 44). Also recorded are the receipt and distribution of livestock – in one year alone, over 28,000 cattle and some 350,000 sheep were 'accounted', some coming from foreign vassals (Oates 1979: 44). There were also lions in cages and pits (Oppenheim 1977: 46).

Many of the later Babylonian and Assyrian kings received wild animals as tribute or gifts, probably sometimes ordering them. Burnaburiash of Babylonia, writing to Amenophis IV of Egypt, praises Egyptian craftsmen, and asks for a model of either a land or an aquatic animal (he doesn't mind which) (Moran 1987: 83). The letter is number EA 10 of another vast collection of tablets, the Tel el-Amarna tablets (Moran 1987). Letters from an Assyrian king, Assur-Uballit I (1365–1330 BC), mention horses he is sending to the Egyptian king as presents, in one case (letter EA 16) two white horses with a beautiful royally equipped chariot (Moran

1987: 106). A later Assyrian king, Tiglath-Pileser I (1115–1077 BC) states that the king of Egypt sent him a crocodile 'which he exhibited to his people' (Olmstead 1927: 65). Tiglath-Pileser was also sent a Bactrian (two-humped) camel by merchants from abroad (Saggs 1984: 63).

Animal tribute or presents may have been so welcome because indigenous large animals were becoming scarce through over-hunting or collecting (Loisel 1912: I, 44). By Tiglath-Pileser's time there were also problems of deforestation (Saggs 1984: 62). Ashurnasirpal II, King of Assyria 883–859 BC, records animal collecting operations in stone inscriptions: apes, lions, tigers, wild bulls, elephants, ostriches, wild asses, deer, bears and leopards were brought in large numbers to his city of Kalach, and 'displayed to all the people of my land' (Grayson 1976: 148–9).

Bulls, wild goats, deer, and gazelles were kept in great parks near the kings' summer palaces, and were hunted with the assistance of Indian dogs, lions, leopards and trained elephants (Loisel 1912: I, 45; Ceram 1952: 255).

The Assyrians also hunted lions released from travelling cages for the purpose – or rather fought them, perhaps more like bullfighters. The strong wooden cages the lions were transported in can be seen in Assyrian low reliefs in the British Museum (Loisel 1912: I, 45). The Assyrian king Assur-bani-pal is shown on his chariot or his horse firing arrows at lions or fighting them on foot with lance and javelin (Loisel 1912: I, 46), the lions prevented from escaping by soldiers with a wall of shields. Obviously the kings liked to show their strength and courage by fighting the lions – a demonstration of dominance with a vengeance! It is striking how the Assyrian sculptures of (say) lions and deer are magnificently lifelike, yet so often of wounded, suffering animals (Olmstead 1927: 409–500; Loisel 1912: I, 46–7).

However, according to Loisel, some of the lions were treated differently. It was lions kept in the large parks which were hunted or fought with. Other lions were kept in enclosures near palaces and became tame – like the tame lions in Egypt (Loisel 1912: I, 45–6). The Assyrians were keen on taming other wild animals too – they tried, but failed, to train wild asses to pull chariots (Rogers 1915: 424).

Apart from all this royal animal keeping, there were also sacred menageries in Mesopotamia, as in Egypt (Loisel 1912: I, 43).

GREECE

There were sacred menageries also in Greece, but the Greeks' most striking animal involvement was a widespread enthusiasm for bird keeping, songbirds especially. Some birds were sacred to Aphrodite, and were given as presents with love letters carried beneath their wings, or bathed in scented water, so that they spread perfume as they fluttered about. Swans, ducks, and owls are often depicted enjoying liberty in gardens, and being fed by hand. Guineafowl were bred by the priests of Athena's temple on the island of Leos, and peacocks by Hera's priests on Samos. Peacocks were expensive and much sought after, and the Athenians seem to have done a brisk trade in them (Loisel 1912: I, 53–8).

Other animals were kept too. Hares could become as tame as dogs, and were hand-fed and caressed on people's laps (Loisel 1912: I, 54–5). Monkeys were often kept in rich houses, and are shown walking around freely with domestic birds (Loisel 1912: I, 57).

Some temples had sacred woods nearby, which were in effect game reserves. Lions and leopards were kept in the temples of Cybele, eagles in those of Zeus, and snakes in those of Aesculepius, god of medicine. To judge from a play of Aristophanes (*Plutus*), snakes played some part in the religious healing process in the temple of Aesculepius (though I hope not as suggested by Loisel, with snakes creeping in to the beds of sleeping supplicants, their cold touch giving them in their sleep the illusion of a divine visitation!) (Loisel 1912: I, 59–60).

It is usually assumed that Aristotle's remarkable biological writings were assisted by observations in a Greek zoo stocked by animals sent back by his famous pupil Alexander the Great from his military expeditions. The main evidence is a comment of Pliny's, written 350 years later. It is probable that animals were actually available for observation in Greece following Alexander's military exploits. For example, a group of his elephants came to the Macedonian court; about this same time the Athenians received a tiger which Seleucus, King of Syria, had given to Alexander (Loisel 1912: I, 62).

In later centuries, in the Roman period, Greece became a staging post for animals such as lions on their way to the Colosseum; Loisel notes, in connection with this, the appearance in

Greek of four words designating transport cages for dangerous animals (Loisel 1912: I, 61–3).

ROME

The Romans contrast with the Greeks – and with almost everyone else – in the extraordinary brutality displayed in the Colosseum and other circuses. The first exotic animal spectacle recorded at Rome was the appearance in a triumph of four elephants captured from Pyrrhus, who was defeated in 275 BC. Twenty-four years later more than a hundred elephants captured from the Carthaginians were similarly brought to Rome. Significantly, the elephants' mahouts 'passed into the Roman service' (Jennison 1937: 44).

In the second century BC Rome's power in northern Africa enabled nobles to display African animals in large numbers (Jennison 1937: 42, 46). It is something to know that such a spectacle as the slaughter of twenty elephants in 55 BC in a show laid on by Pompey revolted not only Cicero but the ordinary spectators (Cicero 1982: 85–8; Pliny 1856: II, 254). Augustus recorded that 3,500 African animals, mostly lions and leopards, were killed in his twenty-six *venationes* (Jennison 1937: 45), and this appalling level of animal slaughter continued into the first century AD (Suetonius 1957: 226–31). There were also performing animals – Suetonius speaks of a knight riding an elephant down a tightrope, which sounds an unlikely achievement – and considerable animal management and handling skills must have been developed (Suetonius 1957: 214).

An illustration of the enormous environmental damage which must have been done by the centuries of Roman animal massacres is another comment of Cicero's about the scarcity of leopards in Cilicia in Asia Minor when he was governor there. To a politically ambitious friend who wanted leopards for his animal shows in Rome, Cicero replied that they seemed to have all moved out to the next province because of their unfair treatment (Cicero 1982: 128).

Animals were sometimes simply displayed, as for example a rhinoceros, a tiger, and a 'serpent nearly ninety feet long' exhibited to the public by Augustus (Suetonius 1957: 76).

The Romans were extremely fond of some animals, for example talking birds. Augustus himself once paid a huge sum for a

raven which had been taught to utter suitably respectful greetings
to a victorious emperor. Ovid wrote a poem of sad farewell to a
friend's dead parrot (Loisel 1912: I, 66–9).

ANCIENT CHINA

A collection of ancient Chinese poetry known as the *Chi-King* (or
She-King) appears to be the only source for the famous 'Intelligence Park' of 'Emperor Wen-Wang' around the eleventh
century BC (Loisel 1912: I, 37). Emperor Wen-Wang was not
actually emperor, not even king strictly speaking, and to confuse
matters further he is sometimes called Wen, sometimes Wan; but
he is a figure of great interest. This is the ode that describes his
famous park:

> When he planned the commencement of the marvellous
> tower,
> He planned it, and defined it;
> And the people in crowds undertook the work,
> And in no time completed it.
> When he planned the commencement [he said], 'Be not in
> a hurry;'
> But the people came as if they were his children.
> The king was in the marvellous park,
> Where the does were lying down –
> The does, so sleek and fat;
> With the white birds glistening.
> The king was by the marvellous pond –
> How full was it of fishes leaping about!
> On his posts was the toothed face-board, high and strong,
> With the large drums and bells.
> In what unison were their sounds!
> What joy was there in the hall with its circlet of water!
> In what unison sounded the drums and bells!
> What joy was there in the hall with its circlet of water!
> The lizard-skin drums rolled harmonious,
> As the blind musicians performed their parts.
> (Legge 1871: 456–7)

The ode is quoted, with interesting comments, by the philosopher
Mencius, a contemporary of Confucius (Mencius 1970: 49–50).
  Wen was the first successor of an advanced (Late Bronze Age)

13

but brutal dynasty, the Shang. Wen was the founder of the Chou dynasty. There is archaeological evidence of human sacrifice on a large scale, as well as animal sacrifice, by the Shang. Wen was the leader of a new tribe, who had come in from western regions, and he was actually a minister under the Shang, but managed to overthrow the last, apparently degenerate, Shang ruler. He was given the title of Wen, a sort of honorary kingship, after his death in recognition of his benevolence and wisdom (Hook 1982: 164–6).

Wen was a leader loved by his people, and a man of peace, and this is suggested in the ode. The translator (afterwards Professor of Chinese at Oxford) comments on the fact that the does were lying down: this 'is mentioned as a proof of their feeling of enjoyment and security' (Legge 1871: 457). The park itself, the tower, and the pond are described by a word translated by Legge as 'marvellous'. D.C. Lau translates it in the version in Mencius as 'sacred' (Mencius 1970: 50). Legge refers to different interpretations by Chinese scholars of the term: 'a Transforming influence that went forth from Wan, as with a spiritual efficaciousness', or 'an allusion to the rapidity with which the tower rose, as if it had been the work of Spirits'. Legge (1871: 456–7) settles for 'marvellous', 'the exact force of which we cannot determine'. What impresses me is that the people seem to have built the tower with great willingness; and presumably enjoyed the park too – perhaps even the band. (Legge (1871: 458) says by the way that, in the Chou dynasty, blind persons were always chosen for the position of musicians because of their acuteness of ear.) The picture of Wen as an admirable and popular ruler is fully supported by Mencius:

> So pleased and delighted were [the people] that they named his terrace the 'Sacred Terrace' and his pond the 'Sacred Pond', and rejoiced in his possession of deer, fish and turtles. It was by sharing their enjoyments with the people that men of antiquity were able to enjoy themselves.
>
> (Mencius 1970: 50)

Wen's park was a peaceful, even a sacred place; there is nothing about its being a collection of animals brought from afar. However, a later animal park was very different. This was the park of the emperor Chi-Hang-Ti, of the Thsin dynasty, who not only filled it with animals and also trees from all parts of his empire,

14

but apparently erected copies of all the palaces of the royal houses he had destroyed (Loisel 1912: I, 37; Mullan and Marvin 1987: 92).

MEDIEVAL EUROPE

In medieval and later Europe large exotic beasts tended to be the property of kings (and were often gifts from one monarch to another), and might be kept in menageries or in deerparks. One famous royal gift was an elephant called Aboul-Abas which Charlemagne (742–814), king of the French, asked for and received from the caliph of Baghdad, Abasside Haroun-er-Reschid, in 797 (Loisel 1912: I, 162). (Baghdad was a city enjoying a kind of neo-Assyrian splendour, complete with lion-pit, into which those who displeased the caliph were thrown (Loisel 1912: I, 185).) The elephant came with monkeys, perfumes and spices, and was to accompany Charlemagne for thirty years. From other Arab leaders Charlemagne received a lion and a Numidian bear, which were added to the peacocks and ducks already ornamenting the gardens of his numerous residences. He also had deerparks. Monks sometimes had menageries too, for example at Saint-Gall in Switzerland, where there were badgers and bears as well as herons and silver pheasants (Loisel 1912: I, 162–3).

We first hear of the British royal menagerie (at Woodstock) during the reign of William II (*reg* 1087–1100), from a chronicler who speaks of his master's receiving a bear from the king. We are told that Henry I (*reg* 1100–35) had at Woodstock lions, leopards, lynxes, camels and a rare owl. The lions (or leopards – there is some doubt which) in the English royal arms date from his reign or soon after. It was probably Henry III (*reg* 1216–72) who moved the menagerie to the Tower, for in 1251 the king received a white bear, whose food the city of London had to pay for. It was presumably a polar bear, as it was allowed to fish in the Thames, secured by an iron chain, a muzzle, and a long rope also paid for by the city. Three years later Henry received an elephant – the first ever in England – from his brother-in-law the King of France, Louis IX. Everyone could come to see the elephant, which was only fair as they also had to pay for its house (Loisel 1912: I, 154–5).

Henry III also received three leopards (Bompas 1885: 281–2) and other beasts from Frederick II (1194–1250), King of Sicily, Holy Roman Emperor, and an outstanding naturalist. When not busy founding the University of Naples or capturing Jerusalem (in the course of the sixth crusade), or for that matter encouraging his court astrologer the great Michael Scot to translate Aristotle's zoological works from Arabic to Latin (Aristotle 1968: 40–2), Frederick enjoyed his '"Vivarium" . . . a large area of marshes and ponds, fed by a well-regulated water supply from aqueducts, and populated by many species of water birds' (Stresemann 1975: 9). Frederick had a menagerie which accompanied him on his travels, but his keeping of animals went hand in hand with a learned interest in them, as demonstrated by his book on falconry (another enthusiasm). The book is in fact an introduction to the whole of ornithology, including ecology, behaviour and anatomy (Stresemann 1975: 10). Frederick's unpopularity with the Church led to his book's not being printed until 1596 and not being noticed by ornithologists until 1788 (Stresemann 1975: 10). His experiments such as those to determine whether vultures find their food by sight or smell, and his careful observations, for example that (contrary to Aristotle's opinion) the leading bird among cranes flying in V-formation changed places during passage, were not to be surpassed until the recent work of Konrad Lorenz himself (Stresemann 1975: 11).

MEDIEVAL CHINA

Frederick II is amazing enough, but for thirteenth-century life surrounded by animals on a quite ridiculously extensive scale – with sumptuous palaces and deerparks all included – we need to go to Kubilai Khan, Mongol Emperor of China, which we can do thanks to the detailed descriptions provided by the Venetian Marco Polo (1254–1324) in 1298. Polo had an eye for mysterious detail, enough to inspire Coleridge's vision in 'Kubla Khan':

> In Xanadu did Kubla Khan
>   A stately pleasure-dome decree:
> Where Alph, the sacred river, ran
> Through caverns measureless to man
>   Down to a sunless sea.
> So twice five miles of fertile ground
> With walls and towers were girdled round:
> And here were gardens bright with sinuous rills
> Where blossomed many an incense-bearing tree;

And here were forests ancient as the hills,
Enfolding sunny spots of greenery.

(Coleridge 1959: 85)

Among other influences on him, Coleridge had been reading a sixteenth-century rewriting (Yule 1871: 269; Holmes 1989: 163–4) of Polo's description of Xanadu (or Shang-tu or Ciandu), where Kubilai had his summer palace, staying there from June to 28 August every year (Polo 1958: 108–9). The 'huge palace of marble' was joined by a wall which 'encloses and encircles fully sixteen miles of park-land well watered with springs and streams and diversified with lawns' (Polo 1958: 108). The park also contained another extraordinary palace – a moveable one built of canes. Near the park was a stud of sacred white horses whose milk had to be poured out as a liberation on 28 August (Coleridge's 'milk of Paradise', from the same poem). In the park were 'hart, stag, and roebuck', apparently kept there partly to provide food for his falcons (of which he had many, especially gyr-falcons). Kubilai would ride through the park, with a 'leopard' (presumably in fact a cheetah) sitting behind him on his horse, to be released to catch prey whenever Kubilai felt like it. (Frederick II similarly used to carry a cheetah on his horse's crupper (Yule 1871: I, 353–4).) One thing Marco Polo doesn't apparently describe in the park is 'a menagerie with quarters for tigers, panthers, and leopards', though Loisel refers to this (Loisel 1912: I, 39). Presumably such a description is found in the French version Loisel refers to. (There are in fact many versions of Marco Polo's travels, none of them wholly authoritative, partly because the account was written in collaboration in the first place (Polo 1958: 25–7).)

Kubilai's winter palace was at Khan-balik (or Cambaluc or Cabalut), where Peking now stands (Yule 1871: I, 333–4). The palace ('the largest that was ever seen') was surrounded by luscious parkland. There were 'white harts, musk-deer, roebuck, stags, squirrels, and many other beautiful animals', as well as ponds with 'a great variety of fish' (Polo 1958: 125–6). There was also an artificial green mound, with another palace (itself green) on top and the 'finest trees in the world' (dug up and transported there by elephants) (Polo 1958: 127). Kubilai had a vast number of elephants, who would all walk in procession at the New Year (Polo 1958: 139). A tame lion was sometimes led into Kubilai's presence, and would prostrate itself before him, and then stay there 'without a chain . . . indeed a thing to marvel at' (Polo 1958: 141). Kubilai would go hawking (from Khan-balik) with 'thousands' of falconers, and would hunt with trained 'leopards' (as at Xanadu), lynxes and 'lions of immense size, bigger than those of Egypt; they have very handsome, richly coloured fur, with longitudinal stripes of black, orange, and white' (Polo 1958: 142) – in other words, tigers, which were presumably unknown in Europe in this period (Yule 1871: I, 354–5). The 'lions' were 'led out to the chase on carts in cages, each with a little dog for company', and 'must always be led upwind; for if their prey caught wind of the smell they would not wait, but would be off in a flash' (Polo 1958: 142).

It was possible for a few more years after Marco Polo's time for Europeans to enter China – until 1368, when the Ming Dynasty replaced the Mongol (Polo 1958: 15). A traveller in 1318, Father Oderic of Pordenone, tells us that he saw three thousand monkeys (probably a species of macaque) in the park of a Buddhist pagoda, which came at the sound of a bell to be fed by a monk (Loisel 1912: I, 40). A little later Mandeville visited China, and he tells us of a closed garden, in a large 'pagan abbey' near Peking, which contained a high mountain, inhabited by monkeys and other animals. Every day after the masters of the abbey had eaten, what was left over was put in gold vessels. The abbey almoner then took a silver trumpet, at whose sound all the beasts assembled around him, and the food was distributed to them (Loisel 1912: I, 40–1).

BRITISH DEERPARKS

We have seen how Kubilai Khan had sumptuous animal parks, and also kept tame cheetahs and tigers, and of course falcons. We have just seen yet another way of keeping animals, having them roaming freely yet apparently so tame a bell or trumpet would summon them to be fed. As we saw earlier with Charlemagne's elephant and his palace parks, and Frederick II with his ponds for waterfowl, a range of ways of keeping animals was to be found also in medieval Europe.

As a normal way in which royalty and nobility often kept larger wild animals – except obviously dangerous ones – deerparks or animal parks are particularly important. The word 'deerpark' probably meant originally 'animal park', for until 1490 or so 'deer' meant 'animal' (it is the same word in origin as the German *Tier*), as in 'rats and mice and such small deer', quoted in *King Lear* from a medieval rhyme (Campbell 1979: 72). About the year 1086 the Domesday Book records thirty-five parks for wild animals and at least one pre-Conquest park, in Ongar (Domesday 1986: 13). John (*reg* 1199–1216) possessed as many as 781 parks (Patrick and Geddie 1923). Deerparks were primarily for hunting and food, and hunting with hounds was not only reserved to the king and nobles but to a great extent was a privilege of the king alone – only he could hunt red deer for example. Their royal status was indicated by special terms for male and female – stag (or hart) and hind instead of buck and doe (Putnam 1988: 156–7). Thus deerparks could only be set up with royal permission (Stenton 1952: 103–4). The red deer at Lowther Castle today are direct descendants of those enclosed when Sir Hugh de Louther was granted a licence to make a deerpark in 1283.

It is hardly likely, though, that royal and noble deerparks, even in this period, were solely for hunting, any more than were Kubilai's parks. From Marco Polo's descriptions, his deer and other animals were also there to be admired, like those happily peaceful does in Wen's park 2,000 years earlier. If deer in British deerparks had not likewise fulfilled some wider role as well as serving to be hunted, deerparks would have disappeared after about 1750 when foxhunting replaced deerhunting. But deerparks didn't disappear; they became mainly ornamental (Patrick and Geddie 1923: 735).

In any case, other wild and semi-wild animals were kept in medieval times in extensive areas without being there to be hunted (Thomas 1984: 276). Notable examples are the swans at Abbotsbury in Dorset, first mentioned in 1393, and the white cattle at Chillingham (and perhaps Cadzow in Scotland). The stone wall surrounding the Chillingham estate (now in Northumberland, almost on the Scottish border) was put up in 1220 (Loisel 1912: III, 61), but it is likely that the white cattle were brought originally from Italy in Roman times (Zeuner 1963: 210). Presumably they were selectively bred by the Romans (or earlier) because of the significance, perhaps sacredness, attributed to the white colour (as with Kubilai's sacred white horses). The extreme antiquity of this reverence for white cattle, and the occasional occurrence of wild white specimens, is suggested by the inclusion of a white aurochs among the paintings in the Lascaux Caves (Zeuner 1963: 207–1) of 15,000 years ago.

One must not underrate, though, the part hunting played in the life of royalty and nobility. How important hunting was is emphasised by the striking fact that 'forest', which now means wild woodland, meant originally an area set aside for hunting – whether or not it contained any woods. In fact the term 'forest' also emphasises the importance of deerparks, which were enclosed areas for hunting, while the essence of a forest (and the derivation of the word) was that it was an unenclosed area for hunting (Gilbert 1979: 19; Davies 1981: 32–3).

Perhaps the enormous enthusiasm of the Norman kings for hunting was no greater than the Saxon kings', or for that matter Kubilai Khan's. But the Norman monarchs certainly took extraordinary steps to extend and protect their hunting interests (Stenton 1952: 108). They kept extending areas of forest, and vicious forest laws came into operation over any 'afforested' area. Domestic animals couldn't feed in the forest; dogs had to be 'lawed' (three claws of the front foot cut); and one could be maimed or executed for poaching, especially killing a red deer (Stenton 1952: 107–8). The cruellest laws were repealed, and newly afforested areas were deforested again, from the Forest Charter in 1217 (Stenton 1952: 106).

An example of an English monarch whose enthusiasm for falconry probably equalled Kubilai Khan's – or Frederick II's for that matter – would be Henry II, who could easily be distracted from court business by the chance of a day's hawking, and who once paid £56 for sending a ship to Norway to buy falcons. Like Kubilai, he especially prized gyr-falcons (Barber 1964: 58). What bird of prey one was allowed to train depended of course on one's rank in society.

LATE MIDDLE AGES AND RENAISSANCE TIMES

Henry II's enthusiasm was shared in many courts in Europe in the Middle Ages and in the following centuries. Philip VI of France (*reg* 1328–50) had lions and leopards at the Louvre. Monkeys and apes were kept in royal courts, often with a collar and a chain attached to a little roller – as seen in French fifteenth–century tapestries, along with various other collared animals (Erlande-Brandenburg 1978) – or to a heavy ball (Morris 1968: 72). Parrots were very popular, as in the Vatican in the fifteenth century (Loisel 1912: 202).

Under Pope Leo X (1513–23), of the Medicis, the Vatican menagerie expanded, with numerous gorgeous parrots, monkeys, civets and other unusual animals portrayed in paintings on walls and ceilings (Loisel I: 202–3). Lions and leopards were sent from Florence, bears from Hungary, and an elephant and a snow leopard, plus tapestries and jewels, from King Manuel I of Portugal. The Portuguese ambassador, the elephant and every-thing else arrived on 12 March 1514. At the window where sat the Pope and court, the elephant stopped, obediently knelt three times to render homage to His Holiness, and then decided the crowd was a bit too pressing. He noticed a nearby tub of water, plunged in his trunk, and everybody from the Pope downwards got squirted. Leo was vastly amused, and also impressed by the other gifts as well, especially the snow leopard and a magnificent arab horse. All the beasts were kept at the Vatican, the elephant continuing as a celebrity, sought out by portrait painters and addressed by poets (Loisel 1912: 202–4).

The cardinals followed the Pope's example. One cardinal kept peacocks and Syrian long-eared goats in his park; another showed off the free-living guineafowl in his garden. And one cardinal, a Medici, kept a troop of exotic foreigners, who spoke more than twenty different languages and were all chosen for their good looks - Moors, Tartars, Indians, Turks and African negroes: a curious parallel, as Loisel remarks, with the human collections to be found contemporaneously on the other side of the Atlantic (Loisel 1912: 204–5).

MEXICO

The human collections Loisel was thinking of were in the zoo of Montezuma II, Aztec emperor of Mexico. The zoo is described by Hernan Cortes (Cortes 1972), who conquered Mexico for Spain between 1517 and 1521, and by his lieutenant Bernal Diaz del Castillo (Castillo 1928). Montezuma tried to prevent Cortes's expedition from reaching his capital Tenochtitlan, but, having failed, decided not to resist. Possibly his reason was a centuries-old legend which foretold the return of a hero-god called Quetzalcoatl from the Gulf region, and the possibility that the Spaniards were divine messengers. Resistance would not have been difficult, his city being protected by a large lake and reach-able only by long causeways with drawbridges. But instead he offered the Spaniards every hospitality (Prescott n.d.: 295–9). His reward, after one week, was to be taken hostage by Cortes, who also insisted on Montezuma's calling to his capital seventeen

Aztecs who had dared to resist another force of Cortes's men. Cortes arranged for these seventeen chiefs to be burnt alive (Prescott n.d.: 341–8).

Cortes and Castillo had every opportunity to view the city and its life, and they provide vivid accounts. Cortes confesses himself lost for words to describe the magnificence of Montezuma's palace, which he says was better than anything in Spain (Cortes 1972: 109). Their accounts of the zoo vary considerably, but they agree in speaking of large collections of birds of prey and of water birds, and also of large cats and dog-like carnivores (Cortes 1972: 109–11; Castillo 1928: 294–5). To this Cortes adds accounts of human albinos, and of deformed humans, who were also kept (quite humanely, it seems), and Castillo describes 'many vipers and poisonous snakes which carry on their tails things that sound like bells', which were kept in 'jars and great pottery vessels with many feathers'. Castillo says that the snakes' food included 'the bodies of the Indians who have been sacrificed', as well as 'the flesh of dogs which they are in the habit of breeding' (Castillo 1928: 295). One wonders how they got the snakes to eat flesh (whether human or dog) as opposed to whole animals, whether living or recently killed. But Castillo's statement about the human food suggests strongly that the snakes were kept for religious reasons. Snake (often rattlesnake) worship, and belief in a plumed serpent god, was widespread in Mexico and among neighbouring peoples (MacCulloch 1920: 401–2). Snakes were associated too with Quetzalcoatl.

Cortes tells us of ten pools for the water birds (Castillo speaks of just one 'great tank of fresh water'). Both were impressed by the care shown for the birds. Cortes said that the sea birds had salt water, the river birds fresh water, and all were given the kind of food they would have in the wild. He speaks too of their having 300 keepers (as well as others 'skilled only in healing sick birds') – and another 300 keepers for the birds of prey and the mammals! Castillo tells us that the birds bred. (He also says the snakes bred, though vipers and rattlesnakes would not actually have laid eggs, as he says they did.) Castillo tells us too of quetzals, with their rich green plumage, and of 'other birds which have feathers of five colours', as well as 'parrots of many different colours', and says that from 'all these birds they plucked the feathers when the time was right to do so, and the feathers grew again'. These feathers were used to decorate armour, hats and just about everything else

– both Cortes and Castillo stress the Aztec craftsmanship in all kinds of beautiful 'featherwork' (Cortes 1972: 108–9; Castillo 1928: 293–4, 296). It is significant that the feathers were plucked, not just collected (as in some recent writers' accounts). For the plucking of particular feathers would have meant the process could be repeated perhaps every three or four months, thus producing a large crop of feathers far larger than would have been possible if the moulted feathers had been collected (moulted feathers would have been available only once a year). The degree of use of the feathers suggests there was a very large supply!

According to Cortes the birds of prey were kept in a separate house from the other birds, 'with a large patio, laid with pretty tiles in the manner of a chessboard', and the birds' separate rooms each had a perch in a covered part of the room as well as another 'outside beneath the latticework'. Cortes tells us 'large numbers of lions, tigers, wolves, foxes and cats of various kinds' were kept in this same house in 'big cages, made from heavy timbers and very well joined'. But according to Castillo the 'tigers and two kinds of lions, and animals something like wolves and foxes, and other smaller carnivorous animals' were in a different building which also contained idols, and he thinks their food probably included the bodies of sacrificed humans. Castillo's account of the carnivore house includes a graphic description of the Aztec sacrifice method, in which the victim's chest was cut open with a stone knife and the still palpitating heart ripped out. However, as we have seen, the horror of such practices somewhat pales beside the extreme cruelty of Cortes himself (not that he wasn't also both courageous and clever). Mullan and Marvin (1987: 104) wonder where the 'lions, tigers and leopards' could have come from, but as other writers realise, these must have been jaguars and pumas – but was there a third kind of big cat, possibly now extinct? This has been suggested.

Castillo, particularly, describes much else of great interest – for example a Tenochtitlan market with slaves on sale ('as many of them . . . as the Portuguese bring negroes from Guinea'), all sorts of merchandise, and 'fowls, cocks with wattles, rabbits, hares, deer, mallards, young dogs and other things of that sort', as well as animal skins (Castillo 1928: 298–9).

But this whole great city and society with its skilled craftsmen and its thousands of ordinary citizens – and of course its animals – were to be destroyed in the course of a long and brutal siege in

1521 (Prescott n.d.: 598–611) – after which Cortes was appointed governor of 'New Spain'.

EUROPEAN ZOOS 1500–1800

Zoos in Europe through these centuries were mostly royal or aristocratic, but not exclusively so, even in the sixteenth century. Manuel I of Portugal, who presented Pope Leo X with his elephant, received monkeys and macaws from South America, grey parrots and baboons from Africa, and six elephants, a rhinoceros, and cheetahs from India (Dembeck 1966: 279). A sketch of the rhinoceros was the basis for Dürer's famous woodcut. Manuel's dealing in animals included selling monkeys (through a middleman) to a merchant in Augsburg. A zoo set up by the Elector of Brandenburg in the late sixteenth century was open to the public, as were menageries in the Netherlands, including one founded by the citizens of The Hague in 1590. So even 400 years ago some zoos were open to ordinary people, thus providing information to them about animals from newly explored foreign lands. The Hague zoo had a cassowary, for example, from Java (Dembeck 1966: 279–80).

On the other hand, an extreme case of an animal collection's being no more than the personal property of a ruler and subject to his every whim was the royal French menagerie at the Louvre (Loisel 1912: II, 274). In January 1583 the king, Henry III, had a nightmare about his animals devouring him. The next day, after hearing mass, he shot his whole collection with an arquebus (Loisel 1912: II, 274–5). (He seems to have been, even apart from this incident, of rather unsound mind.)

Of course this was exceptional, but the arrangement of animal fights hardly was. We have details, for example, of the animals kept at the Tower in James I's reign (these included six lions) from drawings and engravings done of the animals but also from records of fights between lions, bears and dogs provided as a court entertainment (Loisel 1912: II, 13).

A much more serious use of a zoo was to be found with Louis XIV's menagerie at Versailles, founded in 1664, which had a distinguished history on into the eighteenth century, until its problems in the revolutionary period. It was opened both to scientists and to the public, and played a large part in the developing science of comparative anatomy. The Academy of Sciences regularly dissected animals that had died in the menagerie from 1669 to 1690 (Loisel 1912: II, 296–7), starting with a beaver. The various organs were drawn and engraved, and the skins and skeletons were mounted. The most famous of these dissections was that of an elephant, which died in 1681. Important publications were produced from all this work (Loisel 1912: II, 299).

Another royal zoo in France, the Jardin du Roi in Paris, was opened up by Louis XIV to a wide range of visitors. Vienna also had a series of royal zoos, including the one set up by Maria Theresa at the palace of Schönbrunn in 1752 and still there (Dembeck: 281–2).

The seamier side of menageries is illustrated again by events a little earlier than this at the Elector Augustus II's menagerie in Dresden. The Elector arranged, to celebrate a royal wedding, a series of animal fights between bulls, lions, bears, an ape and wild boars. (The only nice thing, from an eye-witness account, is that when a lion, lioness and tiger came in to fight with the bulls, the lion lay down and went to sleep, and looked as if he was just 'a spectator or judge of the combat' – the poor lioness and tiger, though, rushed around looking frightened (Loisel 1912: II, 58–9).)

Jamieson (1985: 108) refers to this incident as an illustration of rulers' occasional demonstrating of their power by 'destroying their entire collections'. This indeed is what Henry III of France had done, as we saw above (but through superstition or madness rather than as a demonstration of power), but it is not, according to Loisel's account, what Augustus II did; it was seven or eight wild boar which he personally shot. I agree with Jamieson about the nastiness of the incident, but it was apparently an extended animal fight, not – as Jamieson describes it – a strict massacre (Loisel 1912: II, 58–9).

The reputable side of zoo-keeping continued also in the eighteenth century. For example, the great naturalist Buffon became director of the Jardin du Roi in Paris in 1739. Buffon was a great friend of Louis XIV who was, according to Nancy Mitford (1955: 94–5, 142–3), extremely keen on animals as well as devoted to hunting.

After the incident when the local revolutionaries marched to the now very run down Versailles menagerie in 1792, the last (unliberated and unslaughtered) animals were sent to the Jardin du Roi (Loisel 1912: II, 161), which about the same time became the Jardin des Plantes and part of the Muséum d'Histoire Naturelle, all directed by the great zoologist Cuvier. This zoo continued as one for the public. It had free entry to all from then on to the present, and was part of a distinguished scientific institution.

MENAGERIES

From the 1770s, there was a second menagerie in London in addition to the Tower, Exeter Change, which gradually became the London base of George Pidcock's travelling menagerie (Altick 1978: 38–9).

By 1793 the Change had a rhinoceros (called a 'unicorn'), zebra, kangaroo, secretary bird, lynx and wolf, and in another four years elephants and tigers (Altick 1978: 39). Twenty or so years later a handbill for the 'Royal Grand National Menagerie' includes a 'Bengal Tygress', hyaena, porcupine, jaguars, monkeys, bison, pelicans, two ostriches, an alpaca, llama, kangaroos, an 'Ouran Outang', boa constrictors and much more (Altick 1978: 308). Obviously the conditions must have been appallingly crowded. Just what it was like was described by Thomas Hood (with a flurry of puns, and in the course of a liberation story in verse oddly reminiscent of the Versailles affair, with a revolutionarily minded monkey doing the liberating, and sadly getting eaten by the lion he releases):

> To look around upon this brute-bastille,
> And see the king of creatures in – a safe!
> The desert's denizen in one small den,
> Swallowing slavery's most bitter pills –
> A bear in bars unbearable. And then
> The fretful porcupine, with all its quills
> Imprison'd in a pen!
> A tiger limited to four feet ten.

> (Hood 1965: 206)

But some of the animals were treated with a kind of consideration for their particular tastes, and were well-known characters of the time, for example a mandrill called Jerry who 'had his own rocking chair, drank gin by the tumbler, smoked church-wardens and was twice presented at Court' (Brightwell 1952: 19). The elephants were popular characters too, including an earlier one whose cleverness a visitor described in 1805 (Altick 1978: 309n.), and also a famous later elephant called Chunie, who appeared at a pantomime at Covent Garden in 1811 (Altick 1978: 310). Tragically, during presumably a period of musth in February 1826, he became wildly disturbed, to an extent which made it necessary for the proprietor to decide two days later to have Chunie shot. But the decision proved appallingly difficult for even a squad of soldiers to execute successfully (Altick 1978: 311–16).

Chunie's body was dissected by a team of surgeons watched by medical students. His skeleton ended up in the Hunterian Museum of the Royal College of Surgeons. The enormous public interest in Chunie and elephants included at least one letter in *The Times* protesting at his confined conditions during life (Altick 1978: 313–16).

Whether or not the animals, such as Chunie, were of any scientific use before death, as they often were after, they were often made full use of by artists (Altick 1978: 310).

Another famous menagerie, a travelling one, was George Wombwell's which became Bostock and Wombwell's in about 1825, and continued until 1931. Just how small and featureless its cages were is shown in photographs, for example of lions and of a hippopotamus, in Newcastle as late as 1930 (Middlemiss 1987: 44–5) – the conditions are unlikely to have been better a century earlier. But many animals including lions were probably very tame and had a close relationship with their keepers (Huxley 1981: 47–8). Animals like elephants and camels obtained exercise and occupation from performing and working (Middlemiss 1987: 16, 50–1). Such menageries' educational role in simply exhibiting animals impossible to see otherwise before the film and television age is illustrated by the royal reception (one of several through the years) given to Bostock and Wombwell's on a visit to Windsor Castle in 1854, when not only the court and all the royal employees but the masters and boys of Eton attended as well (Middlemiss 1987: 44–5).

LONDON ZOO IN THE NINETEENTH CENTURY

The Zoological Society of London was founded the same year as Chunie's sad death, 1826, by Sir Stamford Raffles, newly returned from the East Indies, and its zoological gardens was the first zoo to be explicitly founded as a scientific institution. It was also of course the zoo that gave that word to the world. 'The Zoological Gardens' became 'the Zoo' one night in 1867 when the Great Vance (a music hall artist) sang:

Weekdays may do for cads, but not for me or you,
So dressed right down the street, we show them who is
who . . .
The O.K. thing on Sundays is the walking in the zoo.

(Brightwell 1952: 97; Cherfas 1984: 15)

Originally you couldn't get in at all unless you were a fellow of the
Society or a friend of one. By 1834, the exclusiveness was only
theoretical; tickets could even be bought in neighbouring pubs
(Ritvo 1990: 213). In 1846 or so a businesslike new secretary
opened the zoo to the general public officially (Ritvo 1990: 214).
But Sundays continued, as in Vance's song, as a day of privilege.

The Society's scientific role as perceived originally by Raffles
and his associates sounds today distinctly odd:

> The introduction of new varieties, breeds, and races of
> animals for the purpose of domestication or for stocking our
> farm-yards, woods, pleasure-grounds, and wastes with the
> establishment of a general Zoological Collection, consisting
> of prepared specimens in the different classes and orders, so
> as to . . . point out the analogies between the animals already
> domesticated, and those which are similar in character upon
> which the first experiments may be made.
>
> (Matthews 1976: 281–2)

Domestication and acclimatisation, as here, could have been the
stated purpose of a zoo in ancient Egypt. However the idea that
acclimatising – introducing animals to new continents and releasing them – was a good idea was a scientific mistake of the period,
not of the Zoological Society in particular. And in fact the main
zoological work of the zoo turned out in practice to be mostly, as
with Versailles, and even the Change, the providing of deceased
specimens for dissection. But all reasonable assistance was given
to any scientific investigators. Darwin, for example, was to investigate how monkeys reacted to snakes (Glickman and Sroges 1966:
151–2), and various investigators investigated the animals' olfac-
tory preferences (Cornish 1895: 109–12), or their responses to
music and other sounds (Cornish 1895: 115–38), or the 'speech of
monkeys' (Cornish 1895: 240–7).

The Zoological Gardens were not intended to differ from a
place like the Change only by their scientific role and by their
exclusion of 'the vulgar', but also by the superiority of the conditions they provided for their animals. Sadly, the new institution

was far from fully successful in this third aspiration. The life expectancies of the big cats at the Gardens was about two years, because of their poor housing, and there was extremely strong contemporary criticism, for example in the *Quarterly Review* in 1836 (Altick 1978: 318) of the big cats' conditions and what the animals were missing of their wild existence. Leigh Hunt (about the same year) challenged the keeping of wild animals at all, and certainly 'in a state of endless captivity, their very lives, for the most part, turned into lingering deaths' (Altick 1978: 318).

It is extraordinary to read a newspaper account from thirty years later of how the new lion house was going to be quite different. J. W. Toovey quotes the following words from the *Daily News* of 1869:

Lions at play, free as their own jungles at home; tigers crouching, springing, gambolling, with as little restraint as on the hot plains of their native India – such is the dream of everyone interested in Zoology. We are all tired of the dismal menagerie cages. The cramped walk, the weary restless movement of the head . . . the bored look, the artificial habits . . . . Thousands upon thousands will be gratified to learn that a method of displaying lions and tigers, in what may be called by comparison, a state of nature, is seriously contemplated at last.

(Toovey 1976: 179)

Here is a clear, popular, recognition of the inadequacies of menagerie conditions and of the effects they had on animals like big cats – from over 120 years ago – plus a desire for naturalistic enclosures, which are sometimes still lacking even today. A little more than twenty years later Henry Salt was to protest in his *Animals' Rights* against the cruelty of shutting up a wild animal in a 'cell where it has just space to turn round, and where it necessarily loses every distinctive feature of its character' (Salt 1980: 50), but he recognised that where an animal like an elephant was trained to work, 'the exaction of such service, however questionable in itself, is very different from condemning an animal to a long term of useless and deadening imbecility' (ibid.: 51–2).

Many of the animals, including elephants, did have various activities to perform. The Gardens also had good staff, such as its superintendent for forty years, A. D. Bartlett, who came to the notice of the Society first by his taxidermic skill. Examples of his skill with the management of living animals are the way in which he lanced two abscesses on the massive African elephant Jumbo, without, clearly, losing the animal's trust, and the way in which he organised the transfer of the big cats to new accommodation (by leaving the travelling boxes waiting with food in till the animals were accustomed to them) without avoidable disturbance to animals or humans (Street 1965: 63–6). Bartlett once got an escaped angry hippopotamus back into its enclosure by instructing a keeper he knew the hippo loathed to shout at it and then run for his life – into the enclosure! The animal pursued him in, and the keeper leapt the wall.

On the subject of hippos, the first hippopotamus at the zoo was described in 1850 as 'a fine lively young animal . . . gambolling in the water with great glee' (Darwin 1988: 282–3). Even that is surely enough to remind us that bad as the carnivore and primate conditions must have been, especially in the early days, things were much better for some animals.

CARL HAGENBECK

The Zoological Society of London was followed by the founding in the mid-nineteenth century of other major zoos (Dublin, Bristol, Amsterdam, Frankfurt, Basle, Philadelphia and so on), but major advances in zoo thinking came from a remarkable German animal trainer and trader, Carl Hagenbeck. Jordan and Ormrod (1978: 40–8) provide a useful account of Hagenbeck's remarkable innovations in at least three different fields.

His success was founded on his animal collecting, a highly questionable business morally, though conservationally Hagenbeck's collecting, although vast, was probably 'infinitesimal' in its effects compared to the wildlife destruction caused by 'farmers and sportsmen' (Jordan and Ormrod 1978: 42), and still more by wars. Hagenbeck (1909: 69, 214–15) himself notes the wildlife destruction arising from the war against the Mahdi.

But animal collecting through the centuries, whether or not for zoos, must have caused enormous suffering, and even Hagenbeck accepted the need, for example, to kill accompanying adults when young elephants were captured, and, worse, allowed local Nubian tribesmen who were assisting him to use their own, cruel methods (ibid.: 51 ff.). Giraffes and antelopes would be chased by the Nubians 'until the young, lagging behind, can be isolated from their parents' (ibid.: 57). Hagenbeck had an extraordinary sympathy for the baboons the catching of whom he describes. About half of those captured failed to survive the stress of transportation. Hagenbeck also describes an extraordinary rescue of captured baboons by 'a large force of free baboons' (Hagenbeck 1909: 58–68; Huxley 1981: 149–50).

Hagenbeck's innovations as an animal trainer emphasised the differences between individual animals such as lions, and involved selecting the exceptional animal – the natural performer, as it were – and positively reinforcing what that individual occasionally did anyway. He regarded cruel training as ineffective as well as dangerous compared to his own humane methods (Street 1965: 37 ff.). German zoos have continued to have a much higher regard for animal training, even when taken to the length of circus performing, than do British zoos, and its occupational and psychological usefulness is stressed by Hediger (1968: 117–32; 1964: 158–61).

Hagenbeck also showed that even such delicate animals as chimpanzees and other primates – and many other animals – could adjust, given time, to European winters, and that their health improved enormously with fresh air (Jordan and Ormrod 1978: 43–5).

And finally, in 1907 Hagenbeck founded his own zoo at Stellingen near Hamburg, with moated rather than barred enclosures, and with carnivores and herbivores apparently exhibited (as it appeared to the public) in the same enclosures, in fact separated by hidden moats (Street 1965: 32–7). Prior to setting up the moated enclosures, he carefully investigated the jumping capacities of various animals (Jordan and Ormrod 1978: 46–7). Hagenbeck also displayed humans – whole groups of Lapps, Nubians, Eskimos, and many more (Huxley 1981: 42).

Thirty-six years after its foundation, Stellingen was destroyed in the night of 25 July 1943, by 'a hail of inflammable phosphorus bombs' (Hagenbeck 1956: 217). Hagenbeck's son provides a moving account of keepers humanely shooting cats and bears to save them from death by burning, and fourteen elephants rescued, to take 'refuge in the large pool' (ibid.: 218). It was all rebuilt after the war.

Edinburgh Zoo (1909) was designed in the light of Hagenbeck's innovations. He also had a considerable influence on London, and many other zoos.

WOBURN

The 11th Duke of Bedford is most famous for saving the Père David's deer from extinction. In the years following the deer's description by Père David, a few had been sent to Europe, and some bred in European zoos (Jones and Manton 1983: 1–5). Their extinction in China was to follow a flood in 1894 which breached the walls of the Imperial Hunting Park where they were kept (Jungius and Loudon 1985: 1–2; Jones and Manton 1983: 5). The Duke managed to form a herd of eighteen animals at Woburn between 1893 and 1895, with animals mainly from Paris and Berlin (Bedford 1949: 262; Jones and Manton 1983: 1–5). This herd had grown to 88 animals by 1914, though numbers fell during the First World War (Bedford 1949: 262). There were about 250 by 1945. The Duke for all his earlier foresight, and although he was President of the Zoological Society of London, adamantly refused official requests from its Secretary, at that time Julian Huxley, to transfer any animals to London or Whipsnade for safety (Huxley 1970: 235–6). (Disease could have wiped out the entire world population, as a flood and its consequences apparently did all those remaining in China.) From 1944, his son, now the 12th Duke, began such transfers to other collections, and by 1985 there were about 1,500 animals worldwide (Jungius and Loudon 1985: 1).

The Père David's deer were an addition to an already vast collection of animals at Woburn – a magnificent deerpark in the old sense of 'deer', reminiscent of Kubilai-Khan's Khan-Balik at least! Roaming virtually free were not just deer but llamas, zebus, yaks, ostriches, emus, gnus, chamois, mouflon, American and European bison, tapirs, giraffes, Przewalski's horses, Grevy's and Burchell's zebras, onagers, kangaroos and wapiti, as well as numerous birds (Loisel 1912: III, 71–2). The Duke of Bedford's acclimatisation projects had included the release of the North American grey squirrel (Huxley 1970: 235). The Duke bred too several other endangered species including both species of bison as well as Przewalski's horse (Loisel 1912: III, 79).

The 12th Duke of Bedford, also a keen naturalist who probably knew every individual Père David's deer in the herd (Tavistock 1983: vii–viii), was mainly interested in birds, and 'was the first person to establish a flock and breeding species of homing budgerigars' (ibid.: vii). He also used, each day, to summon the Japanese carp in the pond in front of the Chinese dairy by ringing a small bell, and 'would feed them individually out of his hand' (ibid: viii). I am reminded of the fourteenth-century account of the monkeys in the park in China which were summoned with a bell by a Buddhist monk.

OTHER TWENTIETH-CENTURY DEVELOPMENTS

In 1903 Chalmers Mitchell became Secretary of the Zoological Society of London, a man of forceful personality (Huxley 1981: 41 ff.), who proceeded, by a thorough examination of the animal records, to verify Hagenbeck's findings about animals' need of fresh air and ability to adjust to cold climates. He then took steps to allow many animals previously protected from the London climate access to it (Jordan and Ormrod 1978: 48–50), and thus greatly extended zoo life expectancies.

He couldn't change everything – like the Lion House that, at least in Galsworthy's opinion (Galsworthy 1922: 189–91), among others, had so conspicuously failed to live up to its rapturous welcome in the *Daily News* of 1869.

But Chalmers Mitchell, despite some misgivings about the practicalities of Hagenbeck's naturalistic exhibits (Hagenbeck 1909: ix), was inspired by Hagenbeck's artificial hills at Stellingen (Jordan and Ormrod 1978: 47) to provide much more naturalistic accommodation for many animals with the huge Mappin Terraces (1914–27). Not that everyone, even so, was impressed, at least at the start: a character in Saki's story 'The Mappined Life' still thought in 1914 'an acre or so of concrete enclosure' no substitute to 'a wolf or a tiger-cat for the range of night prowling that would belong to it in a wild state' (Munro 1976: 479–82).

Another far-sighted example of the provision of naturalistic conditions was the opening of Monkey Hill in 1925 with about 100 Hamdryas baboons, including about six females (Zuckerman 1932: 218). It hadn't in fact originally been intended to include any females, but the ones there bred, and it was decided to add thirty more in 1927. A great many deaths unfortunately occurred, some directly through males fighting over females, and from 1930 only males were kept (Zuckerman 1932: 216–23; Street 1965: 75).

And many other animals had opportunities for activity: elephants and camels provided rides; llamas pulled carts; cheetahs were taken for walks (Brightwell n.d.: 101). From the 1920s, the chimpanzees' tea party provided recreation for them (as well as humans), even though the chimps had to be trained to misbehave (Morris 1968: 68). There were unexpected examples of animal–human contact. The 'wolf man' (even if not fully approved of) used to take wolves for walks and wrestle with them in the way that John Aspinall does today with tigers at Howletts (Alldis 1973: 68–9; Brightwell 1952: 20–1).

Chalmers Mitchell's greatest innovation of all was realised in 1931, with the opening of Whipsnade, on an area of 500 acres in rolling Bedfordshire downs, with many extremely large and attractive enclosures (Street 1965: 78 ff.; Huxley 1981: 43–7). Other major zoos today that also run large animal parks, in some cases closed to the public to safeguard undisturbed breeding, include New York, San Diego, Melbourne, Antwerp, Bristol and Edinburgh.

Chalmers Mitchell was succeeded as Secretary by Julian Huxley (1970: 230 ff.). Huxley encouraged various researches, but most of his ambitious plans – a nocturnal house and a Lubetkin-designed elephant house – were overtaken by the war or, in the case of the zoo cinema he wanted constructed, by the Council's concern for 'the prestige of the Zoo as a learned society' (Huxley 1970: 237–40).

Huxley's successor, Solly Zuckerman, maintained London's scientific pre-eminence after the war with the founding of two research institutes in comparative medicine and reproductive physiology, now combined as the Institute of Zoology, just two of a succession of developments under the long secretaryship of Lord Zuckerman.

But in recent years, the exciting developments in zoos have been largely in America and Europe. There, though not in Britain, national or civic zoos have been founded which, thanks to a degree of financial support granted in Britain to museums but never to zoos – not even London – have been able to mount large, naturalistic displays. These include the enormous aviary at the Bronx, New York, or a model Antarctic setting at San Diego with real snow and purified air. Other examples are an African display at Chicago with convincing rainforest and tropical rainstorms, and a polar bear display at Tacoma (Cherfas 1984: 124–44). Sydney's chimpanzee enclosure is just one of many exciting developments in Australia. There is also a marvellous chimpanzee island at Arnhem in the Netherlands. The present director of the Arizona–Sonora Desert Museum has initiated some superbly naturalistic animal exhibits, and has also made plain his scorn for what he regards at the incorrigible British inability to throw off the menagerie mentality (Hancocks 1991a).

British zoos of the last thirty years nevertheless include some fine and individually-minded institutions, such as Jersey, Marwell, Howletts and Port Limpne, all dedicated to the captive breeding of endangered species. Chester, the largest zoo outside London, has become highly professional. The Woolly Monkey Sanctuary at Looe, Cornwall demonstrates how one primate species imaginatively and humanely kept can be not only of scientific interest but commercially successful. Other specialist institutions of real importance are Slimbridge (the first of many reserves of the Wildfowl Trust), the Norfolk Wildlife Park and the Otter Trust.

The Federation of Zoos in Britain was set up by Geoffrey Schomberg in 1966 to raise standards, and, to this end, it introduced compulsory inspections for its members. The passing of zoo legislation, which the Federation was pressing for from at least the early 1970s, was delayed until the 1980s (Durrell 1977: 148–9) by opposition from a rival organisation, the National Zoological Association, representing mainly the safari parks. This opposition, which had been led by Jimmy Chipperfield, then faded away, allowing the two zoo organisations to unite and support the Zoo Licensing Act of 1981 (Cooper 1987: 39).

1966 was also the year in which Jimmy Chipperfield, in partnership with Lord Bath, founded the first safari park at Longleat – in a way a whole new variant on the old-established deerpark (in the old sense of 'deer'!). *The Times* kindly helped publicity by its furious opposition to the very idea of keeping lions and not just deer on country estates, so that the opening of the 'Lions of Longleat' jammed the roads for miles around (Hart-Davis 1991). Safari parks have their enthusiastic supporters (Smith 1979: ix ff.) and also their severe critics (Jordan and Ormrod 1978: 152–7). The advantages of greater freedom for the animals have to some extent been offset by commercial managements' lack of real interest in the captive breeding of endangered species, and perhaps by a tendency to be less concerned for the interests of the animals kept than might appear to the layman. But still the idea of the animals running free and the public confined in cages – their cars – was not only good business, but updated the deerpark concept in at least two ways. At last in the twentieth century large animal parks had ceased to be a source of pleasure and refreshment merely for the very rich. And the safari parks provided a way in which dangerous carnivores could be kept in 'deerparks' – the only large mammals, almost, which even the 11th Duke of Bedford did not keep roaming free at Woburn.

Safari parks and more conventional zoos must work together conservationally, and this may be coming about. Longleat contributed six Père David's deer to a reintroduction project during the 1980s (Hart-Davis 1991). And Woburn of course, long before the addition of its safari park or 'gamepark', was a pioneer conservationally, and is today continuing the 11th Duke's conservational success by regularly breeding bongos, an endangered species of antelope (Tavistock 1983: viii).

Other specialist institutions have included aquaria, dolphinaria and, most recently, butterfly displays (Hughes and Bennett 1991). Dolphinaria raise particular ethical questions (Johnson 1990). In any case, despite some exceptionally fine zoos and animal parks, there have also continued to be many with much lower standards. This is even more so abroad, not least in America (Jordan and Ormrod 1978; Batten 1976), and also notoriously in Japan (WSPA 1991). But even so, a new professionalism and seriousness of aim has become apparent in the zoo world in the last quarter of a century.

3

ANIMALS AND THEIR RIGHTS

ANIMALS THEMSELVES

Animals possess rights (in my view) because of their nature as conscious beings; so we must consider that, briefly. If animals were only remarkable automata, as Descartes proposed (Rosenfield 1968; Cottingham 1978; Clark 1989: 14–15), it would not matter to animals how we treated them, any more than it matters to plants what we do to them (unless, of course, they have a 'secret life'!). I agree with Peter Harrison (1991) that, if we had no good reason to suppose animals could feel pain or suffer in any other ways, there would still be aesthetic reasons for not treating them 'brutally' or vandalistically, and I shall argue in Chapter 8 that there is a very important aesthetic and conservational respect owing to animals, and to anything else natural or artificial worth conserving. But I also believe (unlike Harrison) that individual animals claim our respect because they can feel, suffer pain, and experience pleasure, and because, in short, it matters to *them* how they are treated.

Psychologists and animal behaviourists have assumed for years that we have no good reason to credit animals with consciousness, and that there are good behaviourist reasons for condemning the excesses of anthropomorphism which early animal scientists, following in Darwin's footsteps, are supposed to have committed (Rollin 1990; Tudge 1991d: 200–3). In fact, as Rollin (1990) shows, those the behaviourists were reacting against (such as Romanes and Jennings) were far from unscientific. And in any case, as tends to happen with revolutionary movements, the behaviourist leaders' views were exaggerated or misunderstood by their followers (Rollin 1990: 74–9).

One very influential book in winning back scientific respectability for the study of animals' consciousness, *The Question of Animal Awareness* (1976) by Donald Griffin – himself a pioneer researcher into bat echolocation (Rollin 1990: 251 ff.) – received an extraordinarily unsympathetic review from the philosophically-minded psychologist Nicholas Humphrey (1977), underlining the strength and sophistication of the behaviourist position. Yet Humphrey himself seems soon to have 'changed sides' (Humphrey 1984; Humphrey 1986). Clearly it is possible to attribute too much to animals, to get carried away uncritically with their similarities to ourselves. The biologist Michael Fox (1986), for example, is accused by R. G. Frey (1983: 104–8) of doing just this.

Ironically, computers, and the resulting importance of cognitive studies, have played a part in reinstating the study of animal consciousness (Rollin 1990: 244–6); not only its scientific but also perhaps its philosophical respectability.

We have seen one example of philosophical scepticism about animal consciousness in Harrison's article. Such scepticism about, or at least low evaluation of, animal consciousness and thought stems particularly from Wittgenstein's emphasis on the enormous significance of human language, and how much of our experience – perhaps pain, and certainly thought – could not occur in its absence. Michael Leahy (1991) spells out at length the importance of Wittgenstein's contribution, as he sees it, to how we should perceive animals. Interestingly, Darwin himself was well aware of the argument that, because thought cannot occur in the absence of language, animal thought is impossible (Darwin 1901: 135–6). Darwin replied by quoting the philologist Whitney on how ludicrous it is to suggest that deaf-mutes can't reason until they learn sign language (Darwin 1901: 135n.), and he also quotes some interesting words of Leslie Stephen's: 'A dog frames a general concept of cats or sheep, and knows the corresponding words as well as a philosopher. And the capacity to understand is as good a proof of vocal intelligence, though in an inferior degree, as the capacity to speak' (Darwin 1901: 136). Stephen Clark (1989: 15) similarly argues that to rule out the possibility of thought's occurrence in the absence of language leads to considerable difficulties as to how, 'as a species or as individuals', we ever learnt to talk. People who have a lot to do with animals will probably be astonished that their consciousness could ever have been doubted.

The enormous interest today in the possible ability of chimpanzees and other apes to learn human language, and the discovery of our astonishing closeness genetically to chimpanzees, as well as studies of their behaviour (especially in the wild), have all helped to break down the supposed gulf between us. But whether or not other primates can learn human language (Terrace 1989), we should respect their enormous ability to communicate and the extent to which they seem to share our experience. I see human language as a lucky evolutionary breakthrough, inestimable of course in its consequences for humans, but still something assisted originally by physical factors as well as by mental ability (Lieberman 1991: 53–7), and as something that must have had its origins at least in animal communication.

Wild studies of chimpanzees have shown how many distinctions between us and them aren't in fact significant – using tools, and even perhaps jockeying for position or thinking politically (de Waal 1982)! Leahy (1991: 36–7) will have little of this; he tackles Jane Goodall on her anthropomorphic interpretation (in his view) of an incident she described in *In the Shadow of Man* (Van Lawick-Goodall 1973). He may be right, but it seems unwise to state dogmatically what apes can do and what they can't. Many animals may well have abilities we don't yet appreciate, like a disabled railway signalman's pet baboon in South Africa a century ago who, according to many witnesses, actually worked the signals for him for years (Nisbet 1990).

Of course animals vary – a chimpanzee and a dog are far more like us than either is like a starfish. The mental abilities of animals vary so enormously that we cannot regard them all as mattering equally. But so far as pain is concerned, we should give what are commonly regarded as relatively lowly animals the benefit of the doubt. Crustaceans can most likely feel pain (it certainly sounds like it from an incident described by the naturalist Gavin Maxwell); perhaps insects can (D.W. Morley 1953: 169, 174).

Those who work in zoos – like others who actually know animals, and care for them – appreciate how much their animals are individuals and have personalities, and how well they can express their feelings. If you try too hard to avoid anthropomorphism when you have to look after animals, you are likely to find yourself in difficulties, as the staff of the Yerkes Laboratories of

Primate Biology did, according to an interesting account by Hebb (1946). Another example of the importance of appreciating the individuality of different animals – if your job involves keeping them – was A.D. Bartlett's device for getting that escaped hippo back (Chapter 2).

Animals (to different degrees) have similarities to ourselves. They also of course have remarkable differences from ourselves – for example senses we cannot share, like those of bats, or dolphins (Nagel 1979: 165–80). All these are also a reason for respecting them, as is the recognition of all of the 'higher' animals at least – and it is difficult to say which we should count as 'lower' animals! – as separate centres of consciousness (Sprigge 1979: 118 ff.).

ANIMAL RIGHTS

The animal liberators at Versailles in 1792 came very close to claiming that animals had rights. And animal rights at that time were by no means a new idea. Several writers had already argued for them (Ryder 1979). Indeed in that very year, 1792, a book appeared called *A Vindication of the Rights of Brutes*. But its intention was ironic, to ridicule Mary Wollstonecraft's *Vindication of the Rights of Women* (1975), also first published in 1792.

Obviously the most important thing is that we recognise individual animals as mattering morally, and of course that we actually treat them properly. Does it really help to speak about their rights?

Historically not granting rights to animals meant something very practical and sometimes very cruel, that you could do anything you liked to them, and it did not matter (Linzey 1987: 96–7). This is virtually the position of the Roman Catholic moralist Joseph Rickaby (1976) writing in 1901, and before him of Descartes – though, as we have seen, if Descartes were right about animals' being automata you wouldn't of course be able to hurt them.

Even today to regard animals as having rights may well mean allowing them a higher degree of moral respect, or at least may pose a greater challenge to some of the ways in which we treat them (Linzey 1987: 2; Montefiore 1977; Clark 1977b). However, we must recognise that today many philosophers do not attribute rights to animals, and yet are still extremely concerned about how some of them are treated. Peter Singer, whose book *Animal*

Liberation (1990) is the most influential in the animal rights movement, does not believe in animal rights except in a popular sense. But he argues extremely strongly on utilitarian grounds for vegetarianism as a demonstration against the cruelty involved in most modern animal farming, and because vastly more food would then be available to feed the world's millions of starving humans (Singer 1990: 159–69; Tester 1991: 2 ff.). R.G. Frey (1980) is a philosopher who has argued against attributing rights · or even interests to animals, and he is not himself (unlike Singer) a supporter of vegetarianism. Yet he similarly would oppose factory farming (Frey 1983), and he was prepared to affirm animal rights in a popular sense strongly enough to add his signature to A Declaration against Speciesism (which affirmed animals' 'rights to life, liberty and the quest for happiness') at an important conference on the subject at Trinity College, Cambridge in 1977 (Paterson and Ryder 1979: viii).

To regard animals as having rights seem to me the best way of expressing the moral situation with regard to them. Is it not reasonable to look at animals ('higher animals', anyway) and feel that, from what we know of their similarity to ourselves, that they should be regarded as having rights: rights to be left alone if possible, or unless we have a really good reason for disturbing them; a right not to be killed, unless we have a very strong reason, such as self-defence, or perhaps food (certainly if it is essential food); and above all a right not to be hurt for no very good reason – certainly not for mere pleasure (Regan 1983: 232 ff.)?

Better still, animals should be not just regarded, but fully recognised, as having rights. I suggest that to state that animals should be granted rights is equivalent to stating that they have rights – moral or natural rights. It is to state, in strong terms, that their nature is such that they should not be treated in such and such ways – wantonly killed or hurt, locked up in bad conditions, and so on. To state this in terms of rights makes clear it is a matter of justice, not just of our being kind or considerate. Certain ways of treating animals are unjust, immoral – not just unkind.

Bentham regarded natural rights as nonsense – even 'nonsense upon stilts' in the case of 'imprescriptible rights' as in the French Declaration of Rights (Rollin 1981: 70)! Bentham was a student of the law, which seemed firm and objective, whereas rights were misty – you couldn't look them up. Further, Bentham considered that the law, like morality, should be based on utilitarian principles. Good laws increased the happiness of the majority, the total amount of happiness. Bentham was humane, and included animals within his utilitarian calculus. Their happiness counted too. Utilitarian principles are an excellent general basis for the law – Bentham was right in this. Similarly, indeed, on utilitarian principles much of what we do to animals is appalling, because of the suffering involved, as Singer recognises. But there is still the problem that utilitarian principles do not protect the minority, still less the single individual, whose unjust punishment, whose death even, might in some circumstances increase the total happiness greatly, but would still be wrong (Ryder 1989: 325 ff.). It would be grossly unjust.

Where does justice come from? To me, it is not a mere part of our culture. Do children have to be taught about fairness? Isn't this something a young child cares about without any adult prompting? 'It's just unfair' – to be punished by your teacher for something you didn't do. Now, although actual laws are probably based mainly, and quite rightly, on utilitarian principles, the law is also based on justice. An unjust law does not demand our moral assent. To have disobeyed, if you were brave enough, the former apartheid laws of South Africa, or an anti-Semitic law in Nazi Germany, could have been the morally right course to take.

British law recognises justice as not only one of its sources, but as, in the end, carrying greater weight. A fine example of this is the comment of a judge, Lord Mansfield, in 1777 in the case of a negro slave in England (his master was over from Jamaica) who was lodged in a ship in the Thames, and claimed Habeas Corpus. To a lawyer's argument that slavery wasn't strictly against English law because villeiny, a form of slavery, had never been abolished, Mansfield replied: 'I care not for the supposed dicta of judges, however eminent, if they be contrary to all principle . . . . Every man who comes into England is entitled to the protection of English law . . . whatever may be the colour of his skin' (Wedgwood and Nevins 1942: 88).

Ronald Dworkin (1978) has argued the close relationship of law and morality, and the application of his principles to animal rights is very clearly discussed by Bernard Rollin (1981). Animals should be seen as having moral rights simply because it matters to *them* – as they are not automata – what happens to them. It is not a matter of our deciding to grant them rights.

42

This of course is fine stuff; but who is going to decide what rights animals should have? I can imagine the list my dog Wolf would draw up. In fact he does claim – virtually! – a right to some part of his humans' meals as well as his own (which he usually postpones wolfing till he's seen what's available of ours), walks on demand, freedom to rid the neighbourhood of every cat around, and so on. And beds or chairs to lie on, of course. It's not only domestic animals that take advantage of such luxuries when available. Joy Adamson's lion Elsa used to lie on the bed. Where indeed does one stop?

Or, to be more serious, does it not make a nonsense of rights to grant them to animals and yet regard these rights as not even powerful enough to stop us using them, killing them, even eating them?

Well, unless the use we make of an animal really is, if not actually beneficial, at least not seriously detrimental to it, or essential to us, or better still both, then we should avoid it. Ideally we would not kill them and eat them, though in my view we can still properly use them, and keep them, if the animals concerned indicate that this is reasonably beneficial to them.

After all, human rights are not absolute. Indeed, if we take the American Declaration itself – 'we take these truths to be self-evident, that all men are created equal' – the gulf between fine ideal and reality may strike us. Even the best people have blind spots. Jefferson, who drafted the Declaration, was himself a slave-owner (though he did oppose the slave trade). All *men* created equal? Surely this means women too? But universal women's suffrage in America was only made mandatory in 1920 (Welland 1974: 244).

The right to life is not absolute. We kill people, even innocent people, in war. We do distinguish between better and worse, even in war, and condemn the killing of ordinary prisoners or the avoidable killing of non-combatants. We condemn torture.

Rights put, or should put, a protective fence round the individual (Rollin 1981: 67–86). There are certain depths to which we should not sink even in war, and there are certain things we should not do to animals ever, and other things we should not do to them if we can possibly avoid it. We are hardly going to stop even killing animals if it is a matter of our survival – but we should do it humanely.

Should we eat them if this is not essential? Not at least if this requires keeping them in grossly restricted conditions through life. With scientific, even medical, research, there are certain things we should not do to animals, however important from our point of view. We should not cause continuing, severe pain to an animal. An animal has a right at least to this degree of protection – and not to be hurt at all in normal circumstances.

We regard people as having these rights, and should regard animals similarly inasmuch as their needs are similar to humans' needs, because of simple justice.

ANIMALS' RIGHT TO FREEDOM

The special challenge, for zoos, is the right to freedom. After all, in zoos we don't cause physical pain to animals and we don't usually kill them.

There are several ways in which zoos should *not* defend themselves against the charge of overriding animals' right to freedom.

First, we should not do it by saying that the animals are not really unfree (e.g. in zoos). I agree with Rachels (1976), in a very useful article on the subject, when he notes that a 'bird who is released from a cage and allowed to fly away is "set free" in a perfectly plain sense' (Rachels 1976: 209). Similarly we speak of 'free-range hens', 'liberty budgerigars' (such as the 12th Duke of Bedford used to keep), and so on. Now I do in fact consider that really good captivity is not, to all intents and purposes, captivity at all, and will develop this later (in Chapter 7). But this is not a merely verbal point; it is the conditions which make the difference. It is possible for an animal to be captive – or to be free – in the same obvious sense that humans can be.

Second, we should not do it by saying that we humans are really unfree too, or about as unfree – say, because of the restrictions imposed by our civilisation – as Michael Boorer (1969: 155) puts it in a little book about wild cats. Mary Midgley remarks how she has found her students prone to claim that everyone is unfree because of the restrictions of civilisation, or the like (Midgley 1979: 285).

Third, we should not even do it, it seems to me, by saying that animals are not in fact free in the wild, though I am here disagreeing with a traditional zoo defence affirmed by Hediger (1964: 4 ff.), Hindle (1964: vii–viii), and a host of other writers.

44

What is normally claimed is that animals in the wild state are in fact restricted by all sorts of factors, and not roaming fancy free, as the uninstructed layman is supposed to imagine – and thus they are not free. But they are living their natural lives, however stressful or unpleasant those lives may in some cases be. Living their natural lives is surely the important sense of 'free'. Natural lives are not always unpleasant, as I shall consider in Chapter 5. But even if we thought they were, it would be less misleading to say that animals were actually better off in the unfree state we provide in zoos, rather than to say that that state is not unfree. Again, we can in fact provide conditions, in my view, which provide enough freedom to make life in a zoo 'captive' only in a technical sense. But this is only if the conditions are good. We can't make it captivity merely technically by verbal distinctions or definitions, but by improving the actual conditions. In bad captive conditions, animals are in an obvious sense not free to live their natural lives – and therefore, simply, not free.

Fourth, we should not do it either by clever manoeuvres to make the freedom challenge seem less important than it is. A good example of this approach is the concept of 'the five freedoms' as explained by the veterinary scientist John Webster (1991). Freedom *to* express normal behaviour is listed as merely the fifth of five 'freedoms', the others being freedom *from*, respectively: (a) 'starvation or malnutrition';(b) 'thermal or physical discomfort';(c) 'pain, injury or disease';(d) 'fear or distress'. Now indeed it is highly desirable to be free of these various states or experiences, and inasmuch as captive animals, even battery hens, are free of them, that is a great advantage of their captivity. But they are not 'freedom' in the obvious or central sense – not what those Versailles revolutionaries were talking about when they spoke of the animals having been robbed by tyrants of the freedom their Creator had intended them for. Such 'freedoms' may even be more important than freedom to live your normal life, or at least move about freely. But if we think that, let us say so clearly, not blur the issue by making 'freedom to' just one of five items. In Chapter 6 I will consider several criteria for judging well-being, criteria which are as applicable to humans as to other animals (otherwise I would suspect their validity). But try applying the so-called 'five freedoms' to humans; for example, with the case of an unfortunate guards officer who was imprisoned in Sweden on a drugs charge of which he was probably innocent. He remarked that even if he had been kept in a five-star hotel he would still have been a prisoner, and that was what he hated. He was free from malnutrition, free from thermal or physical discomfort, free from pain, injury or disease, admittedly *not* free from distress, though probably free from fear, and presumably not free to 'express most normal, socially acceptable, patterns of behaviour' (Webster 1991: 160). But by the 'five freedoms', he was hardly unfree at all; yet that clearly wasn't how he himself saw it!

I support Professor Webster's respect for the findings of ethologists and his view that they must decide what animals in fact need, and I applaud his honesty and realism in commenting that society must decide what its priorities are – whether, in particular, it is prepared to pay more for its food in order that the animals concerned are kept more humanely – and in stating that schoolchildren should visit farms, and be shown everything, because hesitation in showing them battery cages suggests we doubt 'the humanity of the system' (Webster 1991: 161–2).

I wholly agree with Professor Webster on the importance of natural behaviour as a criterion, as I shall argue at length in Chapter 6; and it is an important part of my case that if a reasonable amount of natural behaviour is shown by the animals we are keeping then we can reasonably assume that they are probably not missing their life in the wild – that they are not missing, in other words, their freedom in the strictest sense. So I am not disagreeing with him fundamentally. But I still think that the 'five freedoms' concept blurs the issue.

Fifth, how then can we defend zoos from the charge of overriding animals' right to freedom? By showing that we are providing what the animals need, and that our keeping them is in their interests. In James Rachels's interesting discussion of the concept of freedom (1976: 209–10), he shows well how, if humans have a right to freedom, animals should be recognised as having a similar right. But he suggests that both humans and animals need freedom not as an intrinsic good, but as something that serves their interests – both humans and animals should be free because only thus can they flourish. And he gives two examples to back up his view that they can only flourish in a state of freedom and not in zoos: first, the results of a study by Ratcliffe of conditions in a Philadelphia zoo in the 1960s, which showed how poor the health of various animals was (Rachels 1976: 210); and second, an account from a psychology textbook (published in 1967) about 'a baboon colony in the London zoo' in which 'bloody fighting, brutality, and apparently senseless violence' were observed, and generally a completely different picture of baboon society was given from what was found to be the case when baboons were later studied in the wild (ibid: 210).

The first of these examples, the Ratcliffe investigation, is indeed disturbing, but it is referring to conditions of now nearly twenty-five years ago, and there have been considerable developments since then, both in zoo medicine and in the quality of the conditions provided for animals, arising especially from new ethological study of their needs.

The other study is clearly Zuckerman's (1932), a study of the baboon colony at London Zoo which was a pioneering attempt to provide fairly natural conditions, but in which near-disaster ensued – I imagine because it was not appreciated then either how important it is to keep animals in their natural sex ratios (numbers of males to females), or, probably, what the ratios were for baboons. Zuckerman may have been misled about the nature of baboon society. But the importance of sex ratios has long been appreciated, and the incident Rachels is referring to occurred more than sixty years ago (and thirty years earlier than the date of the psychology textbook he quotes); and further, as is made clear by a leading recent primatologist, Alison Jolly (1972: 172, 195), Zuckerman reached conclusions justified by all the evidence available at that time.

So Rachels's demonstrations of how poor zoo conditions are – how badly, as he believes, they serve their animals' interests – do not bear the weight he puts on them. Reputable zoos would be found today, at least in many cases, to be providing conditions in which their animals enjoyed good physical health, and in which their lives were peaceful and in many cases organised in societies clearly similar to those they would have in the wild.

This will not be always true, but for a very striking example of improved conditions for primates, think of the gorilla colonies at Jersey (at which occurred the much-reported fall into the enclosure of a small boy, who was then seemingly protected by the silverback male gorilla), and at Howletts. The baboon problems at London Zoo are far from typical. (And, ironically, they resulted from trying 'too hard' to provide good conditions!)

Rachels having established, mainly by these two examples, just how bad zoo conditions are, goes on to consider what degree of freedom animals need in order that they can live natural lives, or show most of their natural behaviour. A lion, he suggests, would need its actual wild habitat; but hens no doubt wouldn't; they would surely have all they needed in a farmyard – in free-range conditions, in fact, rather than in batteries (Rachels 1976: 212–13).

I agree with Rachels about the hens. But he is assuming that the fact the one is domesticated and the other wild is a very significant difference between the hen and the lion. Perhaps surprisingly, I don't think this difference can be substantiated, as I will seek to show in the second section of Chapter 4. Poultry have retained much of the wild behaviour and natural needs of the Jungle Fowl, their wild ancestor, and therefore have very similar needs, which can be quite well met in a human-provided environment other than wild forest habitat. And similarly lions in zoos, and certainly any bred in zoos, are a little domesticated, and can also have most of their needs met in human-provided environments other than their actual wild habitat.

I entirely agree with Rachels that a lion shouldn't be in a cage in the traditional sense. But that doesn't mean that the only acceptable alternative is East African grassland, any more than, because batteries for poultry are wrong, the only acceptable alternative for them is actual forest.

I will look later at how we judge whether animals are in a state of well-being, and the sorts of ways in which they may be acceptably kept, as well as the serious reasons for keeping animals in zoos other than merely having them 'on exhibit' so as to make money by entertaining people. This is, in a sense, what happens in a zoo, and yet it also seems to downgrade what is happening in a good, modern zoo. Rachels also remarks that 'there is something very *sad* about a grand animal such as a lion or elephant being put on exhibit in a zoo, and being reduced to nothing more than a spectacle for people's enjoyment' (Rachels 1976: 213). When the animal is kept in really good conditions, this is just not the way it strikes me! I don't think of it as 'an exhibit'. I think of the animal as living – in varying degrees – in an artificial environment, but one, nevertheless, which provides (or certainly should provide) its main requirements, and has indeed various advantages over life in its wild habitat. It also has great disadvantages, which I fully recognise, and am in no way endeavouring to underplay – I shall discuss these differences between wild and zoo living in Chapter

5. But the animal (whether lion or elephant or whatever) is living its life in a zoo (not of course usually by itself) with its needs catered for, and where we can admire and study it. And its life there is also, in some cases, helping (in very substantial ways) to conserve its species (at Chester, anyway, if it's an elephant we are talking about). So Rachels's comment seems to me inapplicable to good zoo conditions, though indeed a very proper reaction to the sort of poor conditions we all know of, in the past especially, which are not entirely outlawed today, though they should be.

Rachels gives several other respects in which zoos, as he sees them, are clearly providing very poor conditions for the animals they keep (Rachels 1976: 210 ff.), but many of them quite inapplicable, in my view, to good, modern conditions. He speaks of their 'being taken from their natural habitats'. But this rarely applies today, at least to zoo mammals. Most of them are born in zoos, and are therefore not (as Rachels says) first 'frantic and frustrated', then 'listless and inactive', or 'vicious and destructive' – certainly not if trouble is taken to provide them with the kind of enriched environment that I will mention in Chapters 6 and 7 (Tudge 1991d: 211–40). Rachels speaks of how little they breed successfully, but the success of captive breeding is improving all the time. And he speaks of how many of them die sooner in captivity than in the wild. But this is very far from being the general rule. Rachels (1976: 212) also speaks of 'frustrated, impotent, futile' as an appropriate description for animals in zoos, 'and certainly [appropriate] to the monkeys trapped in the well of despair'. The Harlows' 'well of despair', which Rachels discusses (1976: 211–12), was a demonic invention, and putting monkeys in it for long periods appallingly cruel. But the state of primates and other animals in a good zoo cannot possibly be compared with it.

So I agree with Rachels that animals have a right to freedom, but suggest that 'freedom' may reasonably be rendered as 'being in an environment in which the majority of their needs are catered for' – as Rachels accepts is the case for chickens. And this, while it will certainly include the wild environment, won't necessarily include only this. How far any other environment, and such as we can provide, does provide most of their needs, and whether for 'most of their needs' to be satisfied is enough, is to a great extent a matter for ethological study. We should also recognise our ignorance (even though it is to some extent a diminishing ignorance) about what different wild animals have in their wild environments. But we can go a long way towards providing good conditions in zoos, and this, backed up by the now very serious conservational reasons for keeping animals, means that, given really good conditions, we are not trespassing upon their right to freedom.

4

WILDNESS, CRUELTY AND DOMINATION

WILDNESS

What do we actually mean by 'wild' when we talk about wild animals? The term carries an extraordinary range of senses and associations.

The most obvious characteristic of a wild animal is, traditionally, its being dangerous or fierce. This can of course be the case. To meet a tiger in the wild face to face could be a terrifying experience, though opinions differ on how actually dangerous it might be. Jean Delacour (1966: 122) describes how he nearly stepped on a tiger which quickly bounded away, but adds that he was in no real danger. On the other hand, a recent birdwatcher in Corbett Park had a similar experience and was killed, and many people are killed by tigers annually (Hamlyn 1987).

However, many wild animals are not dangerous, and some are not naturally nervous or afraid of us either (Midgley 1976: 90–100; Diamond 1991: 310). Animals on islands without natural predators often show no fear of man, which is why the dodo was exterminated so rapidly. Penguins similarly are easily caught because they fear potential predators (such as leopard seals) only in the water. Hence their temperamental suitability to life in zoos (and their readiness at Edinburgh Zoo to go on penguin parades close to the public). Those wild animals which are dangerous or ferocious are such because they need to be for survival. Ferocity has not evolved where not needed.

As well as being afraid, reasonably enough, of dangerous animals, we admire them – especially predators – for being dangerous. We are impressed by them as in Blake's Tyger:

What immortal hand or eye

Could frame thy fearful symmetry?

We have seen how ancient and widespread – with the Egyptians, Assyrians and Chinese, and even the Aztecs – is the royal fondness for lions, tigers (or their equivalents!) and birds of prey, and these continue as favourite emblems of kings and states.

Yet although we admire fierce animals, we also tend, with marvellous inconsistency, to blame them for being fierce or dangerous. We imply blame when we use a word such as 'vicious' of sharks or crocodiles, to take examples of Mary Midgley's (1979: 33). North (1983a: 101) gives us an example of even David Attenborough describing a caiman's 'long evil head . . . glaring at us malevolently . . .'. We use terms such as 'brute' or 'vicious brute' or 'wild animal' of an unreasonably violent human, implying that violent behaviour is characteristic of animals – wild animals, no doubt, in particular. We are critical of wild animals for being fierce when we should know that, if they are, they need to be and that in any case they cannot help it.

This popular sense of 'wild' is a hangover from the past. Any blame felt towards a wild animal for being fierce was never justifiable, but is even less so now because of how much more we know about various wild animals – wolves, for example (Midgley 1979: 26–7).

Another synonym for wild is 'untamed'. Again we are perfectly capable of admiring an animal for being untamed. 'Well-named, it is the real untamed and untameable savage', as Millais said of the European wildcat (Mallinson 1978: 137), and as an animal might be described outside an old-fashioned fair sideshow to bring in the crowds. Conversely, 'tame' is often used to mean 'dull' or 'uninteresting'. But at the same time we can use 'untamed' with the implication that the wild animal is in a rather reprehensible state, and could do with being removed from it, with being tamed. Southey caught this sense well, in these ironic lines addressed to a dancing bear:

> Besides
> 'Tis wholesome for thy morals to be brought
> From savage climes into a civilised state,
> Into the decencies of Christendom.
> (Southey 1985)

Another sense of 'wild' is 'disordered, chaotic, structureless'. We can admire this too, as in an expression like 'Let's have a wild party', but we might also use the word disapprovingly of the behaviour of a child showing tantrums or getting too excited. Presumably the word would have been used in this sense in 'wild men', a sense which now seems antiquated because we appreciate that it is inaccurate to speak of primitive people as wild or as savages because they in fact have organised societies, rules to obey, mythologies, cultures, indeed a degree of civilisation (Midgley 1979: 38).

We now appreciate how many animals have structured societies, even in some degree cultures – lions, elephants, primates, for example. Just as we would feel it wrong, as the European slavers did not, or as Captain Fitzroy of the *Beagle* did not, to drag people out of their society and culture, we would now be perfectly right to wonder if we can be justified in removing an animal from the wild – i.e. from the environment, in some cases from the society and culture, in which it naturally lives.

We clearly have conflicting attitudes to animals we call 'wild'. The term 'wild animals', and even more 'wild beasts', still carries suggestions of 'uncontrolled, dangerous, and unlike properly domesticated animals'. On the other hand, 'wildlife' carries all the positive and modern – and romantic – associations of 'wild': animals (and plants) living their natural and proper, uninterfered-with lives.

DO ZOOS KEEP WILD ANIMALS?

It is often assumed that the keeping of wild animals is inappropriate or immoral in a way that keeping domesticated animals is not, as by Jamieson (1985: 109) when he says there is a 'moral presumption against keeping wild animals in captivity' – not any animals. But just how wild are the wild animals zoos keep? Even the distinction between wild and domesticated animals is less real than often imagined. And zoo animals, while they are indeed relatively wild, are also, in my view, slightly domesticated.

Of the few animals that have been successfully domesticated (Bowman 1977: 34–5), most have been changed rather less behaviourally than you might expect. They were domesticated in the first place because of the suitability of their social structure and behaviour. For example, sheep were suitable because, unlike deer and antelopes, they were not territorial and had a single leader. Also, because of being adapted to mountain living, they weren't very fast-running or nervous of predators (Clutton-Brock 1981: 34). Reindeer, exceptionally among deer, could be domesticated because they tended to form large herds and were not territorial (ibid.: 132). Domestic pigs look extremely different from wild boar, but when given a chance to live under natural conditions, turn out to have retained an astonishing number of their natural behaviour patterns (Wood-Gush 1983: 196–8). Poultry similarly have retained a great deal of the natural behaviour, such as dust-bathing, of their wild ancestors, Indian jungle fowl (ibid.: 193–6). There is no great difference between these two kinds of domestic animal and their wild ancestors, nor is there in the requirements for keeping them properly.

Another way in which wild animals are not always so different from domestic animals is in being able to form relationships with humans. Ian Redmond has told us how the late Diane Fossey 'came to be accepted by the gorillas [that she studied in the wild] as a harmless presence and, later, almost an honorary group member' (Redmond 1986: 104). Obviously Jane Goodall has been accepted by wild chimpanzees. Other examples are lions and even a leopard successfully released by Joy Adamson (1962), and John Aspinall's boisterous games with tigers and respectful participation as a visiting primate in a gorilla group at Howletts Zoo (Aspinall 1986), or the meetings between humans and wild woolly monkeys – wild certainly in terms of their social relationships – at the Woolly Monkey Sanctuary founded by the late Leonard Williams (1969: 135).

These days a great many zoo animals have been bred in zoos, and this itself means that they are not strictly wild (Spurway 1952: 11). When animals breed, one is unavoidably selecting, to some extent, for animals that can adapt to captivity. And this clearly is a step towards domestication. So when animals are born in zoos, they are slightly domesticated. At the same time, zoos must try to alter them as little as possible. They should not be selectively breeding.

Where animals in zoos have been taken from the wild, the situation, as Hediger (1964: 154) emphasises, is never really satisfactory until they have settled down, have become adjusted to having people near, and fairly relaxed and tame. The importance of avoiding excessive tameness has also been recently emphasised, even avoiding it altogether where practicable, but the wildness retained, even in much more naturalistic conditions, will still be *relative* wildness (Tromborg *et al.*: 1991). Although this settling down, and becoming in some degree tame, is not a genetic change as such, it is a first stage of domestication. It was as much as elephants and cheetahs ever had in long centuries of semi-domestication.

At the same time, even though the animals are slightly domesticated, there is no reason why it should be impossible in the future in any specific case to reintroduce them into the wild, provided this is tackled carefully. Plenty of domesticated animals have gone feral. It depends on the individual. But it is all the more likely than an animal which has not been selectively bred should be able to go back to the wild, provided, if it is a carnivore, it is given opportunity to practise hunting and killing.

Now if it is acceptable to keep fully domesticated animals in captivity, why is it wrong to keep slightly domesticated animals? I don't of course mean in intensive systems, but these are such as no zoo should even contemplate; and as I have said, hens and pigs show most of their natural behaviour patterns given the opportunity (Cherfas 1987).

It is true that zoo animals have not (or shouldn't have) become genetically adapted to captivity as, in some degree, domesticated animals have. But as I have been showing, domesticated animals are much less changed than we might think (and certainly than, for example, Callicott (1983: 67) appreciates); and this is something zoos must take account of – it is a challenge to them to provide suitable conditions, given that their animals are not very different from their wild fellows.

I may seem to be trying to have it both ways – to say that animals in zoos are not wild and therefore it is acceptable to keep them; and that they are wild, and that therefore it is very useful conservationally, educationally, and so on, to keep them. But this is the situation, even if it is something of a tightrope to walk. There is no hard and fast line between wild and domesticated animals, and many examples of animals in a semi-domesticated state show this when they are in some relationship with humans, such as feral pigeons, robins and many wild birds, storks in Holland (where captive-bred birds have been successfully released), and so on.

Wild animals also have distinctive qualities – most obviously, in many cases, an enormous alertness and readiness to flee quickly; one only needs to try catching a house mouse as opposed to a pet one to appreciate this. But the fact remains that it is much too simple to dismiss the keeping of wild animals as something quite obviously objectionable in a way which is not applicable to domesticated animals.

CRUELTY

Of course animal keeping can be cruel. No one concerned with zoos would dispute this. But in view of the fact that the animals in zoos are relatively wild rather than wild, and as zoo animals and domestic animals have very similar requirements if they are being kept (as we say) captive, there is no good reason to regard *all* wild animal keeping as cruel.

What do we mean by cruelty? We could mean any one of three things:

1 Causing substantial suffering to another unnecessarily and unjustifiably.
2 Causing substantial suffering to another unnecessarily and unjustifiably, and taking pleasure in doing so.
3 Causing substantial suffering to another necessarily or justifiably.

The third kind of cruelty – the sort we must be meaning when we use a phrase like 'cruel to be kind' – hardly concerns us. To the extent that I defend the keeping of animals in this book, I am defending the keeping of them in what I regard as good conditions, such as no reasonable person is going to regard as cruel.

Even less, of course, should the second kind of cruelty – sadism, or cruelty for pleasure – have anything to do with zoos. But we should never forget how people can enjoy cruelty (Ryder 1979: 13–14), and that intentional cruelty – the arranging of animal fights, as at the marriage celebration in Dresden in the eighteenth century, or animal baitings, as arranged for James I at the Tower in the century before – have been one strand in animal keeping down through the ages. Far worse things have of course been done to humans through history, such as often to be almost beyond belief (Wells 1983). And far worse things than even in the worst zoos have been done to animals too (Vyvyan 1969: 27–49; Ryder 1975: 40–1, 82–4), often in the name of science.

Some of this last cruelty would be argued by some to be justified, and I am not suggesting that any of it was (or is) necessarily sadistic, but this is really by the way for our present concerns. What is much more relevant to a discussion of zoos is to realise that the sort of appalling examples given here by Virginia McKenna (1987: 30) are probably unintentional or thoughtless cruelty:

> The bear in an indoor cage four metres by three; the solitary monkey chained within its concrete pen; birds so confined that flight is impossible; the jungle cat crouching in the doorway of its wooden box inside its tiny concrete cage.

No doubt this was also the case with the examples of obvious cruelty in animal keeping in recent times given by Batten (1976) and by Jordan and Ormrod (1978: 160–1, 196–7).

Many acts of cruelty are perpetrated by people who ignore what they are responsible for because they do not see it, or can forget it (Pascal 1986). C.W. Hume's essay 'Blind Spots' offers striking examples of just how humans down the ages have been able to ignore what you would think were obvious cruelties occurring in front of them, from human examples, such as the scandal of child chimney sweeps, which it took 'half a century of agitation' to make finally illegal in 1840, to animal cruelty like the gin trap which only became illegal in England and Wales in 1958 (Hume 1982: 18–28, 45). John Newton, hymn writer and eventual opponent of the slave trade, was actually mate and then master of a slave ship for six years *after* his religious conversion. For those years he just accepted the way in which the slaves were transported – crammed together in irons, so that they could hardly 'turn or move' – conditions so bad that a quarter of the human cargo, on average, wouldn't survive the voyage (Hume 1982: 18–19).

It puzzles me, reading Salt's words in 1894 about London Zoo (1980), or Leigh Hunt's words fifty years earlier (Altick 1978: 318), why, for example, A.D. Bartlett, superintendent of London Zoo for forty years in the nineteenth century as we have seen, and clearly highly competent and humane, didn't feel the same. Did he just accept, was he just blind to the bareness of the cages for the big cats as they were in his day? Perhaps we just can't help having 'blind spots', but it is a possibility we should recognise. People can be admirable (like Bartlett) in much of what they do and yet fail in some particular respect, probably because of the need for us all to accept and follow tradition to a great extent. We can't be innovators in everything.

A related way in which we are enabled to commit actual violence, or simply be unmoved by cruelty of some kind, is by 'compartmentalising' – classifying people, or animals, into different slots, those who matter and those who do not, or those we like and those we don't, and especially those in our group and those who belong to the 'others' – the enemy, the other camp (Steiner 1985: 81; Woolf 1980: 387).

Cruel acts of animal keeping, as I say, are probably mainly a matter of neglect, of people ignoring what they should be attending to.

However, as an example of how inappropriate it is to dismiss all animal keeping whatever (or even all wild animal keeping) as cruel, here is a contrast with hunting. A book on aquarium keeping issues the warning that, if you have to catch a fish, you must avoid 'chasing' it round the tank because of the stress this causes to the fish. If this advice is correct, then pursuing a stag or a fox must be a process of extended stress-causing and thus cruel (Ryder 1989: 123). But the whole point of the advice to fish-keepers is to get them to avoid unwitting cruelty; Roots (1971: 3) gives similar advice about avoiding stressing birds if they have to be held. Avoiding causing stress is not everything. But at least we are in a different world from any where obvious cruelty is being performed; proper animal keeping should involve the greatest consideration for the animals concerned.

I quoted above Virginia McKenna's examples of obviously cruel animal keeping, one of them 'birds so confined that flight is impossible'. One can find Chaucer (1960: 524, lines 163–74), in the fourteenth century, saying that a bird in a cage, even a fine, golden cage and well fed, as you think, would far rather be in a forest eating worms, and the evidence is that he will go if you open the door – 'His libertee this brid desireth ay'. Chaucer is, to all intents and purposes, saying that such bird keeping is cruel. So, if people have a blind spot over this, Chaucer didn't share it. Chaucer is not objecting to the situation because the bird has an intrinsic right to be free. He is rather objecting because freedom would serve the bird's interests much better, and we know that because of the evidence the bird gives us. But suppose we provide the sort of roomy, naturalistic aviary that Francis Bacon, writing in his essay 'Of gardens' at the end of the sixteenth century, recommended: 'For *Auiaries*, I like them not, except they be of that Largenesse, as they may be *Turffed*, and have *Liuing Plants*, and *Bushes*, set in them; That the *Birds* may haue more Scope, and Naturall Neastling' (Bacon 1949: 195). Now if you opened the door of such an aviary, the birds would probably stay; and such a choice by them would surely be pretty good evidence that they were in a state of well-being there, that this sort of bird keeping isn't cruel. There are several criteria for judging whether a way of keeping a bird (or a lion or an elephant) is acceptable – indeed whether it is cruel or not – and these we will look at in Chapter 6. The choice the animal would make, where we can know this, is one way of judging.

A modern writer on bird keeping, Lockley (he is also a field naturalist), would I think agree with Bacon, and with Chaucer. He writes: 'give birds the maximum space you can afford . . . . Nothing is more depressing than to see a bird confined to a single perch in a tiny cage: this is sheer cruelty' (Lockley 1961: 16).

Leahy (1991: 201) disagrees that keeping a bird in conditions where it can't fly is cruel except where the bird gives, say, clear evidence by obviously distressed behaviour. I agree we can't be sure that it is cruel if the bird doesn't give us any indications – as the bird in Chaucer's cage would have done by just flying away, given the chance. But, as I shall emphasise in Chapters 6 and 7, we should give a bird or any animal the benefit of the doubt. The opportunity to move in its normal way, whether or not the animal takes it, is a basic example of this.

We must recognise that humans can be cruel, and the possibility of this with regard to animals, as well as other humans, needs to be guarded against. This is why there is a need for legislation to control animal keeping, for zoo inspections and a place for welfare organisations with a special interest in zoos. Nobody is infallible (Cherfas 1984: 226).

DOMINATION

It seems almost taken for granted these days that zoos are a demonstration of, or essentially motivated by, power and domination. 'Zoos are institutions of power' in the words of *Zoo Culture*, a book by two sociologists (Mullan and Marvin 1987). The point is made particularly eloquently and emphatically by Harriet Ritvo (1990) in her account of London Zoo and other zoos in the nineteenth century.

59

Certainly animals have long been royal and aristocratic status symbols, since at least the days of Assyria and Babylonia. Of course it is no coincidence that lions and tigers, and elephants, were the kind of animals especially prized by past rulers (as we saw in Chapter 2). But then merely having them as status symbols, if they are well looked after, is surely fairly innocent; as innocent as the activity of somebody who keeps an alsatian as a status symbol, but also looks after it properly. And it is an exaggeration to suggest all animal keeping is like this, even for rulers. Consider the British royal family's fondness for corgis, obviously kept because they like them, not because they are status symbols, or show dominance or power. Of course if an animal is kept as a status symbol, even though it is unsuitable to be kept or it is not being kept properly, then this is bad. But it is not the animal's being a status symbol in itself that matters.

Status symbols are no doubt something we all go in for, not just royalty. A ruler's capture and possession of animals as an expression of domination over his people or his enemies seems something rather different. It certainly does sound as if ancient rulers sometimes captured and kept animals to show their power, to judge for example by those boasts of Ashurnasirpal II, King of Assyria, about the apes, tigers, and elephants than he captured, and displayed to his people (Grayson 1976: 149). The first elephants to appear at Rome were in a triumph, and were presumably thought of as defeated enemies. Wild animals have sometimes been thought of as needing taming or subduing. Such an attitude clearly goes hand in hand with one of regarding primitive peoples as similarly needing subduing and civilising: the spirit of imperialism in fact. And the success of empire is well demonstrated by bringing home the spoils, which may include subject people themselves and subject animals. This is one element of meaning in the very word 'captive'. So it is perhaps no coincidence that the great days of London Zoo coincided with those of the empire.

My complaint with Dr Ritvo is that she pushes this kind of thesis too far. For example, she tells us that Raffles's intention in founding the Zoological Society was as a way of continuing his imperialist activities on his retirement from the east (Ritvo 1990: 205). Well maybe, but this seems to me, while theoretically possible as a motive, to be little more significant than the possibility that Ritvo may have had such subsidiary motives in writing her book as displaying her learning or lengthening her publication list. If she did, this matters little. She had more serious intentions, to inform her readers about a fascinating field, in which she succeeds admirably. Similarly, Raffles's expressed intentions were to found a scientific collection of animals. True, this seems for him to have included looking for further species which could be domesticated or introduced successfully to Britain – but this acclimatising was thought at that time to be a good idea.

Raffles's interests seem to have been genuinely scientific (Matthews 1976: 281), and quite enough to explain his possession of a private menagerie and desire to set up a new British animal collection. Gerald Durrell (today a distinguished naturalist and founder of a most seriously minded zoo) has told us in delightful books of his extraordinary passion, as a boy, for bringing home and keeping every sort of creature he could lay his hands on (Durrell 1959). I don't think this is quite an approach we would want to encourage in a child today. We might well feel Durrell shouldn't have been doing it – except, say, with invertebrates, which would hardly notice. But in no way was young Durrell collecting animals in order to dominate them, or show domination over anyone, or show power. He collected and kept them because he was fascinated by them and wanted to study them. And he did all he could to keep them well, to provide them with all they needed. It seems just as likely that Raffles's motivation in keeping animals and founding the Zoological Society was a grown-up version of Gerry Durrell's – he was fascinated by them and wanted to study them. Raffles may have been misguided or unjustified in these aims. But that is a different matter from being motivated by domination or imperialist tendencies.

Keeping animals can show domination or power through bullying them in the course of keeping them. This could mean the display of dominance or power over the actual animals, and by extension, perhaps, a display of power generally of the person concerned. This sort of thing certainly occurs, but it is ludicrous as an account of all wild animal keeping. Rodeos (Serpell 1986: 178–9) and, for example, demonstrations involving manipulations of alligators, which look terribly dangerous though they aren't (Cherfas 1984: 12–14), are clearly displays of human dominance or power over animals.

If zoos were primarily wanting to demonstrate dominance and power just by keeping animals, they wouldn't, for a start, bother to keep lemurs or bushbabies or even camels, still less rabbits, or a host of other animals to be seen in zoos. I grant that keeping gorillas and lions could carry a sort of power message, but I don't believe this is what happens as long as such animals are kept in the sort of conditions provided at, for example, Jersey, Howletts or Chester. For the accommodation or environment provided there for gorillas or chimpanzees demonstrates respect for them, the respect of those keeping them.

No doubt some writers will claim that just about any animal keeping demonstrates domination. That they can't be right seems to me neatly demonstrated by the enthusiasm for keeping budgerigars of Mr Geoff Capes, professional strong-man and champion shot-putter. He, at least, doesn't need to demonstrate his dominance – and if he did, he would hardly do it with budgerigars.

Now Ritvo sees the domination tendency as the driving force behind practically every activity or aspect of London Zoo: the allowing of animal rides (1990: 220–2), putting dangerous animals in small cages (in manicured parks with horticulture displays) (ibid.: 217), laying out the paths in an orderly way (so as to contrast the wild with human civilisation) (ibid.: 217–18), the provision of a guidebook (ibid.: 215–16), allowing the public to feed the animals (ibid.: 220), and the scientific classification of the animals (ibid.: 218).

Museums, as well as zoos, often try to lay out a clear recommended route for visitors, perhaps without realising the rhetoric of domination they are thus enunciating. Chester Zoo has beautiful flowerbeds, presumably also for imperialistic reasons. Where is Harriet Ritvo's evidence for all these interpretations? In my view, certainly, we do tend to dominate over nature too much, e.g. in our over-manicured parks. But it seems unfair to use this tendency in humans as a stick to beat zoos with in particular. The point is worth something, but far less than the weight Ritvo puts on it. London Zoo had numerous faults, as we saw in Chapter 2, but some of those Ritvo enunciates seem almost impossible to avoid!

Domination plays a large part in the management of various animals, such as dogs. To dominate a dog, as must be done for successful training, or even sometimes for mere survival (Mugford 1981), is not improper or unjust, and this is because the dog clearly flourishes in a regime in which he is 'dominated' – kept in order, like children in school, which many psychologists as well as teachers and the children themselves will explain they prefer; they want to be controlled. Juliet Clutton-Brock (1981: 55) notes that it is a 'capacity for active submissive behaviour that enables personal relations to develop between animal and man'. An elephant keeper has to dominate his elephant, though in an acceptable way, a way which goes hand in hand with a personal relationship with the animal, in order to control her; and this is something equally true of elephant keepers since ancient times, and in India and the east as here. This is why it was significant that the 'mahouts passed into the Roman service' (see Chapter 2 above). Only their own mahouts would be able to control the elephants, Romans or no Romans. Similarly with big cats such a relationship is possible. Of course this human-to-animal domination can be taken too far; but this psychological and social relationship is something quite distinct from the sort of symbolic domination zoo animals are supposed to signify, and is an essential part of the management of certain animals. (At least this is my view, but Marthe Kiley-Worthington (1990: 121–6), who as both ethologist and animal trainer is in a good position to know, disputes the need for domination even in circus training.) And domination in the sense of a psychological and social relationship is also part of our dealings with other humans. We are only able to show it anyway (I suggest) because of our own primate nature, which includes a tendency towards domination (and submission) within it.

The urge to dominate, to show one has power over others, is doubtless an important part of human nature, and equally, no doubt, this urge sometimes motivates the capture and keeping of animals. But to regard this as the major motivation behind all wild animal keeping is a wild exaggeration!

5

WILD LIVING VERSUS ZOO LIVING

LENGTH OF LIFE AND VIOLENT DEATH

So far as poor captivity – such as a bird's in a cramped cage – is concerned, Chaucer's statement of the bird's likely preferences could hardly be bettered. But Chaucer was not aware that robins, for example, normally live in the wild a mere tenth of their potential life span and have, any year, only a 50 per cent chance of surviving to the next (Lack 1970: 88–106). Thus it is only too true that captive animals often live longer than wild ones; for many animals it must be true that only with man's protection have they any chance of dying of (as we say) old age.

Instead of Chaucer's miserably confined bird, consider a budgerigar allowed out frequently to fly about the house and enjoying a good relationship with his owner (or one in a roomy aviary at a zoo, or in a garden designed by Bacon). If the actuary's tables for wild-living budgerigars are anything like those for robins, then such a well-cared-for budgerigar has a good bargain in terms of total pleasure or satisfaction from living.

The risks in later life for large mammals like lions or chimpanzees are probably much lower than for small birds or rodents, but lions and chimpanzees will still have a high death rate in early years (as humans did before modern medicine). About 20 per cent of lion cubs survive in the wild to maturity; most cubs dying of starvation.

In view of the high early loss even of animals which are fairly safe once they are mature, it must be the case that many animals in zoos would, in the wild, have died young. If we assume that, at least sometimes, life in a zoo is satisfactory, Rachels's feeling of sadness about it is, at least in these cases, inappropriate. If the animal is living a reasonably enjoyable life and would have been dead if not in a zoo, there seems little to be sad about.

David Jones (1987) has provided an almost awesome account of the dangers, both natural and manmade, faced by wild-living animals. We know, from natural selection, that all animals (like other organisms) have a much higher rate of increase than is necessary merely to replenish their numbers. So most of those born must be dying early from some cause, else population levels would be exploding like those of humans (and, just occasionally, rodents') (Darwin 1968: 116 ff.).

We tend, when we meet an injured wild animal or a dead one, to feel sympathy and regret. We are still recognising injury and death, however necessary biologically, as misfortunes and often causes of suffering to the animals concerned.

Perhaps many animals suffer mentally from their fellows' deaths. A dog can feel the loss of a human, so is likely to feel similarly the loss of another dog. Behaviour is sometimes observed in birds that looks like an expression of mourning; as we know that swallow mates, for example, choose each other, and thus obviously know each other as individuals, it seems likely that they will experience some sense of loss on each other's death (Mead 1987: 360–1). If so, life in the wild is likely to include a good deal of suffering, even if short-lived compared to our own, at the loss of mates or companions.

Of course, not all animals in zoos live to old age, or, sadly, can be allowed to. As the breeding of captive animals improves and approaches the rate of increase in the wild, either birth control or the killing of surplus animals is likely to be necessary (Cherfas 1984: 119, 122). The possibility of animals' suffering from the loss of companions is an additional reason for avoiding killing captive animals as far as possible. But at least if any animal has to be killed in a zoo it should be a humane death. Death in the wild can involve suffering.

Death can itself be violent, or slow, as from injury or disease. Nature red in tooth and claw – even just a mouse caught and played with by a cat – isn't pleasant. A wild cheetah will provide her cubs with a living, injured young gazelle to practise hunting on (Ammann 1984: 111). The horror of violent death is caught by Stubbs's painting of a horse in the moment of attack by a lion, its head turned with a look of absolute terror (Taylor 1971: Plate 61). This may be to get things out of proportion, to assume violent incidents make up the major part of what happens in animals' daily lives, when in fact this cannot be the case. The terrified horse would only be in this state for a minute or two. It might have had frightening near-escapes before, but could not have been caught in the way it had this time, else it wouldn't have lived to be caught again (Midgley 1979: 25 ff.). The violent contrast between the horror and the usual quality of the horse's life may be what upsets us so much. It is also likely that in many cases of violent death, such as a wildebeeste eaten alive by hyaenas, the victim is in a stupor through the action of endorphins or some similar mechanism. This accords with much human experience of serious injury in the heat of battle or the like causing no pain until later (Taylor 1981: 175). But on the other hand, a mouse caught and played with by a cat must feel extreme stress, as presumably any animals do in situations where they are clearly struggling desperately to escape from predators.

So the fact that an animal in a zoo is protected from the violence and other dangers of natural life is not an aspect of captivity to be scorned. David Jones (1987) correctly emphasises how many of the 'challenges' of the wild 'would not usually be tolerated in a captive situation'. We are in some degree conferring on our captive animals the protection from violent death and from disease which civilisation has (to some extent) conferred on ourselves. On the other hand, captive animals have not (usually) 'asked' to be rescued, and the protection we offer cannot compensate for a life of dullness and boredom. If we can successfully compensate for the loss of the purposefulness of wild living, which I will look at further (it is mainly a problem with the more exploratory, opportunist animals, as we will see in Chapters 6 and 7), then the captive animal has by no means a bad bargain.

ARE ZOO ANIMALS HEALTHIER THAN WILD ANIMALS?

Take health first in the straightforward sense of freedom from infection or injury. Wild animals are anything but free from such problems. A single individual can be astonishingly heavily parasitised (Rothschild and Clay 1961: 17). Wild animals can be very much worse for wear compared to their protected, medically attended cousins in captivity; for example a wild lion compared to a zoo or safari park lion (Smith 1979: xv).

Many wild animals must be able to cope with their infections, but those who cannot die. If serious ill-health isn't obvious among wild animals, that is because a seriously unhealthy wild animal is soon a dead one. The middle course open to humans and well-cared-for captive animals is not an option.

Still, mild states of ill-health can cause discomfort without causing death. A successful parasite in biological terms is one that doesn't kill its host – but it may well cause discomfort or worse. Captive animals are clearly well off in that medical aid to ease minor suffering should be available.

But zoo animals can have their own particular health problems. The stress of being captured and transported can make an animal more liable to serious parasitic infection. Conditions in zoos can aid the spread of parasites, or else necessitate the provision of a dull, sterile environment in order to restrict their spread. Ungulates kept in small paddocks are prone to parasitic infection; cats can be, when kept in other than very large enclosures. Until recently, they were thought to require concrete or tiles, easily washed and sterilised – and thus robbed of familiar and carefully deposited smells. It has now been found that deep litter, in addition to other advantages, prevents parasites' eggs surviving (Chamove *et al.* 1982). Primates, being nomadic in the wild, lack the tidy, sanitary tendency of many carnivores, who deposit their droppings in regular spots away from their 'living area'. So in captivity primates have often been thought to need drearily sanitised conditions, but here too the new findings concerning deep litter have improved the situation (Chamove *et al.* 1982).

An animal can also be exposed in a zoo to infections that it wouldn't face in the wild (Dunn 1968). Antarctic penguins live naturally in a highly aseptic climate, but in zoos can die from aspergillosis, to which they lack resistance. Primates, especially apes, can catch tuberculosis and measles from humans. Disease or injury can arise too from zoo conditions. Rhinoceroses can rub their horns against unsuitable objects. Caries can develop from eating the wrong food, as was common in the past, when public feeding was allowed, with bears and elephants as well as primates, and even rhinoceroses (Cave 1985).

So if we regard health primarily as a state of freedom from disease and injury, zoo animals are winners, but not by as wide a margin as might be expected.

Health is, however, quite a tricky concept and not straightforward to define. For example we often use the term 'health' in two different though related senses, which are worth considering in relation to zoo animals.

There is what we may call 'health A', the opposite of being ill (as in the prayer book phrase 'in sickness and in health'). And there is 'health B', to possess which is to have the ability to cope with infection, to keep returning to a state of 'health A' whatever infections, say, occur. Probably we would use the adjective 'healthy' more in the second sense: we wouldn't say 'Are you still ill or are you now healthy?' We recognise that you don't necessarily cease to be healthy by being ill, provided that the latter is a temporary thing, something you are demonstrating your ability to cope with (Downie and Telfer 1980: 15).

Now with regard to 'health A', which can be removed by relatively minor disturbances, well-cared-for zoo animals may indeed be healthier: they have veterinary care to restore them quickly to a state of health, and in any case are mostly protected from situations which cause injuries. But it is only 'health A' which we can be sure they possess – most of the time. Zoo animals may possess 'health B', but their artificially protected situation prevents our really judging.

We would probably regard someone who remains well without aid from their doctor as healthier than someone who remains well but only through frequent medical dosing. Somebody who remains well not only without medical aid but through difficult physical situations – physically or mentally demanding – would be rated healthier again. And indeed, you do not need to remain 'in perfect health' to be judged basically healthy – healthy in the important sense much more than someone who suffers not a scratch but only because they never face situations you can cope with. The wild lion is in the position of a person who faces demanding situations – the arctic explorer, say, or the active sportsman. If we rule these last to be unhealthy because of their 'scratches' or even more serious injuries, we are judging by externals or trivialities, as we are if we rule the wild lion to be unhealthy compared to the artificially protected one in the zoo.

'Health B' is close perhaps to 'fitness' as we would ordinarily use the word. The captive lion, however healthy, is unlikely to be as fit as a wild lion. The captive animal must almost certainly be obtaining less exercise that its wild fellow; it must be less 'in training'. A captive gazelle or lion undoubtedly lacking the fitness of its wild fellow could hardly be said to be healthier. It could be happier; it could be relatively very healthy. But healthier, surely not. Some of the arrangements for carnivores at Glasgow Zoo, such as devices to require searching or even climbing or leaping for food, could do a good deal to increase the fitness of the animals concerned (Tudge 1991d: 223–8).

One way in which the captive antelope, if not the lion, could well be happier is in its freedom from stressful situations. But this again hardly makes the captive animal healthier than the wild one, in that a mild degree of 'physiological stress' is a set of physiological events in the animal which enable it to cope with difficult natural situations (Dawkins 1980: 57; Fiennes 1965: 167).

But severe stress is certainly detrimental: a well-looked-after captive animal is no doubt healthier, as well as luckier, inasmuch as it escapes this condition of extreme stress which will occur sometimes in the wild. (It can also occur in captivity (Fiennes 1965: 170).)

Having no cause, however, to show the milder earlier reactions of 'physiological stress' hardly qualifies the captive animal to be regarded as healthier than its wild counterpart, though it is arguable that it may be happier without this milder stress too. Dawkins makes the point that 'some lesser stress symptoms . . . may be an indication of well-being', and even better physical health (Dawkins 1980: 62). This is perhaps only to be expected with animals, being the case with ourselves: human 'fitness' in the normal 'health' sense includes the ability to respond to at least mildly stressful situations – such as occur in sport. Again, devices which encourage animals to seek for or work for their food are likely to help the captive situation (Tudge 1991d: 211–40).

We might well feel, with humans, that a full definition of good health includes 'leading a full life' or 'leading a normal life' (Brockington 1958: 19). If we would, then a similar definition should be appropriate for any particular kind of animal, in which case the captive animal, obviously necessarily not leading a normal (i.e. natural) life, seems by definition less than healthy in the fullest sense. This should be seen as a challenge to provide the animal with a kind of captivity which approaches or substitutes for its natural life to the greatest degree possible.

FOOD, PLEASURE AND PURPOSE

To be provided with food, even the best, is a mixed blessing. It is a gain not to go short or starve, as many animals in the wild do (D. Jones 1987). But food seeking makes up much of an animal's life: to a great extent its method of obtaining food will have 'formed' it anatomically, physiologically and behaviourally. So having food provided means deprivation of a main purpose in existence, and of likely opportunities to engage in activities whose performance would be accompanied by, psychologically, a sense of purposefulness. This is probably not much of a problem for herbivores such as ungulates, who can continue to spend much time eating as they would in the wild, and are also often occupied, as in the wild, by their social relations. It is opportunists like bears and dogs who are likely to come off worst (Morris 1964).

We must to some extent be depriving predators of a source of pleasure or satisfaction by providing them with food 'on a plate' (not that some – lions, for example – aren't perfectly capable of grabbing any opportunities that present themselves, like a passing owl or even a careless peacock). They don't necessarily 'experience' any deprivation; they just fail to have experiences which would give them satisfaction. Humans' enjoyment of hunting is at least prima-facie evidence for non-human predators' enjoying hunting too.

The whole operation of seeking food, the animal's appetitive behaviour, is likely to be pleasurable or satisfying. And any animal, engaging in any of the 'important business of life' – e.g. feeding, nest building, mating, the establishing of social relations – is probably experiencing a sense of purposefulness.

Our feeling of frustration in failing to complete some task is (like pain, pleasure and boredom) no doubt biologically useful. So it is likely that animals can feel similar frustration to ours – say if a lion has a meal to eat, but keeps being disturbed by hyaenas.

Probably very important also are a sense of security and a sense of belonging. The Harlows' (very inhumane) experiments showed how infant monkeys need a source of security, a source of confidence (Rowell 1972: 135 ff.). Dogs can show their general sense of unease by failing to groom themselves. Of course an animal should be able to enjoy this sense of security, and indeed many other pleasures, in good zoo conditions.

Obviously in the wild there are all sorts of discomforts, problems and very real dangers: parasites, insect bites, problems of finding food – the unpleasantness of sometimes going without or actually starving – and so on. But we have our problems too, and for most of us, most of the time, they are not overwhelming. What often prevents nervous breakdown is a sense of purpose and a sense of security. Although war is a cause of appalling suffering, the suicide rate tends to go down in wartime, presumably because people have more sense of purpose, and of comradeship and belonging, and these more than compensate for the presence of extra hardships in preventing extreme depression. A state of non-depression, a state far from that extreme depression which could lead to suicide, is likely to accompany the state of being very busy: having things to get on with.

It is probably important to many animals, too, to have plenty to get on with, which wild animals obviously normally do, as well as having a sense of security and, where appropriate, companion-ship, a home base and proper relations with one's companions in the case of a social animal. Marian Dawkins mentions experimen-tal findings that sheep are stressed by situations such as being put in a truck or chased by a dog but nothing like as much as they are stressed by simply being separated from the rest of the flock (Dawkins 1980: 59), which bears out what I am suggesting.

And life in the wild is often not all 'business' – essential activities for survival, compensated for only by a sense of purpose such as I have been proposing. There are also plenty of reports of animals enjoying themselves in a direct way – otters sliding down banks, badgers playing leapfrog, and so on.

So in brief, to give the provision of regular food and safety from predators and other dangers, not to mention discomforts, as pure and simple advantages of captivity over against life in the wild is to leave out certain related disadvantages which go hand in hand with such advantages: the loss, in particular, of purposeful living.

A tacit admission that wild life must be reasonably pleasant is that no one (not even those who feel they have a right to capture any animals they wish to, or need to) would suggest it was cruel or unkind *not* to capture any animal, to leave it in the wild (except in cases of certain injured or abandoned individuals). It is agreed that we are not injuring animals by merely leaving them alone (Benson 1978: 547).

However, although it will not do, in view of these considera-tions, to regard captivity as acceptable simply because it is likely to be pleasanter than the wild (Salt 1980: 40–50), we also have many indications that some animals can be in a state of well-being in captivity. In many cases it is possible to provide conditions of captivity which do a lot to compensate for the loss of the positive side of wild existence. But we need to recognise that positive side to realise our responsibility to provide suitably enriched captive conditions.

EVOLUTION AND ADAPTATION

All animals are adapted to life in their natural habitats (the 'wild'). From this we might presume: (a) that they are well off there; (b) that they are not likely to be well off in captivity; or even (c) that it is virtually impossible for them to be well off in captivity.

Point (c) is frequently claimed (Adams 1987); but with regard to many animals it is, for biological reasons, mistaken, as I will now try to show. To do this, I want to look more closely at the indeed indisputable fact that wild animals are adapted to their environment, and consider whether (a) and (b) or (c) do in fact follow from it.

Animals' adaptations are indeed most striking, and are the product, at least in some cases, of millions of years of natural selection. However, the characteristics of animals – their sense organs, body coverings, communication systems, etc. – are by no means entirely the product of the habitat or the environment, as Richard Adams (1987), for example, seems to suppose. Animals' characteristics all have their present form as a result of alterations made to appropriate features of the animals' ancestors, alterations which, as a result of natural selection, have occurred so as to make those features fit the environment, or fit a changed environment, more closely. The alterations which have produced the present adaptations could only be made (by natural selection) on the features which happened to be available. Thus in a way, all the various adaptations of animals – anatomical, physiological, even behavioural – are makeshift arrangements, though often 'inspired' makeshift showing, as it were, the utmost 'ingenuity'. A few 'large-scale' vertebrate examples to illustrate this are gill arches converted to jaw bones, fins converted to legs, inner ears developed probably from something like a lateral line system, and so on. Animals are not perfectly adapted; they are, so to speak, never designed from first principles, but rather themselves 'adaptations', in the sense of 'adaptive alterations', of what went before.

One human example of imperfect adaptation is the tendency to suffer arthritis around the area of the hip bones, partly as a result of our being a two-legged 'vertical' animal converted from a four-legged 'horizontal' one. As de Beer emphasises, animals cannot be perfectly adapted, for if they were, evolution, which is essentially the improvement of adaptations, could not occur (de Beer 1972: 10). In some cases certain species, as a result of environmental changes they fail to adjust to, are in varying degrees ill-adapted (ibid.: 10–13).

Furthermore, all individuals of any particular species differ slightly, having slightly different sets of genes, so that they are not equally adapted, even though to a great extent they are all inheritors of millions of years of natural selection. Even if one could identify a pair of animals almost perfectly adapted to their environment, their young would not be to the same extent, or to the same extent as each other, for all get dealt a slightly different genetic 'hand'.

As evolution is a matter of the differential passing on of genes, so that different genes gradually become more widespread through the gene pool of any particular species, as a result of the individuals carrying them being slightly more successful in reproducing, the welfare of individual animals is hardly going to be benefited by evolution except in that genes aiding welfare also enable the animals carrying them to reproduce successfully, which also includes surviving long enough to reproduce. There seems no way in which the welfare of animals past breeding age can be selected for, except where their welfare assists younger relatives of theirs to reproduce. However, as animals presumably cannot live and reproduce efficiently if they find life too difficult – if they get too disturbed, or too miserable, or are hurt too much – there will be selection of characteristics producing some degree of well-being, perhaps some degree of happiness (Darwin 1929: 146).

Animals (perhaps certain more adventurous or exploratory individuals of a species) will sometimes move into new habitats, or may adopt some new behaviour. This may be a substantial factor in evolution (Hardy 1975: 37–45; Ewer 1953: 117–19). In the new habitat or the new niche, selection will operate to improve adaptation to it, but this will be a slow process, and the development will be occurring in a population, not in any single individuals. Some or all individuals may well be rather ill-adapted in the early stages of moving into a new habitat or a new niche, as in the situation of an environmental change which forces upon a population a need to adapt, if it has enough genetic adaptability. Failure to adapt in such circumstances is likely of course to result in extinction (de Beer 1972: 5–6, 10–13).

Animals, perhaps partly because they are all (including humans) 'previous models' 'updated' with numerous adaptations, have varying degrees of adaptability. Some move readily into new environments created by man (like cities); others cannot adapt so easily. Here I am thinking mainly not of genetic adaptability, but of cultural or behavioural (or physiological) adaptability, an animal's ability to adjust to changed circumstances within its own lifetime. Some become tame easily, some can be trained easily, others not. Some can change their habits easily, for example, switch to different kinds of food (of course, within limits); some (like koalas) cannot.

Sometimes an animal which moves into association with man is moving into a new niche evolutionarily, as with sheep and dogs. Although our domesticated sheep and dogs are to a great extent the products of artificial selection, what man does in selecting certain characters and as a result increasing greatly the numbers of certain genes can be seen as a way in which those genes are manipulating him (not of course in any sense consciously or voluntarily). If we measure evolutionary success in terms of numbers of individuals of a particular species, as we well may, then we can see dogs as enormously successful where their wild conspecifics are failing (Clutton-Brock 1981: 191). This does not mean that domestication is necessarily morally right. But it cannot be regarded sensibly as 'biologically' wrong, and we might regard it as biologically successful, of course depending on how we decide to measure biological success.

Therefore, although it is true that animals are adapted to their natural habitats, and to their ways of life in those habitats, and although it is likely that if we take them out of their natural habitats and keep them in captivity they are likely to have much less of what they need for well-being, this is far from being an absolute rule. It is unlikely that any animals require all the features of their habitats. Some may be vital; all hardly can be, if only because all animals are likely to be somewhat adaptable.

We should not regard ourselves as having *carte blanche* to collect or capture any animals we like. As a working rule, we should assume an animal is well off in the wild, is best off there, and is likely to be much less well off in captivity. But this does not mean we know that such applies to every case. It is quite possible that some animals can be kept quite well or very well in captivity; and we can only really judge by various evidence and approaches such as I attempt to outline in Chapter 6.

6

JUDGING WELL-BEING

People sometimes comment that we cannot know whether animals are in satisfactory conditions because they cannot tell us. But they do tell us, by their health, the readiness with which they breed, how much of their natural behaviour they show, and how much abnormal behaviour they engage in, as well as by what can be called 'direct indications'. Weighing the findings of the criteria against each other, we can establish pretty well how satisfactory any particular conditions are, and whether any particular kind of animal shouldn't be kept at all.

HEALTH

Of course zoo animals should receive proper veterinary attention: we have a responsibility towards them to care for them as best we can. Ill-health and injuries are presumably unpleasant for them as for us. Good physical health is a sign of conditions being at least fairly good. It is an indication of general well-being, in some degree even of mental health.

Length of life is obviously relevant; occasional individuals may die early, however good the conditions. But as the zoo situation is free from the dangers of wild life – predators, possibility of starvation, drought, and so on – animals ought to live out pretty well their potential life spans. If animals of a particular species have generally short lives in captivity, or certain kinds of captivity, this would be an 'indictment' under the health criterion.

Important though physical health is, we have seen how some animals can be provided with hygienic conditions which are dull and sterile. It is bad if our keeping them in good health requires such a cost. There was over-emphasis in the 1960s on the need for

76

great hygiene and the danger of infection. This was one reason why chimpanzees tended to be kept only in pairs. Today it is recognised that it is better to have chimpanzees in a group, even at a higher risk of infection; but luckily such a choice does not have to be made, thanks to developments such as the proved effectiveness of deep woodchip litter as a bacterial inhibitor as well as a 'behavioural enhancement' (Chamove *et al.* 1982). But we must be responsible and put the animals' interests first; hard standing may be very good for horses, because of hoof wear as well as helping to avoid parasite build-up. They should not be kept on grass just to please the public (Tong 1973: 53). But presumably they ought to be on grass sometimes.

Mental health is likely to include the living of a satisfactory life: this connects with the natural behaviour criterion. Vets are much more concerned now than formerly with all aspects of animals' well-being, not just their physical health in a narrow sense.

We don't want an animal to be unduly stressed. But as we have seen, while serious stress is detrimental, an occasional mild stress is quite good for health, and the ability to show a mild stress reaction itself part of health. It is a problem what exactly we can do for zoo animals in this regard, but the matter should be given attention.

Stress can be measured physiologically, and physiological indications could well be regarded as another important criterion of well-being, as Dawkins gives them as a criterion of suffering (Dawkins 1980: 55–68). I prefer to include them as a supplement to health, in regard to zoo animals, because zoos tend to avoid interference of a 'laboratory' kind with their animals as much as possible, though anaesthetising, often by dart gun or blowpipe, by a veterinarian is sometimes necessary. But such physiological evidence as a rise in the heartbeat, or a build-up of adrenalin, would be useful and important.

Physical health is one very important indicator to be used in conjunction with the other indicators I look at below (and it overlaps with some of them, such as natural and abnormal behaviour). To judge an animal's health accurately requires the fullest knowledge of that animal's biology, natural behaviour, natural way of life and environment, that we can manage.

BREEDING

How far does the fact an animal breeds inform us, or our desire to encourage it to breed dictate to us, what the animal's conditions should be? And how far does an animal's breeding indicate that it is in a state of well-being?

Hediger speaks of breeding as the 'only one criterion for suitable biological conditions', even suggesting it is like 'arithmetical proof to the mathematician' (Hediger 1964: 37). This weights breeding as a criterion too highly, but it is still very important, for several reasons:

1 Breeding is an important and central part of natural behaviour, part of the 'full life' of an animal (though not all animals would breed in the wild).

2 It can be very difficult to get 'wild' animals to breed in captivity. Domestic animals presumably became domesticated partly because of their readiness to breed in captivity or close to man, but very few animals ever have been domesticated. With an animal that has not, by selective breeding, been adapted to life in captivity – even though there must be some adaptation, necessarily (Spurway 1952) – one is most likely to achieve success (if it does not breed readily) by study of its breeding in the wild, and by varying the captive conditions as seems appropriate or promising. Thus one is here either providing conditions like the wild, or else an effective substitute for the wild.

3 Many animals can be easily put off – for example, they may kill their young if disturbed or upset – so their successful breeding is some indication that at least the parents are relaxed. (A cheetah, for example, can be put off from breeding if leopards are near.)

4 Successful breeding is some indication that the animals concerned are not deleteriously inbred.

Some problems with breeding as a criterion

First, breeding as a criterion is hardly applicable to domestic animals, both because it is likely that an initial readiness to breed close to man was one condition leading to their domestication in the first place, and because they will have been selectively bred to breed well in captivity. Bitches breed very readily even in bad

78

conditions: hence the scandal of 'puppy farms'. Gerbils, for example, even though only recently domesticated, and to a much lesser degree, still have become domesticated partly because they breed so readily. Again some domestic animals such as pigs and poultry not only survive but breed in horrifying conditions (Singer 1990 107–19; 125–9; Johnson 1991). A sort of 'forced breeding' can be practised with domesticated animals; its occurrence is the very opposite of any indication of their conditions being good. Now we are likely (unwittingly) to be selectively breeding our relatively wild zoo animals precisely for breeding in captivity (Spurway 1952) so perhaps this point about domesticated animals could apply in some cases to zoo animals.

Second, some animals breed in apparently bad conditions, for example lions in 'rabbit hutches' (Keeling 1984: 3; Bareham 1973: 93). Hediger gives examples of lions and certain other mammals, such as an anteater, in small 'menagerie-type' cages, and also birds of prey in cages they cannot fly in (Hediger 1964: 37–8). Leonard Williams once spoke of Rhesus monkeys which bred readily at London zoo as being comparable to the Victorian working class in their ability to breed in slum-type conditions (Williams 1969: 21 ff.). The lions must at least be relaxed to be breeding, so their conditions must be good to that extent.

Third, breeding could actually be a response to bad conditions (as in some protozoans). Presumably the proverbial high human birth rate in slums can be seen as a response to such conditions, or more directly to any combination of despair, boredom or ignorance. It does show that even slum conditions are not as bad as they might be; they are not 'rock bottom'. Given poor enough conditions, as for the poor in some parts of Europe in the seventeenth century, partly as a result of a deteriorating climate, human breeding falls off. (Calhoun's work on overcrowding in rats is of interest here (Bleibtreu 1968: 204 ff.).) We could (unwittingly) be selectively breeding for breeding in bad conditions: presumably the animals concerned would have to be good captive breeders to start with, as lions seem to be, and perhaps Rhesus monkeys (in view of Williams's comment above).

However, the situation with animals is more complicated still. Caracals, for example, probably come into oestrus as a result of poor conditions suddenly followed by an improvement, as in the desert: that is, a rather poor diet suddenly improved. Again the female may come into oestrus very quickly again if her young cubs are taken away, even while she is still lactating. Thus a high breeding rate would hardly in this instance demonstrate good conditions. With ring-tailed lemurs, on the other hand, there is evidence that an improved diet increases the chance of male young being born (males being, as it were, a comparative luxury to dispense with in lean times). Similarly, with Grevy's zebras, it seems that the better the condition of the female, the more likely she is to have male young: a way in which the zebras respond to better or poorer conditions; a female has a much higher chance of mating and breeding than a male, so in poor conditions it is better just to have female young, which still stand a fair chance of breeding.

Fourth, breeding in captivity could even perhaps just be out of boredom. Certainly masturbation can be, and perhaps mating, but it seems unlikely that successful breeding – that is, the whole cycle of courtship, mating, birth, perhaps nest-building, and rearing of young – could be, both because so many animals are highly 'fussy' about the right conditions for successful breeding, and because breeding, as a centrally important occurrence in animals' lives, and likely, for reasons of natural selection, to be highly satisfying, can hardly be seen itself as a response to boredom.

Fifth, breeding in captivity sometimes only occurs with 'artificial' assistance from us. We can distinguish between artificial and 'natural' breeding. Only natural breeding will do as a criterion of good conditions, though artificial breeding may still be conservationally desirable.

Sixth, a problem – though rather with the public function of a zoo than with the application of breeding as criterion – is that many animals breed much better away from the public. Obviously it is up to zoo personnel to ensure that breeding animals are not disturbed by the public, as they should try to prevent any animals being disturbed.

Seventh, one may get more breeding as a result of interference with the natural grouping. Capuchins are highly social, but if you keep them in pairs you may have those various pairs breeding successfully, while if you have them in a more natural large group you may find that only a dominant pair breeds. Certainly it has been found with marmosets that, in the wild or in captivity, only a single dominant female breeds, as her aggressive behaviour suppresses the ovarian cycles of her subordinates (Wiseman 1986). So here breeding by only one female in a group as opposed to breeding by more of them is a direct indication of natural social conditions and presumably good conditions, if we assume conditions are better the more they approach those natural to the species. We might feel this was an exceptional case where women's lib (though it would be 'lib' from the influence of the dominant female) could well be extended to marmosets. At any rate, while breeding by the dominant female would here be a criterion of natural or good conditions, breeding by the other females would not be: it would indicate we were keeping them in unnatural groups, that is, separate pairs. It could be similar with a very different species, alpacas: with these, if they are kept in a presumably natural herd, only one or two young a year will be produced; kept, less naturally, in pairs, the breeding would greatly increase. A similar situation could apply with porcupines.

What these examples show is that degree of breeding by itself is not a reliable criterion of good conditions; the criterion should be breeding as it would occur in the wild. We may well object to an excess of captive breeding, as we would to the way in which some domestic animals are forced to breed, e.g. bitches on 'puppy farms'. This is not to say that it may not be acceptable, even highly desirable on conservation grounds, to increase what would be the natural rate of breeding. But such a policy should be cautious, and its success should certainly not be claimed as a definitive demonstration of the suitability of the conditions.

But despite this qualification and the other problems with breeding that I have mentioned, breeding remains a major criterion of good conditions in captivity, to be used alongside the other criteria.

NATURAL BEHAVIOUR

Why should display of its natural behaviour be a criterion of a zoo animal's well-being or otherwise? (Natural behaviour is very desirable in a zoo because it makes the animals much more interesting to watch, but this isn't the point here.)

There are several reasons, but the main one perhaps is that we know humans have various natural needs and can hardly dispute that certain animals have them also (Midgley 1983a: 155). Solitary confinement is a severe penalty for a human because we all, in varying degrees, need some contact with other humans. Some natural needs are to express certain behaviour – feeding and social contact, for example. Dogs obviously have certain similar needs to ourselves, including some behavioural needs such as eating and contact with other dogs.

Even such basic needs could be challenged. The need for food could be met by some technical substitute for feeding. Intensive pig systems allow certain farrowing sows almost no opportunity for locomotion. However although behavioural scientists may seek experimental demonstration before granting the truth of even such basics, few would want to challenge the comment of Julian Huxley, 'that it is the frustration of activities natural to the animal which may well be the worst form of cruelty' (Harrison 1979: 125; Ryder 1989: 265).

Suppose someone challenges the need to feed (not of course the need for food) and suggests that, if a particular animal is fed intravenously, the lack of need or opportunity actually to eat in the normal way won't be a deprivation. The process of feeding is normally pleasurable to us, and presumably to many other animals, because for us and them, that serves the biological function of ensuring that eating occurs. But to eat, an animal has to find food, which in some cases involves searching for it, pursuing it and killing it. It seems inherently likely that such appetitive or seeking behaviour will also be pleasurable, or if not itself pleasurable, will at least be directed by drives whose frustration will produce dissatisfaction. For it is easy to see how such devices for ensuring that food is sought for will have been selected. Similarly it is likely that the performance of other vital behaviour – social, reproductive and so on – selected for through millions of years will also be ensured by drives or pleasurable experiences.

To seek to judge an animal's well-being by its behaviour is a good approach for another reason. We can actually judge a fellow human's well-being more reliably by their behaviour than by what they tell us: they may lie or may deceive themselves or may not wish to trouble us with an accurate account in what they tell us. But if we know their normal behaviour from the past, then we are likely to be able to judge their well-being quite well; we will have good indications perhaps that they are now going through a period of depression, or that they seem to be as happy as previously. We are comparing their behaviour now with formerly. Their behaviour tells us what we are seeking to know. Now much as people vary, their behaviour is circumscribed by behaviour common to the great majority of humans, natural human behaviour in other words, such as could be studied by an ethologist (Jones 1967). But much basic human behaviour is so familiar to us that we don't need an ethological study to identify it for us. Thus when we judge some person's well-being by their behaviour, our basic terms of reference are going to be our (obviously intimate) knowledge of natural human behaviour. Thus we might be concerned because our subject seemed to be departing from the natural norm – locking themselves away for long hours, say, for no understandable reason, and ceasing to communicate even with close members of their family (though of course we have to keep due regard for variations in behaviour among individuals). Similarly we can judge the well-being of an individual animal that we know well – our dog, say – by comparing his present behaviour with his normal. We would be greatly aided, even with an animal we knew well, by knowledge of that species' natural behaviour, and this would apply still more, if anything, in the case of a relatively wild animal in a zoo (though I have stressed the often striking closeness of behaviour in wild and domestic animals). We can hardly avoid taking that species' wild behaviour as a norm, even though we must be aware too of variation in individual members of that species and of the fact that life in the wild can involve suffering (see discussion of point 3 below).

Natural behaviour as a criterion defended

Marian Dawkins, discussing how we assess suffering in domesticated or at least artificially selected animals, disagrees that natural behaviour is a most important criterion. She gives three reasons for doubting the validity of the wild as standard:

1　Wild and domesticated animals are very different, and even different breeds of the same species of domesticated animal differ greatly (Dawkins 1980: 41–8).
2　It cannot be assumed that captive animals suffer through not performing, or being unable to perform, particular natural behaviour (ibid.: 51–4).
3　Suffering occurs in the wild.

(ibid.: 51–4).

None of these seems a substantial objection to natural behaviour as a criterion, though the third poses real problems. I will discuss them in turn.

Point 1, even if it is the case, wouldn't apply to judging the well-being of zoo animals, most of which are relatively wild. But she gives no convincing evidence of large differences between wild and domestic animals, and some indications of the contrary, such as an intriguing experiment in which Wood-Gush and Duncan released domestic hens on to a Scottish island. They lost them all to mink very quickly, but they gave a second batch of hens preliminary 'commando-training'. These birds successfully selected 'inaccessible and extremely well hidden nest sites' which they approached warily (Dawkins 1980: 45). Dawkins mentions Hughes's view that there seem to have been as many genetic changes in chickens in the last 100 years as in the preceding 4,500 years, and that behavioural differences between 'modern broiler strains and modern egg-laying strains are greater than those . . . between a "primitive" breed such as brown leghorns and ancestral junglefowl' (ibid.: 44). She doesn't say what breed the birds receiving the commando training were, but they don't sound very different from ancestral jungle fowl if they could adjust so readily to dangerous wild living. Dawkins stresses the need to find out whether there are genetic or environmental differences between wild and captive animals before using the wild as a standard for the welfare of captive animals, but the fact that there are going to be inevitable differences seems far from a demonstration that the differences are really significant, that they amount to fundamental differences in capacity for finding satisfaction, for instance.

To illustrate point 2, that captive animals are not necessarily suffering in not showing, or not having opportunity to show, natural behaviour, Dawkins gives only one example, that of their lack of opportunity to show the kind of behaviour by which they would respond to the presence of a predator. But this is the one clear example of behaviour or experience which we would be inclined to feel a captive animal was well off without; and Dawkins herself gives some interesting evidence to suggest that even missing predators isn't a clear advantage, because it appears that animals will 'seek out stimulation even when it puts them in danger': Kruuk's account of how, for example, some African mammals will move so close to their predators they get killed by them, and Humphrey's example of monkeys choosing to see 'horror films', i.e. voluntarily pressing a lever to see films or photographs which frighten them when seen the first time (Dawkins 1980: 49).

With regard to point 3, Dawkins mentions first of all Lack's figures about robins and other song-birds, which may well indicate some degree of suffering as well as mere shortness of lives. However, the situation is probably different with adult lions or chimpanzees, as Lack suggests in a comment that Dawkins quotes: 'We ourselves would be shocked if half our friends died each year' (Dawkins 1980: 52). I have already mentioned another example Dawkins gives to illustrate suffering in the wild, that of animals eaten alive by hyaenas, but the comment of Kruuk that she quotes – 'It is rare that the victim puts up any significant active defence' – suggests the animal is in a stupor, like Livingstone's dreamy state when caught by a lion, despite injuries he was aware of after his escape (Dawkins 1980: 52; Livingstone 1910: 11; Jordan 1979: 150–1) (see Chapter 5 above). Still, the fact a good deal of suffering does occur in wild living presents a real problem for the use of natural behaviour – behaviour such as would occur in the wild – as a criterion of well-being. After all, how can a suffering animal be the standard for an animal in a state of well-being? I suggest, as a solution, that our standard should be the successful wild conspecific. For not only does the wild present high risks for most individuals; it may be particularly stressful for the less successful animal of any species, the one lower down the peck order, and that is bullied by its fellows, or that does not succeed in staking out a territory, or in securing a mate (Fiennes 1965: 174–5). It must of course succeed in finding food, else it could not survive at all. We have to recognise that there are degrees of well-being in the wild, just as there are more and less optimal habitats. But the successful wild individual – the one who dominates, who wins territory, who mates successfully, and so on – seems to me the right standard. In as much as the captive animal shows similar behaviour to them, we have a strong indication of well-being.

Finally, Dawkins is concerned with how we tell whether an animal is suffering; I am concerned with a wider issue: how we tell whether it is positively well off, or in optimum conditions. Even in the narrower issue, the wild as a criterion is far from being invalidated by Dawkins' criticisms; in the wider issue, it is still more likely to be useful.

Relevant kinds of natural behaviour

I mean roughly by the 'natural behaviour' of a specified animal (A) behaviour such as we have observed, or have good reason to expect that we could observe, being carried out by conspecifics of A in their natural habitat in a state of non-interference by man. I am thinking mainly of groups of related actions (such as the various actions involved in building a nest). There will be an enormous variety of separate actions and even of activities, but we can still pick out certain main categories of behaviour which are likely to be distinctive of a particular species, and which may be in some degree innate in all or many members of that species:

1   Characteristic forms of locomotion: walking, running, leaping, climbing, brachiating, swimming, gliding, flying, etc., and also burrowing.
2   Feeding, and more than this, appetitive behaviour: the preliminaries of looking for food, and catching it in the case of a predator.
3   Mutual grooming, and self-grooming, and any other maintenance activities.
4   Behaviour connected with the establishing of relationships with conspecifics (and in some cases possibly non-conspecifics), such as the establishing of territory and of dominance hierarchies or peck orders.
5   Breeding, i.e. courtship, nest-building, mating, young-rearing.
6   Play behaviour.

These categories are only intended to be approximate, and are not necessarily exclusive. The first, locomotion, is rather different from the others, in all of which it is likely to play a part. Few would dispute the importance of its being at least physically possible for a captive animal to engage in its characteristic forms of locomotion, but flying, and to a lesser extent swimming and burrowing, tends to be treated as an exception. With all of these ways of getting about there is clearly a great difference between minimal and adequate provision: should not animals have space to run as well as walk? To swim, if they do swim, more than a few metres? To perform more than a token climb? Most kinds of animal can use two or more means of locomotion. Are they all essential requirements? Clearly we should err on the side of over-provision; we should give the animal the benefit of the doubt. On the other hand evidence that, in the wild, an animal never or hardly ever moved in a particular way, however much one might expect it to at a first glance, would make a difference. But to argue in such a way would be a very different matter from arguing that a pig or a fowl needed little opportunity to move around because its physical health was good. This is not a matter, one hopes, of any direct relevance to zoos, where the provisions for locomotion, even probably in the worst remaining menagerie-type cages, are better than those still regarded as acceptable in intensive husbandry systems. But animals are much the same anywhere, and the same general principles for how they should be kept should apply to selectively bred as much as to relatively wild captive animals. The natural behaviour criterion should be pre-eminent in that at least minimal requirements set by that criterion alone should not be able to be overruled by the application of any other criteria, including health. On the other hand it may well be that provisions which seem desirable on the natural behaviour criterion but which are well beyond the minimal requirements may be realised to be inessential in the light of the application of other criteria.

Play is particularly interesting because it doesn't need the necessities of living as a motivation. It is thus 'tailor-made' for life in a zoo, and it would be both unsurprising and undisturbing to find that any animal played more in zoos than in the wild (Markowitz 1982: 7).

Different ways of keeping animals, especially ways which provide opportunities for them to behave naturally, will be looked at in the next chapter.

ABNORMAL BEHAVIOUR

Abnormal behaviour, ranging from stereotyped pacing and weaving to self-mutilation, manipulation of faeces, and so on, may well seem the clearest possible indication of bad captive conditions (Hediger 1964: 75–7; Morris 1964: 603–30; Meyer-Holzapfel 1968: 476 ff.; Stevenson 1983: 184–8). It may seem obvious that where this sort of thing occurs, conditions must be improved until at least the abnormal behaviour ceases, or else the animals must just not be kept. There may seem no possible appeal from the indictment of the conditions to other criteria such as health and natural behaviour. This is the opinion of Stefan Ormrod (1987). David Jones (1987) assumes there is such an appeal.

There is no dispute that abnormal behaviour such as is documented by Meyer-Holzapfel, Morris and others is regrettable, to say the least, and that it has been widespread in captive animals in the past, and is by no means unknown even in some good zoos today. It is likely to be uncommon today in zoos with large and/or well-furnished enclosures, but it is well-known how prevalent pacing and weaving is among, for example, captive polar bears and sometimes elephants (Jordan and Ormrod 1978: 158 ff.).

However, abnormal behaviour is not always an easy criterion to apply, or even define (Stevenson 1983: 179), though no less useful or important on that account as a warning sign, even as a potential reason for condemning some particular captive conditions strongly, and certainly as an indicator of something wrong that needs to be remedied.

It can really only be defined as 'behaviour which we have good reason to suppose does not occur in the wild and which we believe to reveal a disturbed state in the animal displaying it'. Thus it is a matter of far from infallible judgement to identify any particular behaviour as (in our defined sense) abnormal. Take, for example, stereotyped behaviour. How do we decide that this indicates a disturbed state? Not simply because it is stereotyped. Stereotyped or ritualised behaviour plays a large part in many animals' courtship, for example. We can agree that stereotypies we would expect to see under wild conditions are not abnormal. But neither are other stereotypies, necessarily, such as that of a polar bear that swims in a precisely regular way (in a particular part of her pool, one way on her front, then back on her back – as a particular female used to at Glasgow). She did not seem thereby deranged, any more than this piece of behaviour seems disturbing. Humans, like other animals, can get into the habit of performing series of actions not only regularly but identically every time. Somebody swimming in their private swimming pool each day might do this (like the bear). Kant's neighbours are reputed to have set their watches by his afternoon walks with their clockwork regularity. On the other hand, a polar bear's weaving is similar both to the behaviour of deprived children in institutions, and to that of young rhesus monkeys experimentally deprived of their mothers' support, and therefore reasonably regarded as a sign of a deprived situation (Rowell 1972: 135 ff.). Take, as another example, the manipulation of faeces by great apes, even the throwing of them at visitors. The latter is presumably pleasurable (for the ape concerned), and its use hardly an indication of abnormality, if there is nothing else available; in any case faeces could be the best material for getting a response from humans. Humans would use it for the same reason (Morris 1964).

It may be difficult to identify a likely piece of behaviour as abnormal, or to assess how serious its abnormality is, because it is often not easy to know the precise cause or causes of such behaviour. Sometimes the cause of, say, a stereotypy is the conditions in which an animal was kept, or the way in which it was treated, in the past. Hand-rearing may be a cause, or the fact that an animal was, perhaps for a brief period after capture, kept in a confined area, or kept in more confined conditions in a circus. Habits earlier formed may prove ineradicable later, however great the improvement in conditions (Stevenson 1983: 184–7). One example is of polar bears caught near Winnipeg, because of wandering into town repeatedly. Stereotypies then acquired during a short period of close confinement may continue, however spacious and interesting later captive conditions are. In cases like this it is clearly as unjust as it is inaccurate to blame those now responsible for keeping the animal, or the conditions they provide, for the animal's abnormal behaviour. Sometimes there seems to be a hereditary factor; for example, only one of three Glasgow polar bears showed substantial stereotypic behaviour. Another example is that of a stereotypy occurring in some black leopards and known as 'stargazing'. The tendency to engage in this appears to be inherited. In both these cases it seems, therefore, that the stereotyped behaviour is only partially caused by the captive conditions to which it is a response.

Abnormal behaviour such as stereotypies does not itself indicate physical or even serious or continual mental suffering, or at least not necessarily. The behaviour may give satisfaction or comfort through the release of endorphins, though of course the environment ought to be so stimulating that the animal does not need to find satisfaction in this way.

Obviously the degree of abnormality makes some difference. An animal may show a little or a great deal of pacing or weaving. Any is no doubt a warning sign; but that is not to say that a little pacing occurring only occasionally (on the identification of this as abnormal, opinions in any case differ) is a reason for condemning wholly the conditions in which the animal concerned is kept (Stevenson 1983: 184–6).

It is not necessarily correct or justified to call an animal which shows stereotypic behaviour psychotic or mad. A self-plucking parrot can go on doing this in the company of other parrots (the original cause having probably been confinement in a small cage) and can be apparently all right otherwise. The feather plucking is obviously regrettable, distressing (at least to us), and a sign of something wrong, but it may be apparently impossible to cure, and it would hardly be wrong to go on keeping the parrot, despite its condition, if this seemed the kindest thing to do and the parrot gave signs of being (otherwise) in a state of well-being (Stevenson 1983: 186).

In general, apart from when actually physically harmful (e.g. self-mutilation), even abnormal stereotypies are probably adaptive, in that they help the animal to survive, to cope with its situation (perhaps through releasing endorphins). The animal, of course, should not be in a situation where it needs to behave abnormally in order to survive, to keep, perhaps, its sanity. But that its abnormal behaviour may serve that very function seems a rather good reason for not calling the animal mad. That the conditions, whether past or present, which caused the behaviour stand condemned (if we can only pinpoint them) is obvious enough.

It is perhaps important to show that the occurrence of abnormal behaviour is not an unanswerable indictment of any particular captive conditions. One reason is that abnormal behaviour may be shown in what seem to be and may indeed be very good conditions, such as those of the polar bear enclosure at Tacoma Zoo. This was praised by Cherfas but found fallible by Ormrod, because he, to his own surprise and disappointment, observed stereotyped behaviour by one or more of the bears (Cherfas 1984: 139–40; Ormrod 1987: 24–5). It may be that one of the bears had acquired a stereotypy long before being in that enclosure. In any case Ormrod's observations, though they cast a serious doubt over whether the enclosure is good enough – perhaps over whether polar bears should be kept at all – do not settle the matter. Another reason is that a zoo may accept that its polar bear facilities are not good enough and may decide not to replace its present bears after their deaths, but still have the problem of what to do about the bears it has. It may well feel the best thing to do is to continue keeping them as well as possible, with whatever improvements can be made. Others may feel that, in such a situation, it would be better for the bears to be humanely killed (if, of course, they cannot be sent to better accommodation elsewhere). The considerations above should help to decide the best course in such a situation, and make it likely that a decision to keep the bears for their natural lives is the best course.

DIRECT INDICATIONS

The bogy of anthropomorphism

Barnett remarks that 'the sight of a large mammal or bird behind bars is distressing', but that this tells us 'nothing of the needs or feelings of the animals themselves'. We can indeed be misled by attributing human feelings and wishes to other animals; we must be careful to avoid unwarranted anthropomorphism (Barnett 1970: 25). Even expert zoologists can make mistaken assumptions about what animals actually prefer: on investigation, hens turned out to prefer 'fine gauge hexagonal wire' cage floors, not heavier mesh as assumed by the Brambell Committee (which investigated factory farming for the government in the 1960s) (Dawkins 1980: 88).

But anthropomorphism is a term easily misused, as Mary Midgley (1979: 344–51; 1983b: 125–9) shows us. We can make false assumptions about the mental abilities of other animals: we can do the same about humans (Barnett 1970: 25–6; Midgley 1983b: 130). An exaggerated fear of anthropomorphism is as unscientific as being unaware of the need for caution in attributing feelings and intentions to other species (Hume 1982). Is Hediger (1964: 51–2) right to assume that an eagle flying up into the heavens is only concerned with finding food below, that only humans can enjoy soaring for its own sake? Perhaps enjoyment of such a thing requires humans' imagination and capacity for abstract thought. But it is more scientific to keep an open mind on the matter than to assume that humans, in this as in so much else, stand on a pedestal. Hediger himself (1974: 100 ff.) is well aware that there is sometimes quite a lot to be said for anthropomorphism!

While we need to be careful about anthropomorphism, animals clearly give by their actions various direct indications about their satisfaction or otherwise with their captive conditions.

Escaping

To us 'a cage is a prison – something from which to escape' (Barnett 1970: 25). Couldn't it be a prison for an animal too? An animal's apparent attempts at escape – a leopard tearing at the bars or a lizard scrabbling at the glass – may be just what they seem. We may not always be justified in reading the intention of escaping into such actions, but an animal clearly can have such an intention. Take the extreme case of a very small or otherwise very unsuitable cage: a large box, for instance. If we put a dog into this, he would scrabble around, frantically trying to get out. Would we be less justified in thus describing his reactions than in similarly describing a human's reaction to the same situation? Would it really be anthropomorphic, would it not just be obvious, that the dog as much as the human was trying to escape? So at least a very small cage would be a prison to an animal as to a human.

It is striking how we use the term 'escape' of an animal as readily as of a human. Not only is it partly because of our animal, indeed our primate, nature, that confinement in a prison cell (or a cage) is so unpleasant for us. Probably our human nature – our ability to introspect, think abstractly, and so on – enables some of us to cope with this situation. In as much as we are animals, we just want to get out like any other primate, or for that matter like the caracal in David Garnett's short novel *A Man in the Zoo* (1985). Leahy (1991: 201), discussing Garnett's novel, suggests that a caged human's fate is worse than an animal's because of the human's self-consciousness and knowledge of what they are missing. John Cromartie in the novel becomes a representative human in the London Zoo primate house by his own choice, but had he been compelled to be there, he might still have found solace in reflection, presumably unlike the unhappy caracal (Garnett 1985: 47).

Any animal's escape is a 'criticism' of the captive conditions; it speaks for itself, at least in suggesting the 'escaper' is dissatisfied with conditions, or perhaps is aware of being confined. Michael Brambell (1973: 45) suggests that the 'general aim [in zoos] is to provide an environment in which the animal, if it could, would not know that it was in captivity'.

Conversely, an animal who makes no effort to escape from a cage or enclosure is giving some indication of satisfaction with it. Of course, he might have given up in despair trying to get out; he might just be tired; he might be just getting used to it. But in the absence of other indications, the fact of clearly not trying to escape is worth something as an indicator of well-being. With certain enclosures at Glasgow (those for Axis deer and for camels, for instance) the animals could probably get out if they tried very hard; we assume this will not occur unless they are badly stressed, which we try to avoid.

Sometimes in zoos animals are allowed out from any enclosure, so that they could escape if they wished, though there could be some mental or behavioural restriction on their doing so. Monkeys at the Woolly Monkey Sanctuary are let out occasionally (except for mature males) into trees outside their enclosures but do not make a run for it; presumably this is some demonstration of satisfaction with life in the Sanctuary, though, having little or no experience of fending for themselves as under wild conditions, they could be afraid to venture into unknown territory. Just as likely, they simply have no need to go, having a known food source, good social relations in the Sanctuary, and no pressure from, say, a too concentrated population. This is clearly extremely different from the kind of menagerie set-up where the animals probably wouldn't hesitate to get away from their confined conditions (like humans in jail) if they could.

Peacocks (such as at Glasgow Zoo) are often kept unconfined; of course their behaviour as pheasant-type birds which mostly stay close to the ground and scratch a living from the soil makes them unlikely to go, as does their being territorial; if we didn't know they were unlikely to depart, we could not keep them like this. Still, the fact remains that they stay through choice. And, as I say, this would apply to some of the other animals too, even though they are kept in enclosures.

Many animals that do escape come back, as in certain examples that Barnett discusses. Where an escaped bear, say, returns he may be doing it because of fear at the unknown environment outside, like one bear alarmed by the noise of the planks a workman he met dropped in fright before running for help (Street 1965: 219–20); he might be choosing the lesser of two evils. But at least his enclosure is a place of retreat for him, of security in the face of the unknown, so such an occurrence is also worth something as evidence for his well-being there. (And perhaps the occasional effectiveness of a little bribery shows that an animal has no intense dislike of his conditions, as with a Himalayan bear that used to escape regularly at Whipsnade, and

93

was equally regularly recaptured with some aid from condensed milk kept for the purpose (Street 1965: 221–2).)

Choice tests

Specific choice tests for animals, such as those arranged by Dawkins to test whether hens prefer batteries or not, would give specific information on animals' preferences in regard to enclosures and their furniture. It has been found, for example, that pigs prefer moderate lighting both to very bright conditions and to darkness (Dawkins 1980: 88 ff.). On the other hand, such a test might only be telling us which was the lesser of two evils. In some cases natural 'choice tests' occur: certain animals arrive and lodge themselves with us by free choice. Zoos offer good food sources for many wild birds. Waterfowl can be attracted by the creation of suitable ponds.

Direct communication

Animals can give other indications of how they feel about their relations with us. They can communicate their feelings directly to us, as when a cat purrs, lets herself be scratched or stroked by a human, or instead snarls; as when a primate lip-smacks at us, even lets himself be groomed by us or grooms us in return, as a baboon called Emma used to do at Glasgow with her bearded keeper. These are direct signs of happiness, or at least pleasure, or of the opposite. I accept that these could signal short-term moods hardly reflecting the animal's long-term well-being or otherwise. They are still worth something. If we had good reason to think the lions at London Zoo really roared at night, as supposed by the novelist E.H. Young (1949: 172), with 'the awful indignation of the wrongfully imprisoned who have no redress', this would be a direct indication too; but this seems unlikely. Even a bear begging, or otherwise communicating with a human, and an elephant having a joke – grabbing somebody's umbrella and pretending to be about to eat it (Alldis 1973: 122) – are some indication of well-being: they would not occur if the animals did not in some degree accept their relationship with humans. (It could be said that they had no alternative; but they have one, to remain untame, unrelaxed (Huxley 1981: 22; Burgess 1968: 204).)

We do not always understand what animals are communicating. The chimpanzee 'grin' is a sign of unease rather than pleasure. We must be ready to be corrected by ethological study. But the fact remains that with species familiar to us, such as dogs and cats, we can interpret signs of pleasure or of distrust very easily, and need to do so in managing animals (Hebb 1946: 88 ff.).

Indirect communication

There are various actions animals perform, where they are not actually communicating or seeking to do so with us, which also reveal a good deal of their state of relaxation, or the opposite. Examples are a cat's washing herself, a dog's grooming himself (and a great many animals groom), and animals playing. This could be either play with us, or play which we observe. One example of play with humans would be that of Aspinall and some of his keepers with gorillas and with tigers (Aspinall 1986: 11–19; Aspinall 1976). Interestingly, play itself is an interspecific activity – something that certain other mammals understand, as we do – and can involve the use of such interspecific signals as the primate play-face (Loizos 1967: 181 ff.) Animals' engaging in play among themselves – the normal occurrence in zoos – is quite a strong indication of their well-being. There is evidence that more time is spent on play in the wild in optimal than in suboptimal conditions, so the occurrence of more play in a zoo than in the wild, is an indication of good conditions (Stevenson 1983: 181). This puts play in a special category: judging by the natural behaviour criterion, we would regard play's occurrence in zoos as a favourable indication, but hardly its occurrence to a greater extent than in the wild.

Taming

All the favourable indications mentioned above only occur following an animal's becoming in some degree tame; their occurrence may be just what we mean by an animal's becoming tame. Tameness itself is an important indication of an animal's well-being, and probably necessary in some degree for well-being in captivity (Hediger 1964: 154 ff.; Tromborg et al. 1991); it is something distinct from natural behaviour, by which we mean precisely what an animal would do in the wild state, although it is also significant that wild animals can sometimes become tame extremely quickly, or be tame already (see Chapter 4). Becoming tame includes not fleeing from humans, becoming relaxed in their presence, and probably aware of friendly signals from humans, plus the giving of friendly signals to them. More than a certain degree of tameness may not be desirable in zoo animals, not being an advantage in reintroductions. But it may not matter even then: the lioness Elsa became in various respects wild, yet remained friendly towards the Adamsons (Adamson 1962: 122–3); it was similar with a tigress released by Arjan Singh (1984: 98–9).

Training

That an animal can be trained, although this only happens with certain animals in zoos, is also an important and interesting phenomenon. It is widely appreciated how dogs respond to a skilled trainer, presumably because of their wild nature as social, hierarchical animals who would be submissive towards a pack leader (Hearne 1987). Perhaps humans are capable of having the relationship they can have with dogs only because they too are by nature hierarchical.

Some relationships between animals and keepers in zoos approach the dog–human relationship. Despite (nearly always) having been born in the wild, elephants are usually managed as domesticated animals, and trained by keepers at least to lie down, lift up a foot (as would be necessary for veterinary examination) and so on. It is striking how through history there have been comments on the need of elephants to be managed by the keepers they know, as in Keith Thomas's comment (1984: 277): '"There is an elephant given to the King", notes an early Tudor schoolmaster, "but none can guide him but they that came with the present."'

There is a close relationship between training and taming, but the training relationship, in its own right, can be a useful indicator of an animal's well-being, or itself a respect in which the animal is in a state of well-being. That is, the animal is likely to find the relationship satisfying (Kiley-Worthington 1990: 111 ff.).

THEORETICAL ASSESSMENT

This last criterion for assessing well-being is simply the consideration of any other factors that seem to be relevant. We need to view the animal in the light of its natural environment, and whatever behaviourally, ecologically and otherwise is known about it, and consider accordingly the likelihood of its being all right when kept in particular conditions or in a particular way.

The matters discussed under the heading 'Evolution and adaptation' in Chapter 5 are particularly relevant: the fact that degrees of adaptability vary greatly, so that certain animals have much more specific requirements than others, and that some may be unsuitable for keeping at all. Desmond Morris's distinction between specialists (such as lions) and opportunists (such as dogs and bears and primates) is very relevant (Morris 1964). The tendency of opportunists to explore and investigate for long periods makes them much more difficult to cater for in zoos, and more obviously in need of behavioural enrichment, than specialists who may be naturally attuned to doing nothing very much for a good deal of the time. Also relevant is the fact that certain animals in zoos can have a special relationship with humans and be kept more or less as domesticated animals (or indeed are domesticated animals, like llamas and camels). It is important for many animals to be looked after by the right people, the presence of and contact with whom tend to relax their charges (like the effect of sympathetic people on children) (Miller and West 1972: 893). There are several different approaches to keeping animals, any of which may be acceptable, and these will be considered in the next chapter.

Feeding and food animals

It is an important responsibility of a zoo to provide the right food for its animals, indeed the best food it can manage, just because the animals are likely to have – through our decision, not theirs – no opportunity to find food for themselves. Deciding on the best food is not without its problems, but involves balancing the demands of nutritional value (which may be best served by a synthetic product) against those of interest of food, of exercise for jaw muscles and roughage provided (e.g. for cats with whole dead animals to consume), and also such physiological needs as those of cattle, adapted as they are to digesting plant food over long periods with the aid of internal micro-organisms rather than consuming apparently better-quality, more concentrated food (Kiley-Worthington 1990: 189).

There are widely diverging views on the virtues of synthetic food, such as the 'Radcliffe diet', as contrasted with more natural but less nutritionally rich foods (Hediger 1974: 133 ff.; Durrell 1977: 69 ff.).

There is an obvious clash between our responsibilities to carnivores like cats, who benefit from the provision of dead rabbits and chickens (say), and our responsibilities to those rabbits and chickens themselves. There are three particular problems: live feeding; killing; and the quality of life of the food animals.

Live feeding

This is in Britain legally not an option except for the feeding of, mainly, live rodents to snakes, and for the use in feeding of various live invertebrates, such as locusts or mealworms. The feeding of live vertebrate prey to snakes must be a grey area legally, such feeding to any other animal clearly being an offence under the 1911 Cruelty to Animals Act. It is rare in any British zoo now, probably because of realisations of its moral questionableness strongly backed up by considerations of public relations, though no doubt regarded as acceptable by many private keepers of snakes. (Snakes take live prey far more readily than dead prey, which is why this particular problem arises with them.)

The practice seems morally objectionable, legal considerations apart, because, although rodents and birds would of course be taken by snakes in the wild, that is not our responsibility, whereas what we do in a zoo is. Earthquakes cause many human deaths, but that is no moral (or legal) excuse for murders. There may be other reasons why we should regard live vertebrate feeding as objectionable, such as the fact the 'prey' would be in a more confined space than in the wild, perhaps that it would not be getting a 'fair chance', and as a public spectacle there is an obvious danger of veering towards a mini-Colosseum. Probably little suffering in fact is caused by the live feeding of snakes: for example, a mouse is probably unaware of the threat to it until virtually the moment of seizure by the snake (in the case of a constrictor like a boa or python), and death occurs within a few seconds (unlike, obviously, the deaths of many mice caught by cats). Some argue we should recognise the reality of carnivores' nature as well as the obvious enrichment of their lives from the provision of live prey (Smith 1979: xiv; Hancocks 1980: 171–2; Markowitz 1982: 13–14; Cherfas 1984: 133).

The law offers little protection to invertebrates. It may be necessary to use live invertebrates as food (e.g. for other invertebrates such as scorpions), or at least impracticable not to. This matters less than would similar use of vertebrates in that we have good reason to regard invertebrates as less aware; but, if only in view of Morley's comments about ants' feeling pain (1953: 169, 174), we should minimise any use of live invertebrates as food, and still more of injured or incapacitated invertebrates. We should give them the benefit of the doubt with regard to suffering.

Killing

This is regrettable but unavoidable if carnivores are to be kept. As they need meat, there is no additional moral problem in killing chickens or rats or rabbits in a zoo, when meat from cows or horses is being used anyway – i.e. from animals killed elsewhere. Obviously, any killing must be as humane as possible, and such factors as animals' probable awareness of the deaths of other animals should be remembered.

Quality of life

The quality of life of animals to be used for food is as important as that of any other animals in the zoo. We should not be intensively rearing mice or chickens or any other animals, difficult though this may be for reasons of economy or practicality. We should do as much as we can to provide naturalistic and/or enriched environments for any food animals. In a zoo we should be setting an example with regard to all our animals, including those for food and any others 'off exhibition'.

Being seen and being stared at

With many animals, the better the captive environment provided, the less the public are going to see the animal. Small mammals don't sit around being seen in natural conditions. They hide away. This applies still more to snakes who, if not hunting or basking, would probably stay in a burrow in darkness and in as much tactile

99

contact as possible with their surroundings. Enclosures for smaller mammals designed like mini-habitats – as at Palacerigg Country Park or the Highland Wildlife Park – can make it difficult to spot the occupants. One answer here is education. Spotting the animal in a really good enclosure is a little like spotting an animal in its actual natural habitat – which is in some ways better educationally and more interesting. The essential, unfortunate, paradox which faces us here – the better the enclosure for the animal, the less you see of it – is compensated for by an important aspect of enrichment in which animal and human interests coincide: the more you can stimulate the animal to behave naturally (e.g. hide a Fennec fox's food so that he searches and digs for it) the more interesting his zoo life is for him, and the more interesting it is for people to watch him.

The problem with staring is that this is in a way the essence of a zoo, but that staring with many species, including ourselves, is a threat (Midgley 1979: 11 ff.). This probably applies particularly to primates. One solution is large enclosures which the public can't get very near to, but which they have to observe to some extent in the way necessary in the natural habitat, like the chimpanzees in their outside enclosure at Edinburgh, who are unlikely to be aware of being stared at. Perhaps primates get used to being stared at, and so are not discomfited by it, but this should be investigated (it seems not to have been). One-way glass could be tried.

Stress

Stress should not be caused by the basic captive conditions, but as we have seen, an absence of stress is not natural. Some stress will arise from relations between social animals kept in natural groups. This is desirable, provided there isn't an excess, for example from an animal's being unable to get away from a dominant conspecific as it would in the wild. Refuges, screened areas and other devices are important for primates, particularly. In view of the evidence that some animals will voluntarily seek out stressful situations, an ideal arrangement would be to provide a way for primates, among others, to subject themselves to mild stress if they choose.

Need for natural items and surroundings

We humans often get particular satisfaction from being among trees and other plants, perhaps because we are evolutionarily programmed to get satisfaction from being in the kind of places which are likely food sources. If so, this would apply to other primates too. In any case, the fact that we enjoy contact with plants suggests that other primates may, and perhaps other animals. Domestic dogs visiting the country presumably don't admire the view but perhaps get richer supplies of smells than in the city. (Or perhaps they don't, as there are so many dogs in cities all busy marking their territories.) Significantly, prisons are associated for us with concrete and bricks, as well as bars. To be imprisoned with access to a garden would for many humans be a considerable amelioration of their situation. It might be assumed that humans' mental capacities lead to their enjoyment of nature, and that this doesn't apply to other animals other than, of course, when natural things are an actual food source (as for herbivores). But this may not be so. Usually natural objects, such as branches, are more interesting in several ways than artificial substitutes, with more varied shapes and bark to pull off with the likelihood of juicy invertebrates underneath. All this is already strong reason to provide real branches, rather than artificial substitutes. But grass underfoot or other vegetation, real trees and bushes may be attractive to animals in the kind of ways they are to us too.

There are difficulties in the provision of real trees and even other plants in enclosures in some cases: that they last only a short time because of damage from the animals. Whatever solution is reached, it shouldn't be that of some elaborate naturalistic displays with pseudo-provision of real vegetation, which appears to be in the enclosure but merely surrounds it, or is protected from animal contact by electric wires (Ormrod 1987: 23, 25–6).

7

THE KEEPING AND DISPLAY
OF ANIMALS

SIX WAYS OF KEEPING ANIMALS

There are several acceptable approaches to keeping animals. Six can be usefully distinguished, though they overlap.

Natural and/or free-living conditions

For some animals we can create artificial habitats that are probably no different, so far as the animals are concerned, from their natural ones. In some cases stocking is unnecessary because the animals just arrive. Examples are ponds for wildfowl, such as those of the Emperor Frederick II, or of Sir Peter Scott and the Wildfowl and Wetlands Trust. Some of the wildfowl will arrive in the course of migration. Artificial ponds can probably be even more the real thing for freshwater invertebrates, as well as amphibians and fish. Diving beetles and the like arrive of their own accord, once a suitable pond has been created.

The keeping of deer in a large deerpark will not be quite as natural as this. The deer won't be preyed upon by wolves, where the occupants of a pond will be predators and/or form prey for others, as part of an almost natural ecosystem. But in other ways deer in a large park may be living almost naturally. The Père David's deer at Woburn were in a very large area with lakes and marshes, and bred well, but also faced such natural hazards as a high loss of young born in particularly bad weather. The numbers of the Chillingham wild cattle fell to thirteen during the extreme winter of 1947 (their recent peak was fifty-nine in 1982) (Allison 1987: 102). This is the cost of not having housing provided as in mainstream zoo-keeping.

THE KEEPING AND DISPLAY OF ANIMALS

Parrots may be kept free-flying, remaining around a park because of the availability of food, like conures and macaws at the Loroparque in Tenerife, or for that matter the peacocks at Glasgow Zoo. As we saw, the 12th Duke of Bedford kept 'liberty budgerigars'.

With indigenous animals it seems the ideal arrangement to provide a habitat so attractive that the animals you want to keep drop in and stick around by choice (Tudge 1991b: 161–2) – like the members of a long-established colony of jackdaws at Glasgow Zoo. A free-living colony of Night herons at Edinburgh Zoo escaped years ago, and have remained by choice where they are well off. At least once a wild Roe deer has leapt into the Axis deer enclosure at Glasgow Zoo, quite a compliment to the enclosure.

Most animals cannot be kept in such virtually free and/or wild conditions, and in many cases should not be, not least because of the danger of escapes and establishment as free-living but un-welcome additions to our wild fauna. (Attitudes have changed since the days when acclimatisation, even to Gustave Loisel eighty years ago, seemed a good idea.)

Semi-naturalistic enclosure

A main way of keeping animals in zoos is in a semi-naturalistic enclosure, which may suggest the wild habitat to some degree or in some respects, but will not simulate it very closely: hence 'semi-naturalistic'. The more naturalistic it is, the better. But in any case it should provide whatever features the animals need to allow and stimulate a large portion of their natural behaviour, certainly including whatever means of locomotion – climbing, burrowing, swimming, and so on – they would normally use in the wild. For many animals, such as various ungulates and wallabies, their needs may be met by little more than a field suitably enclosed (Duncan and Poole 1990: 220). Rodents such as prairie-dogs or porcupines may need only an enclosure of reasonable size allow-ing burrowing: they will create for themselves what else they need, and will be fully occupied by excavations and their social relations. Lions, specialists as we have seen, may also be suitably catered for with an appropriately furnished large enclosure: they seem able to adapt to what is only a somewhat extended version of their long leisure periods even in the wild (and the males usually rely on the females to do the hunting in any case). However, the

103

effects of various kinds of enrichment on lions should be investigated. (I take it for granted that all these animals also have inside accommodation for night or retreat from the weather.)

With this kind of relatively straightforward animal keeping, we are likely to observe enough natural behaviour to give us (along with the application of the other criteria) reasonable indication of the animals' well-being.

Even with animals quite easily catered for, there is always room for improvement, especially in the light of their wild behaviour, guided by careful monitoring of the animals' behaviour in the enclosure (Duncan and Pool 1990: 222–3).

Enriched semi-naturalistic enclosure

Such improvement, or enrichment, becomes much more urgent with the more 'difficult' animals – the highly intelligent, exploratory, opportunist and sometimes also (to make it worse) physically powerful animals, such as bears, dogs, primates (especially apes) and perhaps pigs. I am identifying this as a third possible approach to emphasise how greatly animals' requirements differ.

Especially needed here is ingenuity in doing everything possible to make the animals' lives more interesting, in particular whatever can be done to elicit their natural behaviour. The obvious deprivation of zoo animals is the occupation of food-seeking which, in many cases, would occupy them for long periods in the wild. The remedy is to hide food, so that it has to be searched for, or provide it so that it has to be worked for in some way. Some primates, for example, will, by choice, work for their food rather than merely receive it (Markowitz 1982: 7). As before, it is usually a matter of providing a more or less natural-looking area. But where an area something like the natural habitat will probably be enough for wallabies, this may be far from enough, even with a tree or a climbing frame or two, for chimpanzees. A wooded enclosure the size of the chimpanzee island at Arnhem (de Wall 1982) is a different matter. Where an area like this is not available, it is still desirable for the enclosure to be as natural as possible or at least have natural elements, such as a grassy area and plants; but it is still more important to provide what will stimulate the animals, which may be, for example, an artificial termite mound into which they can stick straws to extract not termites but honey. The significant thing about this example is that it is provided in the light of knowledge of what chimpanzees do in the wild.

Knowledge of the animal's wild habitat and behaviour is the best source of ideas for what can be provided to enrich its captive environment, and naturalistic enrichment – features identical to those in the natural habitat which would stimulate the animals' natural behaviour, or simulation of wild features – is probably the best approach. Many examples of such enrichment at Glasgow Zoo in the Himalayan Black bear enclosures (O'Grady *et al.* 1990), with the cats (Law 1991), and with the polar bears while these were still kept at Glasgow (Law *et al.* 1986b) are described by Colin Tudge (1991a; 1991d: 223–8).

To achieve breeding for the first time is often a matter of altering the captive environment – perhaps keeping male and female normally apart (as in cheetahs), or adjusting the photoperiod (Law and Boyle 1984: 192–3), or providing certain nest materials – to make it accord more closely in some significant respect with the wild.

Markowitz has pioneered several more elaborate devices to elicit animals' natural behaviour such as flying meatballs for servals to leap to grab (Markowitz 1982: 175–9), or self-operated shower-baths for elephants, and trunk-operated switchboards giving a reward for the right combination (ibid.: 86–93), and arrangements by which polar bears or primates can perform some task and thus produce food (ibid.: 46–55). As mentioned above, he has found that many animals will voluntarily work for their food in preference merely to being given it, which is eloquent evidence of the need of some animals for occupation and even creative activity. Markowitz himself is aware of the criticisms some of his work has received, such as that it conditions animals to respond (perhaps in artificial ways) to artificial stimuli, and thus may be rendering animals ill-equipped for reintroduction to the wild. He advises those who find some of his suggestions impractical, or distasteful because of their mechanical nature, to work to the same end in whatever ways they feel are more appropriate, the end being the provision of a rich, stimulating captive environment (Cherfas 1984: 128 ff.; Campbell 1979: 213). There is great room for, on the one hand, learning from study of the animals' wild behaviour, and, on the other, exercising ingenuity in how to simulate or substitute for features of their wild environment in the captive one. So there may be ways by such methods of

105

'behavioural engineering' of supplementing the more natural ways of enriching the captive environment of (especially) opportunists.

The criterion of natural behaviour will still be important here in evaluating the desirability of any such devices, whether elaborate or very simple. Where it is clearly natural behaviour which is being elicited this will be in such methods' favour; we may still be uneasy if the device seems itself distinctly unnatural. Ideally we want natural behaviour elicited by natural stimuli, or something closely related to natural stimuli. On the other hand, some behaviour not obviously natural at all may, when we judge by the other criteria (like health and direct indications), seem perfectly acceptable and desirable. An extreme example would be the driving of motorcycles and electric jeeps by chimpanzees at St Louis Zoo in America, which Hediger (1968: 136–7) describes. His own feelings of 'repugnance' were replaced by the undeniable evidence of his eyes that the chimpanzees, like a crowd of 'fidgety naughty schoolboys', loved the whole business, which they had utterly mastered, despite the fact you would have thought that it was 'beyond the extreme limits of the animals' capacity' (Hediger 1968: 137).

Enriched non-naturalistic enclosure

Sometimes animals may be kept in an enclosure which is frankly non-naturalistic but which is highly suitable for them, even so, because it succeeds in supplying what they need.

A paradigm example of an enclosure of this sort, though not in a zoo, is the 'enriched pig pen' developed at the Edinburgh School of Agriculture. Domestic pigs were studied in semi-wild conditions for many months and (very significantly) much natural behaviour was observed, almost exactly typical of that of wild boar: even to the very details of what sort of place the animals chose to nest in, the sort of spot they would defaecate in, the way a sow behaved when she farrowed. A pen, obviously covering a tiny area by comparison with the hillside, was then designed so as to include the right features to elicit most of the behaviour which had been observed in the larger area – nest-making, rooting, defaecating (in an imitation of a path between bushes, rather than a cul-de-sac), and so on. And this approach worked: most of the pigs' wild behaviour still occurred in the 'enriched pig pen'

(Wood-Gush 1983:196–8; Huntingford 1984; Duncan and Poole 1990: 209–13). This is in at least one very important respect exactly the right approach to adopt in a zoo with any 'difficult' animals (i.e. those for whom it is very clear that merely putting them in a fairly natural-type area is insufficient for their well-being). Zoos will normally have much more space available than, for commercial reasons, would have been appropriate for the 'pig pen'; indeed a zoo would ideally provide an enclosure more like the semi-natural hillside where the first part of the pig study leading to the design of the pen occurred. But the wild study leading to the identification of the essential stimuli for eliciting different parts of the animals' behavioural repertoire, and then the careful providing either of those stimuli or of substitutes for them, is a fine demonstration of how an enclosure can be improved – or designed from scratch – in the light of study of the wild behaviour of the species concerned.

Howletts' gorilla enclosure is a good example of a non-naturalistic enclosure which yet meets the animals' requirements admirably, as is borne out by their breeding success. The enclosure looks more like a sort of gymnasium than a bit of rain forest – a sort of health club for gorillas, indeed, or a holiday camp. According to John Aspinall himself, he would probably have gone in for a more naturalistic enclosure had American-type funding been available. But the fact remains, it is an excellent enclosure for the actual gorillas. The Woolly Monkey Sanctuary's linked, and varied enclosures, are another example, though some of the enclosures are semi-naturalistic – and for that matter, on occasion some of the monkeys are allowed out completely into the trees. But the enclosures in no way simulate the Amazon forest.

Fully naturalistic enclosure

Again, there is no sharp line between this approach and the 'enriched, semi-naturalistic enclosure'. This is clear from the writing of a leading spokesman for elaborately naturalistic enclosures, the architect and zoo director David Hancocks. Hancocks has long emphasised the need to provide conditions in zoos where animals can express their natural behaviour and be kept free from any need to indulge in stereotypies or other abnormal behaviour (Hancocks 1971: 185). He recommends naturalistic enrichment very much along the lines above, emphasising the animal's need for more complexity in its environment than (to put it mildly) has been traditionally provided (Hancocks 1980: 167). *Temporal* change is needed too (ibid.: 168), and varied feeding, made far more interesting and stimulating for the animals (Hutchins *et al.* 1984: 35–7). He notes how easily and cheaply, with a little research and ingenuity, an existing enclosure can often be enormously improved by (whenever possible) natural materials (ibid.: 30).

But Hancocks goes further, seeing such naturalistic enrichment of enclosures as an interim measure. He advocates enclosures which simulate the wild habitat to a remarkable extent, such as two elaborately naturalistic enclosures for gorillas (ibid.: 33) and for Lion-tailed macaques (ibid.: 35) at Woodland Park Zoo in America, both modelled closely on areas in the animals' natural habitats.

Hancocks is enormously concerned with the welfare of the animals. In no way are these naturalistic exhibits provided merely for the public, though their interest and stimulus for the human visitor are also very much Hancocks's concerns. I shall look at his approach from the human point of view, rather than the animal's, below (113 ff.).

However, as we have seen, some highly naturalistic displays are not necessarily satisfactory for the animal occupants, or at least may be much less suitable than appears to the public. Animal occupants of beautiful exhibits sometimes have far less space than appears and can't reach the plants. The periodic changes in enclosures recommended by Hancocks are unlikely to be feasible in vastly expensive displays with fibreglass trees and the like.

With Hancocks's own exhibits, my only reservation is with his unwillingness to use non-naturalistic objects under any circumstances. I have already emphasised the advantages of natural materials – actual branches, leaves, and so on. His gorillas seem very well off. But suppose it appeared likely that they would enjoy climbing ropes, or would enjoy tearing up cardboard boxes. If there wasn't a natural substitute to use instead, there would be a clash here between the interests of the animals and the aesthetic aspect of the enclosure. (Those jeep-driving chimps at St Louis weren't worried about aesthetics or naturalness; they were too busy enjoying themselves!)

Trained, 'domestic animal' approach

A very different approach to keeping animals is training them to perform various tasks and generally treating them as domesticated animals, which camels and llamas are, as we have seen, and perhaps elephants too, though only partially. To have llamas pulling carts and camels giving rides, where possible, seems, in view of their being domesticated animals, unobjectionable and likely to be good for their mental as well as their physical health. To Hancocks (1971: 184) the training of animals in zoos is quite inappropriate, except to the minimal extent needed for medical treatment. But a recent defence of the training of animals, on all sorts of levels from that of management to the possibilities thereby provided for public instruction about the cognitive abilities of animals, has been mounted by Marthe Kiley-Worthington (1990). Hediger (1968: 133–9) would clearly support her.

Training seems less appropriate with obviously wild animals, such as the carnivores; though of course training here is often perfectly possible, not least with bears, including polar bears (Grzimek 1966: 204), even though this is not an option normally considered in zoos, at least in Britain. But it hardly seems objectionable with falconry, no doubt because much of the falcon's behaviour remains very obviously natural. The case of dolphins is more difficult, but the fact that they respond so readily to training, and obviously develop a close relationship with their trainer, makes it difficult to condemn out of hand. In some respects the keeping of dolphins has often been very seriously inadequate, as made clear by W. Johnson (1990).

THE AESTHETICS AND PURPOSE OF ZOO DESIGN

Let us now look at ways of keeping animals, not from the point of view of their interests, but from the point of view of zoo visitors – though in the end these two cannot be fully separated.

I have purposely been speaking of enclosures rather than buildings, not because the buildings aren't obviously very important – whether the animals are kept entirely within them or whether they have outside enclosures as well – but because zoo architecture often seems to have been a rather misguided pursuit, aimed at pleasing human taste instead of serving the animals' own interests. However, we can hardly ignore the numerous zoo buildings of architectural importance, not least at London Zoo.

London has had striking buildings from the start, and contains no fewer than nine listed buildings, including five for animals: Decimus Burton's Raven's Cage (1828) and Giraffe House (1836–7), the Mappin Terraces (1914–27), and Lubetkin's Gorilla House (1932–3) and Penguin Pool (1934) (Victorian Society 1992: 1–2). Many of its other buildings are architecturally interesting and, as the zoo as a whole has conservation status, the Victorian Society has been able to save various unlisted Victorian buildings which the zoo wished to demolish in 1985 as part of its development. The Thirties Society has a strong interest in Sir Hugh Casson's Elephant and Rhino House (1965) and the Snowdon Aviary (1962–4) (Victorian Society 1992: 6).

Let us consider the '"heavy", blank-walled concrete' Elephant and Rhino House (Victorian Society 1992: 6), whose 'appropriate brutality' architecturally can be seen as continuing London Zoo's long tradition of reflecting 'contemporary styles for human habitations' (Victorian Society 1992: 1).

We often regard animals as beautiful or magnificent, as I shall discuss in the next chapter. Let us for a moment think of animals as rather like magnificent pictures such as we would display in an art gallery. To display a picture or a sculpture properly is itself an aesthetic matter, requiring judgement about the most effective, tasteful and even respectful way of displaying it. A picture's frame needs to be appropriate; a picture could be framed in a way that made it look ridiculous, just as it could be hung in a situation so inappropriate as to be insulting to its quality.

It is desirable for an art gallery itself to be a work of art, and the best case for Casson's Elephant and Rhino House at London Zoo would be to see it as a way of displaying elephants (and rhinos) in a manner which does honour to them as magnificent works of nature, like displaying a great master in an art gallery to the best advantage. As another architect sees it, the building

> shows a freedom in concept using a sculptural form to reflect the occupants and designed to display them in the most dramatic way. The rough texture of the walls is not unlike that of an elephant's hide. Internally, the timber joists arch overhead like trees in a forest . . . giving the appearance of animals standing in bright toplit clearings in a forest.
>
> (Wylson 1984: 107)

110

The aesthetic aim is appropriate and creditable, and whether it is achieved is a matter of aesthetic judgement which does not affect the case. But obviously the animals' needs should have come first, as is well put by the comment of an anonymous 'distinguished continental zoo director' whom Gerald Durrell quotes (1977: 28–9): 'What for the roof so high, uh? They think sometimes maybe the elephant is meaning to fly up at night and be roosting?' Of course if the animals' needs had been met, and the aesthetic demands as well, this would have been ideal. One could argue that they have been, for, as Eltringham (1984) remarks, stables have not needed much change through the centuries and elephants, regarded as domestic animals, perhaps just need a large stable. As such, the Elephant House is no worse than one without the towering pinnacles. However, even aesthetically speaking, something more obviously suited to the elephants themselves would have been more appropriate, and to show this I want to mention another example, also at London, that of the Lubetkin Penguin Pool.

This, designed some sixty years ago by Berthold Lubetkin, 'is certainly a masterpiece . . . and a work of art' (Gardiner 1987). It was inspired by the shape of an egg, which Lubetkin saw as 'one of nature's most perfect shapes . . . here was a single idea . . . flawlessly executed, and that somehow possessed, as if in diagrammatic form, all those fundamental principles of design upon which architecture depends' (Gardiner 1987).

Significantly, the same article remarks that 'It was functional, economic and practical, enjoyed by onlookers and penguins alike'. This is significant because the pool, despite this overwhelming praise, has been claimed to be rather unsuitable for penguins, in particular not to be deep enough to allow proper swimming (Lambourne 1990). Because of the pool's architectural merit, some thousands of pounds were granted to restore it in 1987 to its original splendour. There was no question so far as I know, despite the money available, of the pool's being deepened in the interests of the penguins, but probably not because of the conservation order on the pool. If this was the reason, it was a bad one, despite the fact that (in my view) it is right we should have a system under which something of special architectural merit can have such protection. Fine works of art are clear examples of items which should be regarded as belonging, in the final instance, to the whole community or to mankind, and even protected from their owners if necessary (as we will see further in the next chapter). I don't think the protection order was necessarily the reason here, for the Victorian Society, for instance, is clearly prepared to support the alteration if judged reasonable of a listed building (Victorian Society 1992: 5). Again, it is not clear that the pool needs to be any deeper, though Lubetkin himself is claimed to have said that originally the zoo authorities required the reduction of the pool's depth to save costs, despite the keepers' protests that the birds preferred deeper water for swimming (Aitken 1990). But the present Curator of birds at London, Peter Olney, has said that Black-footed penguins (the kind kept in the Lubetkin pool) prefer shallow water and go in for surface-swimming (Olney 1990). He also reminds us of the breeding success of the colony. And at least one change has been made, the inclusion of larger nesting boxes in the restored pool (Victorian Society 1992: 2). One solution of the depth problem would have been to give the penguins the benefit of the doubt – a deeper pool just in case they preferred it. At any rate, where there is a clash between animal requirements and aesthetic considerations, the needs of the animals on welfare grounds should be recognised as completely superseding any aesthetic requirements. The enclosure (or pool, or whatever it may be), being a functional piece of architecture, would itself be aesthetically flawed in as much as it failed to meet biological requirements. One odd consequence of this fact may seem to be that the quality of a functional work of art must then change through time, as (in the case of architecture for animals) we learn more of their requirements. But it is rather that, with such a work of art, a final judgement upon its quality must wait upon the acquisition of the fullest understanding of the biological factors involved. And in as much as we will never reach perfect understanding of these, so we will never be in a position to give a final judgement upon such a work of art's merit.

At least in theory, there should be no conflict, when designing a building or enclosure for an animal species, between biological and aesthetic requirements, because the aesthetic requirements must in fact include the biological requirements, first and foremost, and perhaps other non-aesthetic requirements such as the enclosure's not giving misleading messages to the public about how it should regard the animal. However, the challenge to the zoo architect or designer becomes an even more interesting one if they appreciate the need to meet the biological needs of the animal (as well as other important, non-biological requirements). For all artists work under restrictions, under rules, and part of an artistic achievement is the way the artist solves the problems of those restrictions, achieves so much within them. It is interesting that sometimes even works of art as such, like Henry Moore's sculpture, *King and Queen*, or many of the works of art in the Burrell Collection at Glasgow, have been presumed to be set off to advantage, or set off best, by a background of the natural world, such as trees and grass. It is more than likely that for most animals a really aesthetically successful enclosure or building will be naturalistic or at least incorporate a natural area. The message for zoo architects, on aesthetic grounds alone, seems clear.

THE AESTHETIC OF THE NATURALISTIC

So it seems likely that the best enclosures aesthetically will be naturalistic, as David Hancocks maintains, but as many others have realised also, including the designers of the Mappin Terraces at London, which itself was modelled on a similar construction by Carl Hagenbeck at Stellingen.

Where Casson's Elephant House and Lubetkin's Penguin Enclosure are a little like art galleries displaying pictures and inviting our admiration for them, enclosures such as those for gorillas and for Lion-tailed macaques at the Woodland Park Zoo, which David Hancocks describes, are like theatre. Hancocks is keen for a degree of naturalism which gives the illusion of seeing the animals in the wild. As the visitors know they are at a zoo, he is aiming presumably for the sort of strange suspended belief that operates when we watch a play or a film: we get caught up in the performance and almost think it real – otherwise we wouldn't care about the characters and what happens to them – and yet at the same time we somehow know it isn't real (else we would react to a stage murder as to a real one).

A great deal of the 'furnishings' of the enclosure are, or may well be, for the animals' benefit as well as ours. Not entirely, for some of them will be 'backcloth' – imitation cliffs or banks rather than real ones – but these will be at a minimum (Hancocks 1989a: 260) (at least in one of Hancocks's enclosures – by no means necessarily in some other elaborate naturalistic displays, as we have seen).

But Hancocks does not rest with the enclosure itself and its content. He is concerned with the 'supporting programme', the surroundings of the enclosures, as well as the arrangement of viewing areas. He provides (in a series of Australian architectural articles (Hancocks 1989a; 1989b; 1990)) detailed directions for how to maintain the visitor's state of suspended disbelief and ensure the quality of the viewing experience.

Primary routes, handling many people, and where kiosks and the like are situated, are sharply differentiated from secondary routes, which lead to viewing areas and contain no public services to destroy the suggestion of naturalness. There are even small tertiary routes, for the most intimate viewing experience, where even seats are banned (other than 'a rock, or a log, or a tree to lean against') so as not to detract from nature (Hancocks 1989a: 265–6). When you actually view the animals in their enclosure, there must if possible be no bars or walls or anything of the kind visible.

The windows or viewing areas themselves must be arranged so that you do not see the whole enclosure. This makes it look bigger and more interesting. At no point must visitors at different viewing points have overlapping lines of sight; you must not see other people looking; for this too would spoil the illusion of seeing the real thing (Hancocks 1989b: 421).

Now all this is in many ways superb. Clearly Hancocks's enclosures are informing us of the nature of the animals' natural habitats, and explaining their relations to it. They are likely to stimulate our respect and admiration for the animal – Hancocks (Hutchins *et al.* 1984: 33–5) notes the responses of visitors to the gorilla and macaque enclosures. Clearly there is not a trace of the 'visiting prison' feeling which a gorilla enclosure can sometimes impart, neither is there any encouragement to the public to view the animals as clowns to be laughed at – an all too familiar reaction to primates at least from very young children. He notes the hushed tones of admiration. Clearly also these enclosures are as likely as any to stimulate visitors to support with their pockets the protection of actual wild habitats, and visitors may well be receiving also such a satisfying experience of almost-real nature that many of them will have no need to experience any actual wild habitats – and this, the taking of pressure off wild habitats, and of course the stimulating of concern about them, are two important supplementary conservational roles of zoos (one of which especially I will discuss further in Chapter 9).

So Hancocks is here advocating (and creating) animal enclosures whose aesthetic quality includes, as it should, very important conservational and educational elements. But strangely, Hancocks regards these as the entire conservational role of zoos. He minimises, in fact, the importance of zoos' conservational captive breeding (Hancocks 1991a; 1991b). This is particularly strange in view of his remarks about the Lion-tailed macaque enclosure (Hancocks 1989a: 264), where he actually says that they breed so well, and the species is under such pressure in the wild, that these macaques may go extinct in the wild, but will survive without doubt at Woodland Park. Again, he recognises the captive breeding role on occasion (Hutchins *et al.* 1984: 28), yet stresses that it is inadvisable to combine zoo-keeping, where public viewing is essential, with serious breeding (Hancocks 1991a). This would seem, were it true, to be a serious indictment of the possibility of providing good conditions in a zoo. Yet he has demonstrated himself, as we have seen, just how good conditions *can* be provided in a zoo (the macaque enclosure for example) and also how well the animals breed. So Hancocks is rather inconsistent.

He is demonstrating the most marvellous aesthetic and educational possibilities of zoos, yet he is excluding a role which may yet prove vastly important. One hopes it won't, but the indicators are not good.

And again, as we saw above, Hancocks himself advocates the improvement of existing enclosures by all the naturalistic enrichment possible, while recommending still more highly the extreme naturalistic enclosure created from scratch. He has every right to be critical of other zoos and their dilatoriness in providing enrichment, yet his criticism is in some cases ludicrously extreme. As I mentioned in the Introduction, Hancocks is one zoo director who welcomed the apparently impending closure of London Zoo (Hancocks 1991a; 1991b; 1991c), at the same time dismissing almost every other zoo in Britain as valueless also (1991a). And why? Because they are not following his dictum that an enclosure is valueless unless it is fully naturalistic, and because, unlike him, they are advocating captive breeding as a conservational tool (Hancocks 1991a).

He observes himself that there is a dichotomy of views on the whole approach to zoo display, and that it is a dichotomy in museum display also: whether they should be 'object-driven' or 'story-driven', as he puts it; in his view most zoos and museums are 'object-driven' and quite wrong: 'they select an object and then choose some way to display it, rather than select a path of information and then choose the objects that will illuminate it' (Hancocks 1991c: 3). Hancocks's 'story-driven' approach is fine as long as it is seen as one possible approach for a museum or zoo, but near disastrous when it is claimed, as by Hancocks, as their *only* proper role (Hancocks 1991c: 3). A museum, like an art gallery – itself a kind of museum – should have as its prime function the 'conserving' of valuable objects: that is, it looks after them, and also studies them and displays them as best it can to the public. No one, I think, has been so inspired yet as to propose some other role for art galleries – no doubt somebody will in time. But this is advocated for natural history museums, so that the Natural History Museum in London has banished many of its 'works of nature' – its actual valuable objects which used to be displayed – to the basement and instead concentrates upon mounting informative displays – about ecology or other highly important subjects – incorporating some of the objects. My only complaint about the mounting of the informative displays is that it greatly diminishes the space for showing the actual objects (hence the banishments to the basement). It is as if an art gallery, such as the Burrell in Glasgow, having been entrusted with Burrell's lifelong collections, should hide most of them away and just display a few as objects illustrating exhibitions *about* the role of art or the like.

Even as an educational vehicle, the 'story-driven' approach is in a way slightly insulting to the public – or the student, for that matter. It does not display, as it were, the precious object directly, inviting the public to respond to it as they will, while giving them whatever aid in the way of interpretive information is possible; instead it takes the response out of the hands of the public: it makes the response for it, putting (just a few) objects into an informative display. The wonder – the numinous quality, almost, of some of the objects – is thus a little diminished; and the public are a little insulted. This applies particularly with animals, whose appeal as amazing creatures – sometimes, even, almost as numinous objects: objects to be responded to with awe – has been a large part of zoos for centuries. Of course, the animals should be kept as well as possible, and far better than they were in the past, and Hancocks is making a great contribution to the theory and practice of how they should be kept. But the fact remains that the animals are principally there in their own right to be admired and studied, not to form part of displays which are informing us about, even, ecosystems and the balance of nature and pollution problems.

Furthermore, of course, the direct conservation role of zoos – of breeding animals as part of managed captive populations and so on – is becoming more and more important and parallels museums' importance as conservers of precious objects as such. Zoos really are, as we shall see in the next two chapters, conserving those very special living precious objects called animals.

This dichotomy of approaches has been apparent in recent discussions about the future role of London Zoo. Some would turn it into a kind of theme-park, with just a few large displays about conservation, pollution, and so on, in each case incorporating a few illustrative animals; these are following the 'story-driven' approach. Those who recognise the zoo's central role as that of keeping animals, especially for conservational purposes, are following the 'object-driven' approach, and they appear to have won. Of course there is a need for all the imaginative displays possible, but it is now particularly important to tell the public about the actual animals zoos keep. All aspects of them, including the zoological and the ecological, should be included, and why captive breeding programmes are now so important as a supplement to the protection of natural habitats. (Ecology, of course, is a part of zoology, as of botany, although Hancocks (1991a) does not seem to appreciate this.) Hancocks's contribution, provided it is seen as one approach among others, is superb; but to try and make it the exclusive approach, as he does, verges on the mischievous. It denigrates what is likely to be an inestimably important role of zoos.

Very elaborate zoo exhibits – reconstructions of tropical forest and the like – are very expensive. One example of just how expensive is a set of animal and plant exhibits – the 'Cleveland Metroparks Rainforest' – scheduled to open this year at an estimated cost of $25–30 million (Taylor 1990). Many other zoos would probably question whether expenditure on this scale – on constructing an imitation rainforest, not on saving the real thing! – is necessary, though it will clearly operate as a magnificent educational device for the rainforest and will no doubt itself assist the raising of large sums for actual rainforest conservation.

London doesn't have this kind of money, though interestingly, according to Hancocks himself (twenty years ago), 'government assistance [for zoos] is certainly necessary' (Hancocks 1971: 189). This is interesting because Hancocks implicitly denied in 1991 that London's problems had anything to do with its lack of government funding (Hancocks 1991a), though indeed some of the Zoological Society of London's own fellows would agree with Hancocks that London has not in recent years made the best use of some substantial sums of money that it has had. But Hancocks actually makes the extraordinary judgement that the value of an institution is to be identified with its financial success, remarking (in 1991) that the fact London Zoo was facing closure showed it wasn't any good and that it wasn't worth trying to buttress up (Hancocks 1991b) – a strangely materialistic judgement from one of Hancocks's artistic abilities. If London Zoo had closed, this would of course have indicated financial, perhaps management, perhaps political, failure. But in no way would it necessarily imply scientific, conservational, or educational failure, any more than the closure of, say, the Royal Opera House, Covent Garden – which would probably occur immediately if all government subsidy were withdrawn – would demonstrate musical or artistic failure.

Again, it is interesting that the 'Cleveland Metroparks Rainforest', with its astronomical cost (by British standards), is calculated to increase attendances to 'well over a million visitors a year' (Taylor 1990). London Zoo, without such marvellous displays, still has an attendance of well over a million – much less than 40 years ago no doubt, but still enough to make it a very substantial tourist attraction. This fact tends to be ignored by fashionable denigrators, who include even the authors of an editorial and a very interesting study of Lubetkin's work in a recent issue of the *Architects' Journal* ('Astragal' 1991: 14; Reading 1991: 29, 37). The Victorian Society and Thirties Society, on the other hand, note how successful London Zoo still is, and comment also on what they see as the absurdity of the way it is starved of funds by the government (Victorian Society 1992: 2–3). That London Zoo's lack of government funding is anomalous in view of its world importance conservationally and scientifically, the support given to comparable national institutions (such as major museums and Kew Gardens) and the funding regarded by foreign capital cities as appropriate for their zoos, was also recognised by a recent House of Commons Environment Committee Report (House of Commons 1991: 5–6).

I mention all this to emphasise that the age-old attractions for people of seeing animals are not gone; it is worth adding that a good many displays at London are of course at least semi-naturalistic, notably the Snowdon Aviary and the enclosures in the Charles Clore Pavilion for Small Mammals, and the present accommodation for large cats. The Hancocks philosophy has a lot to contribute, but it has not superseded all other thinking, or all other practices, in the zoo world.

IS IT CAPTIVITY?

We saw in the first section of this chapter several different ways of keeping animals. Some of them are often referred to as 'captivity'. 'Animal captivity' is a convenient and useful term in that it readily marks off one state of animals – that of being kept by humans – from another state – that of being entirely free-living or wild. But on the other hand, anything that can be called animal captivity may seem, in the eyes of anyone prepared to grant animals a minimum of consideration, to be self-condemned by the very term 'captivity', surely of necessity an oppressive treatment only justified if at all for some human criminals. But is the keeping of animals in acceptable ways, such as we have considered, captivity? Does it indeed have anything in common with human captivity? Let us see what is involved in a human's being captive, and then consider how much of this applies also to animal captivity, and in particular to good animal captivity. It should then be possible to establish both that 'captivity' is used here as a technical term without very much of the meaning and overtones which it carries in the case of human captivity, and more importantly that at least some forms of what would normally be counted as animal captivity should also be regarded as acceptable.

Aspects of human captivity

The following aspects of captivity seem important as far as human captivity is concerned:

1 Movement restriction. A captive's movements, especially travel, and to some extent other actions, are prevented or restricted.
2 Dullness of conditions. The captive is frequently confined within dull, bare accommodation – the traditional prisoner's

cell in fact. Dull or plain food, even poor food, has often been a feature of captivity.

3 Communication restriction. Their freedom to communicate with their family and friends or other people is restricted.

4 Reproduction restriction. They are not normally able to carry on family life and/or have children.

5 Possibility of non-physical captivity. While the normal means of their being kept captive is by means of prison walls, locked doors, and so on, they could be kept captive without any restrictions being placed on their actual travel if they were controlled by drugs which they were forced to take, or by some sort of wiring in, or cerebral manipulation, or hypnotism, so that they were not acting freely, even though there were no bars or actual physical barriers restricting their movements. If we thought some application of indoctrination or training quite excessive, and forced upon someone against their wishes, and particularly perhaps if we considered that it was such as to change their nature or personality, we might call this captivity.

6 Restriction by outside agent. The restrictions must be necessarily imposed by an outside agent. Not to be able to travel or communicate or generally live one's normal life because of physical or mental illness, or a rail strike, or living in the country, would not make one strictly captive. The effects might be the same, but it would not be real captivity just because there was no outside agent purposely restricting one's freedom.

7 Intentional unpleasantness. Captivity is normally, or at least very often, intended to be in some degree unpleasant.

8 Imposed as punishment or as treatment of enemy. A state of captivity is inflicted or imposed either as a punishment or, more likely, as appropriate treatment of a defeated enemy in war, or a member of a subject and perhaps (in the view of the captor) inferior race.

9 Captive's awareness of their state. The captive will normally be aware of their state, and such awareness is part of or involved in their captivity, and it may be part of the pleasure of the captor – as in a Roman triumph, with prisoners/captives paraded.

Aspects of animal captivity

Now let us see how many of these are aspects also of good animal captivity:

1 Movement restriction. Yes, but . . . . The movement restriction applies, and in some degree the restrictions on other actions. However, as we have seen, the animal ought to be kept in such a way that as many as possible of its natural activities occur.

2 Dullness of conditions. No, but . . . . Animal accommodation has only too often been like a prisoner's cell, though not invariably so, even historically, as we have seen. But in none of the acceptable ways of keeping animals I have outlined would the conditions be cell-like. The importance of enrichment is now widely (and indeed should be universally) recognised. The food provided should of course be enormously better than traditional 'prison fare', and even historically probably was often far superior.

3 Communication restriction. Yes, but . . . . This applies, though the animal should be able to communicate with other animals in its group in the zoo, if not usually with others in the wild. (This could occur, e.g. in the case of swans at Slimbridge.)

4 Reproduction restriction. No, but . . . . A main point of modern animal captivity is that breeding should occur. Although it occurs at best less freely than it would in the wild, it often does not or cannot occur, and this was very often the case in zoos historically.

5 Possibility of non-physical captivity. (Yes.) This does, or rather it could occur: we could wire up an animal so as to manipulate it through its brain (Lausch 1975: 78, 94), or use drugs, etc. More to the point, we could change an animal just by taming it and also by training, and by selective breeding; though in this last case it would be on the animal's descendants, not on the animal itself, that the effect would be produced. The wiring up and use of drugs examples do not, of course, normally occur in zoos; they are merely theoretical possibilities. Taming in some degree does, as does in some cases training. It is an accepted responsibility of zoos to endeavour to avoid selective breeding, but, as I argued in Chapter 4, I do not think a rigid distinction can be drawn between 'zoo animals' (or even fully

wild animals) on the one hand and domesticated animals on the other.

6   Restriction by outside agent. Yes. The animal's situation is indeed brought about by an outside agent, who also belongs to a different species from the captive.

7   Intentional unpleasantness. No. The captivity is not intended to be unpleasant, or, if it ever is, most certainly ought not to be, though in some cases it is perhaps likely to be, and expected to be. But this is mainly so only of the actual capture of a wild animal and the period ensuing until it has adjusted to captivity. Many animals are born in zoos, and capturing is in any case more difficult to justify than mere keeping captive: I shall look at it in Chapter 13.

8   Imposed as punishment or as treatment of enemy. No. Again, the captivity is certainly not normally imposed as a punishment or appropriate treatment of a defeated enemy. However, this may have been the situation in the past, and it is possible that it could be today in some cases.

9   Captive's awareness of their state. No. It is unlikely that the captive animal will be aware of being captive, or at least it should not be if its captive conditions are adequate (Brambell 1973: 45). However, it is not anthropomorphic, as we saw in Chapter 6, to assume an animal is aware of being restricted in a very confined cage. But many zoo staff reasonably believe many of their animals are well enough off not to escape if they could.

So at least (7) ('intentional unpleasantness'), (8) ('punishment') and (9) ('aware') do not apply in the animal situation; (2) ('dullness') and (4) ('reproduction') do not apply today in good conditions; (1) ('movement and action') and (3) ('communication') are applicable, but only in some degree; (5) ('technological') is a special case which I will leave out of this particular calculation; and (6) ('outside agent') certainly does apply to animal captivity.

So animal captivity is at least substantially different from human captivity, and we could well regard the word 'captivity' in connection with good zoos as a technical term. Some will feel that the unquestioned fact that the animal's state of captivity is brought about by an outside agent, a member of another species indeed, is so important, and so regrettable, that all the other points fade by comparison, and animal captivity remains well named by that term and is irretrievably wrong. This seems to be the position of the travel writer Jan Morris (1990) in an oddly extreme article about the wickedness of London Zoo. One of the drawbacks of her position, if we take it seriously, is that, having exhausted all her derogatory superlatives in describing the keeping of animals at London Zoo, she would have no stronger terms available to describe animal keeping in obviously worse conditions such as hens in batteries or even primates in the unspeakable 'well of despair' of the Harlows (Rachels 1976: 211–12). So Morris's position will be, for most people, an unreasonably extreme one, especially in view of all the positive aspects of good zoos and their animal keeping. Not that capturing itself in the wild doesn't seem particularly difficult to justify, as I recognise by reserving it for consideration until Chapter 13. By good zoos I mean ones that are providing good conditions for their animals in the light of the fullest knowledge available of what their needs are, and this is something very different from what any human prisoner or captive is likely to be provided with. Replacing the term 'captivity', if we could think of a suitable substitute such as 'keeping' or 'holding' perhaps, would not be, with regard to good zoos, the mere adopting of a euphemism.

I am not justifying or defending the sort of captivity which could reasonably be called prison-like. We now have ways, and know how to set about discovering new ways, of keeping animals so that their real needs are fulfilled, as we have seen. There is another important point, and that is that, if we insist on calling keeping animals 'captivity', there are obviously grades of it. Nobody would call the first of my six ways of keeping animals captivity, but even this first forms a continuum with the others: there is not necessarily any sharp division between them.

8

WHY CONSERVATION IS A MORAL MATTER

Of course how we treat individual animals is a moral matter – starving your dog is morally blameworthy (to say the least). But I want in this chapter to show how caring for animals in another way is also a moral matter – caring for animal species (and for individual animals, of which species consist) as remarkable things (for want of a better word). We will see how caring for various kinds of precious thing is a moral matter, and then note how animals are very striking examples of precious things.

CARING FOR OBJECTS

Some physical objects demand respect from us. Innumerable examples are possible, but here are two or three. Consider a book – not just any book, but a handsome one like a volume of the *She-King* (the collection of Chinese poetry that contains the account of Wen-Wang's Intelligence Park in ancient China) in an edition edited by James Legge. It is beautifully bound, contains, as well as the Chinese characters, a translation and careful notes, and is fairly old (1871). Even if it belonged to me and not a library, I should have no business to throw it out, and would deserve censure if I did. Lady Churchill appears to have destroyed the portrait by Graham Sutherland of her husband, a portrait he disliked. Arguably she should not have done, even though it was her property. The owner of a magnificent mansion could be criticised if he suddenly had it pulled down (because he wanted something more comfortable, say). The owners of grand houses, and of land, often recognise they have a trustee-status – that their ownership is not absolute. They hold their houses or land in trust for their descendants, and could well feel they are also held in trust for the community or the nation. Many such buildings have passed to the National Trust.

My concern here is not the question of whether any fine or beautiful object has an intrinsic value, a value independent of its usefulness to or appreciation by humans. I am merely noting that the respect due to fine objects goes beyond a respect due to them as someone else's property, or, if they are yours, is such that you have not a complete right to do anything you like with them. It is not just a matter of not destroying something of value. It is a matter of caring for it, in the appropriate way. This caring is what we mean by conservation. There are all sorts of things which ought to be conserved.

There are also all sorts of things which do not need to be conserved (in fact more strictly cannot be, in as much as the term conservation contains a built-in value judgement). Many things are rubbish, or become rubbish as soon as you have used them, and had better be thrown out. It would be crazy to try to conserve all buildings, and advisable to be selective too with anything else you are tempted to keep. (As a hoarder by temperament I know the problems.) Selecting and evaluating are essential to conservation. Some kinds of thing do not need to be conserved; and different things of the same kind should be recognised as being of greatly differing value. A painting by Graham Sutherland probably should not be destroyed, even if it is yours and you do not like it; this does not mean that every painting by anybody who cares to try their hand needs to be conserved.

The sorts of thing which demand to be cared for or conserved tend, for obvious reasons, to be unique rather than easily replaceable. A painting, an original anyway, is unique. A tool or piece of equipment which could easily be replaced, does not demand quite the same respect. Obviously a rare specimen of Elizabethan telescope, or even an early model of vacuum cleaner, is different. (Still more a vastly expensive and vital piece of medical equipment.) Though it is important to throw away to avoid clutter, it is also very desirable to have quite a high degree of respect for such everyday objects as, for example, motorcycles and cars, especially if you have to maintain or use them (Pirsig 1976: 24–6). A woman social worker, who is also an expert mechanic, instils young car-stealing delinquents with the skills of motorcycle care and an ensuing respect for motorbikes and cars, including other people's (Levin 1979). On the general virtue of caring for things I am struck by the following – somewhat exaggerated! – comment from a book on boating: 'The satisfaction of having your ship really clean . . . confers a spiritual calm "beyond the power even of religion to bestow"' (Housley 1928: 90).

What we conserve or should conserve is very often what is useful to us, like, historically, rivers, sewers, and forests (which the *Shorter Oxford English Dictionary* mentions under 'conservation'), and animals for hunting. But it is not only useful things, not only resources, or at least not only 'things' of practical use or economic importance (like coal and oil), which should be conserved. Things which are especially beautiful, or are just fine works of art, or are of special historical interest, should be conserved too.

I have said the conservation of something is just caring for it. However we are only likely to care *for* something – or conserve it – if we also care *about* it. Caring about, appreciating, recognising the value of, being moved by the wonder of – these are the driving force, the motivation, for actually caring *for* whatever it may be. The real mechanic cares about motorcycles – he appreciates them – and this is what motivates him to maintain them well. Also essential is his understanding of them, his professional knowledge and skill and so on – but for this too the 'caring about' is a motivation. So caring about is also very important for conservation; indeed we could see it as part of conservation, with the other part being the caring for – putting our caring into action.

DIFFERENT WAYS OF CONSERVING

Because there are great differences between some of the kinds of thing which can or should be conserved, they require different kinds of conservation. Conservation in a museum or art gallery means doing whatever is necessary to keep the specimen or picture in good condition – so that it does not rot, or get infested by woodworm, or encrusted with grime.

But suppose that it is not paintings but music that we are concerned to conserve – say Beethoven's symphonies, or Beethoven's Fifth in particular. It may seem unlikely that this would need conserving, but let us assume it does; let us suppose that Beethoven's Fifth is beginning to be neglected or ignored. Now with the painting it is clear what we are talking about, but less clear with the symphony. Do we mean the performances, or a particular performance (Wollheim 1970: 20–6)? We could conserve that, in a way, by recording it, but we are hardly talking about a mere recording. Neither are we talking about the score of the symphony, for it has to be played – or at least read by a skilled musician – to be music. Still less do we mean Beethoven's manuscript, desirable though it would be to conserve that. In fact we would be talking about performances of the symphony, for it exists in the truest sense only in those. And conserving those would involve conserving quite a lot of other things – first and foremost the actual skill and art of playing, and then various institutions, including orchestras, and concert halls, and musical academies (significantly sometimes called conservatories or conservatoires) where the understanding and study and tradition of Beethoven's music are nurtured. Conserving drama – Shakespeare for instance – would be rather similar to conserving music. The music (or drama) example illustrates, as well as the fact that a piece of music is a kind of 'thing' which exists fully only in its various performances, that we can conserve skills, and ways of life (such as that of the professional musician) and institutions as well as objects in a more obvious sense.

Note also that conserving Beethoven's symphonies would not mean conserving exactly the same kind of performance, and this would be still more obvious with conserving music in general – or Shakespeare or drama. We would only be conserving these properly if we were providing the conditions in which they could change and develop. Indeed it is a rather general characteristic of conservation that it involves caring for something so that it remains active and continues to develop (if it is that sort of thing – obviously a picture does not develop, though the art of painting does), or remains alive (if it is something living). 'Conservation' contrasts with 'preservation', which suggests keeping something in mere existence, like a fly in amber, rather than as something still usable, or developing, or alive.

It may be already sufficiently obvious that caring for valuable things (of very many kinds) is moral – that it can be very important, not just a matter of taste, and we deserve credit for engaging in it, and discredit for neglecting it. But the moral nature of conservation is brought home most clearly by considering its opposite, vandalism.

VANDALISM

The concept of vandalism demonstrates how we do not regard wanton or careless destroying of something of value as merely a way of behaving that we do not care for; we condemn it as in itself immoral. Vandalism includes the stupid damaging of things of vital importance (crops or food supplies or telephone boxes someone's life may depend on) and it is easy to see why damaging these could be a moral matter. But even if beauty or historic interest or great age is what we value something for, we still regard wantonly damaging it as an immoral act.

Sometimes there will be disagreement about whether something is vandalism. I would be inclined to call Lady Churchill's destroying of the Sutherland picture vandalistic, but she had her reason, her husband's intense dislike of the painting. The explorer Richard Burton's widow destroyed his life-long journals on his death to protect his reputation. This seems vandalistic, but she thought she was serving his interests (Brodie 1971: 18). A Mrs Radcliffe destroyed the series of letters on his metaphysical system that Bradley had sent her (Wollheim 1969: 15); well, if he was foolish enough to write to her in these terms, perhaps he had only himself to blame if she didn't bother to keep them. But if she had put them aside as meaningless to her but possibly of interest to someone else, this would have been a creditable 'conservational' or 'respectful' attitude: that of anyone who, though unappreciative of something themselves, yet recognises and respects someone else's appreciation of it. I should add that vandalism can be committed by governments or powerful individuals as well as by groups of young delinquents. For example, an obituary supplement in *The Independent* recorded a council leader's blatantly vandalistic destruction of 'Kensington's opulent Victorian Town Hall' when 'he got wind of an impending preservation order' (Glancey 1989).

If destroying fine things is, in varying degrees, immoral, it seems likely that caring for fine things is moral.

ANIMALS AS NATURAL WORKS OF ART

We have seen that particularly fine or outstanding objects – including works of art – merit respect (even from their owners). Now I want to discuss animals' claims upon us, first their aesthetic claims – in as much as they are rather like works of art – and secondly some of their striking characteristics as animals, and how these characteristics are all reasons for conserving them and in some cases guides to how we should conserve them.

You might think such a discussion was superfluous. Is it not obvious that everyone agrees animals should be conserved, so that the only question remaining is how to do it? Strangely, this is not the case, as a few examples will show. In 1981 John Burton, secretary of (no less!) the long-established Fauna and Flora Preservation Society, told *The Times* that money should not be wasted on captive breeding of the giant panda because it is a 'post-pleistocene relic', doomed to extinction like the mammoth (Samstag 1981). Clive Hollands, a leading animal welfarist, has observed on two occasions (Hollands 1979: 205; 1985: 170) that, if whales go extinct, the loss will be man's not the whales', who will suffer no more at man's hands. To be fair, Hollands in the later comment emphasises the importance of the conservation groups' work, and qualifies his comment about whales by 'so far as suffering is concerned', but at least in the earlier comment he is contemplating with equanimity what to me would be an appalling act of vandalism. There are businessmen who would view the extinction of whales as a result of their actions with equanimity because the extinction would have been a price worth paying for the short-term profits which could then be invested (Cherfas 1986). Businessmen in Taiwan today are apparently stockpiling rhino horn (a report in *The Times* says they have an 'estimated ten tonnes of it – the equivalent of 4,000 dead rhinos') ready to trade in 'once the species becomes extinct' (Pitman 1992). Lord Zuckerman, in the concluding address of an international conference on conservational captive breeding in 1976, made some odd comments about the ill-advisedness of reintroducing rare animals to the wild (Jordan and Ormrod 1978: 56–7) and even – as I recall – that there was no point in conserving certain animals, such as the coelacanth. (His comments were understandably not included in the printed version.) So, as it is not obvious to everybody that animal species ought to be conserved, let us consider animals' aesthetic claims upon us.

Animals are not actually works of art, for it seems essential to the nature of a work of art to be made by man; after all, the derivation of 'art' is the Latins *ars, artem*, i.e. skill. Clearly works of art usually are made, and with skill, though it is arguable that an object's selection alone by an artistically-minded person could qualify it as a work of art, like a gnarled root, or polished pebble, picked up on the shore and displayed on the mantelpiece (or in an exhibition). In this case there would still have been skill exercised; skill in selecting rather than in actually creating the object in question (Miller 1986: 255). The eminent sculptor Henry Moore 'always paid great attention to natural forms, such as bones, shells, and pebbles, etc.' (Moore 1968: 593).

In any case, the term 'work of nature' exists, which suggests that we readily think of natural objects as similar enough to works of art to merit these similar terms. We might also regard animals as works of God, as in the comment on the hippopotamus (Behemoth) splendidly described in Job 40: 15–24, 'He is the first of the works of God', or, less appreciatively, by Macaulay on seeing the first hippopotamus to arrive at London Zoo: 'I have seen the hippo both asleep and awake, and I can assure you that, asleep or awake, he is the ugliest of the works of God' (Blunt 1976: 111).

If we do regard animals as works of God, this is pretty well equivalent to regarding them as divine works of art. There is the problem here that it is doubtful if God could (or would need to) exercise skill, being omnipotent. But perhaps it is the act of intentional creation (or at least selection) that makes something a work of art, and this could apply to God as much as to man. At any rate, we readily think of animals as being like works of art, and human animals similarly. 'What a piece of work is a man . . . the beauty of the world! the paragon of animals' as Hamlet said (II.ii.303). 'Piece of work' here means 'masterpiece' (Spence 1980: 255), and of course a masterpiece is a master work of art.

True, animals move around independently and live their own lives, which may seem to disqualify them from being in the slightest degree comparable to works of art. But a doll's house whose occupants appear to be living actual lives, as in a story by M.R. James (1970), might seem (as well as a source of unexpected moral problems) a fantastically fine work of art, incredibly correct to the last detail. For that matter, all evolution could seem a divine entertainment, as in God's comment at the end of Mephistopheles' summary of the history of the world at the start of Bertrand Russell's essay 'A free man's worship': 'it was a good play; I will have it performed again' (Russell 1953: 51).

Animals 'function' aesthetically in another way. They, thanks to their genes, are the opportunity for a kind of living sculpture engaged in by selective breeders. Darwin commented that

'Breeders habitually speak of an animal's organisation as something quite plastic, which they can model almost as they please.'
He also said, 'Not one man in a thousand has accuracy of eye and
judgement sufficient to become an eminent breeder' (Darwin
1968: 90–1). The breeding can be either for practical reasons, as
with our familiar domestic animals – dogs, horses, sheep, pigs – or
for amusement or a delight in creating new and ever odder
varieties, for example of pigeons — carriers, tumblers, runts,
barbs, pouters and many more, all described by Darwin (1968: 82
ff.). I am not here approving or disapproving of these activities,
though I would condemn the production by fashion of animals
with problems in living properly (Fox 1971: 204–5). I am simply
pointing out that people do regard animals, when so domesticated, as a kind of artistic medium, and the animal varieties they
produce as their creations. So it is hardly a wild extrapolation
from this to regard wild animals as rather like works of art.

Taxidermy is another example, well illustrated by Bartlett's
work, and how he saw it, 'preserving specimens of Nature's most
beautiful work', and their display in a museum (as Bartlett's
reconstruction of a dodo was displayed at the Crystal Palace) is
analogous to the display of pictures in an art gallery (Street 1965:
53; Bartlett 1899: 4).

As animals have been viewed aesthetically since ancient times,
and in view of the various remarkable features of animals which
modern science has greatly extended our appreciation of (I will
sketch these below), we are eminently justified in viewing some
animal species – oryxes or condors for a start – as being valuable
aesthetically like a great work of man such as the pyramids or the
Taj Mahal: as something obviously precious that we should
conserve.

ANIMALS AS ANIMALS

I shall note seven features of animals that are unique to living
organisms and two more that are unique to animals, and consider
these as guides both to why animals merit conservation, and to
how they should be conserved.

An animal's intricate mechanism and delicate harmony

W.S. Gilbert once commented:

131

I don't think I ever wittingly stepped on a black-beetle. The mechanism of life is so wonderful that I shrink from stopping its action. To tread on a black-beetle would be to me like crushing a watch of complex and exquisite workmanship.

(Pearson 1950: 128)

Gilbert's response of wonder at the 'workmanship' of a beetle is even more appropriate today: every one of an animal's millions of cells is (in the neurobiologist Steven Rose's words) 'the most completely automated factory we know [with] thousands of reactions' occurring within it (Rose 1966: 188, 190). Claude Bernard, the great French biologist whose concept of the *milieu intérieur* is the foundation of modern physiology, praised 'the harmony of a living organism, and [described] it as the consequence of a reciprocal harmony between all its parts so delicate that to disturb one element is to produce a perturbation in the whole' (Vyvyan 1969: 47). (Bernard, despite his appreciation of the organism's harmony, was a notoriously cruel experimenter.)

An animal's relationship to its environment

Animals have a close relationship to their environments, being to different degrees anatomically, physiologically and behaviourally adapted to them, and forming, along with all the other living beings and non-living materials of those environments, different ecosystems. Thus every animal is not only an enormously complex mechanism; it is part of a complex system, or many systems, according to how we choose to analyse the situation.

The transitoriness of individual animals

Each animal is born or hatches (or buds off in the case of a coelenterate such as a hydra) and, after a limited length of life, dies. So animals are constantly being replaced; all seem part of a cycle of life.

Between 'birth' and death animals change; they develop (a process which starts normally from fertilisation). Lengths of life vary a great deal, corresponding very roughly with an animal's size. We tend to feel more respect for an animal when it is very long-lived, and similarly for a plant, such as one of the great trees. There is conservational sense in this, since long-lived organisms are not readily replaced.

Animals make up long-lasting species

Animals come in 'sets' that we call species, sets of very similar though not identical specimens. Thus an individual animal such as a tiger does not, in a way, require the protection that a picture does, because the latter is unique where the tiger is not. What is unique is the species, and this is not only comparable with a work of art but, you might think, incomparably more valuable in numerous respects; for example, the first two features listed above. Actually, most people apparently don't think this – if they did, it would not have been easy in the 1970s to raise half a million pounds to purchase Henri Rousseau's famous painting of a most untiger-like tiger (admittedly in a magnificent jungle) but extremely difficult to raise a similar sum to save tigers themselves from threatened extinction (Mountfort 1973: 79). The tiger species (and every other species) is analogous aesthetically to a piece of music such as a symphony, which, as we saw above, exists in many transitory copies, the actual performances.

At the same time the individual tiger is different from every other tiger, and, just as the symphony fully exists only in its performances, so the tiger species exists only in individual tigers. So although every individual (conservationally speaking) is dispensable, this is only true in some degree. Some individual tigers are (conservationally) more important than others.

Other taxonomic groups are like musical sets of variations

Animals can also be arranged in and appreciated as members of an indefinite number of sets (genera, families, orders and so on) of increasing size or generality. Related species, and related genera and so on, are themselves rather like a set of musical variations on a theme: they can be appreciated in the same way to some degree. The variations here would be not only anatomical but behavioural.

I am less reluctant to suggest analogies between music and organisms – including the comparison of a symphony with a species! – in view of the distinguished biologists who have suggested similar analogies. The anatomist Sir Gavin de Beer (1971: 8), echoing Bernard's recourse to musical terms to express the subtlety of the organism's design, writes of the limb as 'a pattern . . . transposed over the long axis of the vertebrate body, like a tune that can be transposed over the keys'. Gregory Bateson

(1980: 18) notes that the 'anatomy of the crab is repetitive and rhythmical. It is, like music, repetitive with modulation'.

An animal's 'construction' is directed by its genes

Many features of animals are controlled by their genes, paired sets of highly variable complex molecules, which are duplicated in every one of an organism's millions of cells, and which are 'shuffled' in the process of formation of every egg and sperm, and occasionally some of them altered chemically, so that every new organism has slightly different sets from its parents. This feature of animals is closely connected with the next.

Animals are part of evolving populations

Animals evolve, or rather are part of populations or gene-pools that evolve. This gives the species, considered as a work of art, a time dimension: it develops through millions of years, and the fact it changes and will probably eventually disappear (or be transmuted into something else) is all part of its development (Hull 1978; Clark 1988). This again is a reason for not feeling we have to preserve every individual member of a species, but at the same time is a reason for reluctance to let the species itself go extinct. All living things are the product of a thousand million years of evolution; they are the inheritors probably of two or three preceding billions of years of bacterial evolution (Margulis and Sagan 1987). Individual animals, and especially individual plants, with very long life-spans rather similarly command special respect.

Animals are sentient

Animals are sentient, and many of them must have consciousness or awareness; many must be able to suffer and to experience pleasure.

Many animals have individuality, even personality

Certain animals are virtual persons, though we tend to restrict the concept of personhood to humans. Many are at least individuals. Some non-human animals have personal relations with us, and many must have rather similar relations with each other.

WHY ANIMALS MERIT DOUBLE RESPECT

These last two features of animals are significantly the only two of the nine features listed which apply exclusively to animals rather than other living organisms. They are particularly important because they are not merely reasons why animals are of value to us as remarkable 'furniture' of our world; they are reasons why animals are of value to themselves.

It is because of the sentience of animals, especially their capacity for suffering and positive pleasure, and the fact that some of them are perhaps virtual persons, or at least individuals, that we should respect them on welfare grounds, and further, that we should regard higher animals at least as having rights.

So, at this point, reasons for conserving animals and reasons for regarding them as having rights coalesce. Thus we should have for at least higher animals, any we have reason to regard as being conscious (not just self-conscious), a 'double respect': (a) respect for them as fine and remarkable 'things'; and (b) respect for them as sentient beings, who can both suffer and experience pleasure.

This is my solution to a problem which is posed clearly by Rodman (1977), and by many others such as Baird Callicott (1983: 54–8) – how to reconcile 'animal rights' concern for sentient animals with 'environmental ethics' concern for the whole natural environment.

Rodman appreciates Peter Singer's demand that animals require our concern because they can (in particular) suffer, but at the same time is dissatisfied with the implication of Singer's view that we should feel no concern for non-sentient beings and other parts of the environment (Rodman 1977: 84). Rodman tells us about his own concern for the protection of a particular area – as it happens, of no great ecological or other obvious importance (just 'sagebrush, scrub oak, and cactus'). It turned out that this area was inhabited by dusky-footed woodrats, which of course provided a reason on Singer's principles of concern for sentient higher animals for protecting it. But Rodman tells us that he knows he would still have wanted to protect the area even if it hadn't turned out to be inhabited by dusky-footed woodrats or any other comparable animals. He finds it 'odd to think that the plants have value only for the happiness of the dusky-footed woodrats'. As I see it, Rodman was right to feel that the plants had a value independent of their usefulness to the woodrats. The plants had a value (at least for humans) because of their beauty and complexity (as well as any possible usefulness as food, say, for humans or woodrats). The woodrats, in addition to having a value as things of beauty and complexity (whatever other usefulness they may have, perhaps ecologically) also matter from their own point of view because of their capacity for pleasure and satisfaction. This provides an additional reason for conserving them. They should be conserved for their sake (at least unless there are overwhelming considerations preventing this). (J.J.C. Smart (1984: 155n.) similarly recognises whales' sentience, and their own and their descendants' future happiness, as a reason for conserving them.) The woodrats' sentience is also a reason (whatever other considerations there may be) for treating them as humanely as possible.

I should call the kind of respect that follows from the various aesthetic aspects and biological features of animals that we have looked at, an 'aesthetic/conservational respect', or, for short, 'conservation respect'. The respect due to higher animals, on account of their sentience and individuality, is a respect for their rights as individuals, or, for short, 'rights respect'.

The combination of animals' aesthetic characters and biological characters (some of them analogous, as I suggested, to music!) should be more than enough to make us regard the causing of avoidable animal extinctions as serious vandalism.

Rights respect is appropriate for higher animals, including humans. Conservation respect is especially appropriate to animals – in view of the various features we have noted – but it is also appropriate, as we have seen, to a considerable range of other kinds of things:

1 Precious objects, including works of art of various kinds and buildings
2 Skills and practices
3 Traditions and ways of life
4 Institutions
5 Other living organisms
6 Ecosystems, natural areas and non-living natural objects
7 Resources, including energy resources.

Before we turn to considering how zoos can help the conservation of animals, the subject of the next chapter, a few points about the conservation of practices – and of animals – need to be made.

Obviously there are bad practices which should not be conserved, such as cockfighting and dogfighting, despite the enthusiasm shown for these two by, respectively, the President of the Old English Game Club (Finsterbusch 1980: 13) and by Richard Stratton (Hearne 1987: 219–23). It is more difficult to make a judgement on hunting, in view of its good elements as well as bad, and its historic role in wildlife conservation.

Hunting demonstrates how one can separate conservation respect and rights respect. The unenlightened hunter shows neither. He takes potshots at anything, and was responsible for almost unbelievable massacres like those of the American bison (Willock 1991: 1–2) and the Passenger pigeon (Willock 1991: 7–8). The enlightened hunter shows a high degree of conservation respect, together with a low degree or absence of rights respect. He shows conservation respect in appreciating the special conservational requirements of animals: that to ensure their survival, you must protect the breeding stock, and must protect or provide 'great woods or coverts for the secret abodes of wild beastes and . . . fruitful pastures for their continual feed' (as John Manwood wrote in Elizabethan times about royal forests (Stenton 1952: 98–9)).

Hunters appreciate, as laymen often don't, that there is no contradiction between conservation and hunting. Historically, hunting provided the motivation for wildlife conservation.

Even conservation respect, though, contains elements which would challenge hunting. To smash up a beautiful mechanism seemed vandalistic to W.S. Gilbert, and it was conservation respect he was showing: he didn't say the beetle had a right to live, or would be hurt by being stood on, but should be respected as a marvellous mechanism.

Also, conservation respect should include recognition of animals' sentience and individuality, and that animals should be conserved for themselves as well as to suit us. Of course hunters in some degree do this; their protection of the 'great woods or coverts' (Stenton 1952: 98) is in the interests of the animals, even of individuals actually hunted, in as much as they have lived acceptable lives up to that point. (But hunters have often done anything but conserve, have instead actively persecuted, their non-human rival predators, such as stoats, weasels and birds of prey.)

Again, either from conservation respect's recognition of animals' sentience and individuality, or from some degree of rights respect, decent hunters are humane. They kill their prey, but don't extend its dying unduly, and certainly not in the crassly heartless way described by a nineteenth century elephant hunter who stops in the middle of killing an elephant to make coffee (Carrington 1962: 156–8; Midgley 1983b: 14–16).

And hunting often involves much appreciation of nature and even the prey species, apart from any enjoyment of the killing. If the latter is there at all, it may be mainly pleasure in success and the exercise of a skill. (Hence perhaps Corbett's misgivings over shooting a sleeping tiger, though a dangerous man-eater; he also couldn't help regretting not giving the tiger a 'sporting chance' (Corbett 1955: 161–2).)

A distinction can be drawn between acceptable hunting, where the prey is simply killed (as in skilful shooting), and hunting with hounds, where the prey is pursued and so stressed for a long period – surely cruelly, as we saw in Chapter 4.

Obviously there are practices we should not conserve, though it is not always easy to decide which; we must distinguish and evaluate as in any other conservation. We shouldn't and can't conserve everything!

Should any animals not be conserved? The 'African Convention' of 1900 (the first international protection for African wildlife) excluded crocodiles, poisonous snakes and pythons (Lyster 1985: 112–13). The tsetse fly might seem an obvious non-candidate for conservation. As it happens, attempts at its eradication have been conspicuously unsuccessful and destructive of vast numbers of large mammals (Willock 1991: 128–9), and the tsetse fly has greatly assisted the unintended but effective conservation of much African wildlife (ibid.: 127–30). We in Britain are very quick to tell people in India to conserve their tigers. One can imagine the outcry at any attempt to reintroduce wolves or bears in Scotland or England! But clearly we now recognise, at least in theory, that all animals should be conserved.

Hunters at their best appreciate wildlife, even the animals they hunt (sad though it is that such appreciation cannot more often be transmuted into pure respect for animals). Such appreciation or 'caring about' is an essential element in conservation, as we have seen.

Zoos can help to inculcate respect, even awe, for wildlife (especially indeed where animals are shown in such marvellously naturalistic conditions as those pioneered by Hancocks). Wonder at and respect for the natural world is what we need if we are going to have much chance of conserving other species in today's overcrowded world (overcrowded, that is, by humans). Such awe is an emotional reaction any sensitive person should feel, and it is founded in a perfectly reasonable recognition of those aesthetic and biological aspects of animals that we have looked at.

9

ZOOS AND CONSERVATION

CONSERVATIONAL CAPTIVE BREEDING

There is a strong moral demand on us to conserve species if humanly possible – though we cannot conserve all, and some species mean far more to us than others. All merit conservation respect; the individuals of some species merit in addition rights respect.

Conservation respect is owed also to ecosystems, which are each made up of innumerable species: animal, plant, bacterial, viral, and anything else going. If every species is complex and intricate, every ecosystem must be even more so.

Furthermore, if we can conserve any particular animal species as part of its ecosystem, we conserve not just the species itself but its way of life, and do not disturb its links with other parts of its ecosystem. And we may wonder how far we can conserve species properly outside their ecosystems.

So obviously we should conserve ecosystems by preference. There is no controversy about that (Tudge 1991d: 1).

But many ecosystems – many natural habitats – we cannot conserve complete and undamaged, or cannot be sure we can indefinitely. Almost all are threatened in the end by the human population explosion, from a billion people around 1850 to two billion around 1930, four billion around 1980, and the prospect of eight billion looming very near (Ehrlich 1971: 2–3). Whatever threats to habitats are with us now – demands for rainforest timber, or for agricultural land or building space – or simple human greed for a quick and considerable profit from rhino horn, ivory, whatever – will intensify as humans multiply.

In any case, large animals tend to disappear long before their habitat suffers severe damage (Foose *et al.* 1985: 20–1). Predators, such as cats, at the top of food chains, tend to be particularly threatened. Often there is a direct human threat to particular species, as with the Arabian oryx, the Californian condor, and to some extent gorillas (Bertram 1980; Wheater 1985). There is sometimes no way the natural habitat can be made safe in the first instance for a particular species. Many countries where mega-vertebrates happen to live are unstable, with some perennial danger of war or revolution. Hagenbeck's (1909: 69, 214–15) misgivings about the survival of large game in Africa are echoed by Moorehead (1962: 111–12) in 1957 and by Dubos (1980: 67). Dubos also notes the environmental damage done in Meso-potamia and in the Lebanon (once famous for its forests, 'now almost barren'), by South American civilisations, and in China (Buddhist monks were responsible for much deforestation) (Dubos 1980: 64–6).

And this is where zoos' conservational captive breeding comes in. They can keep in existence, at a safe population level, particu-lar species which are under extreme pressure or facing extinction in the wild. Individuals can be reintroduced either to refound an extinct population or to strengthen a threatened one.

Most species under threat are so because of habitat damage, and here there is no point in seeking to reintroduce members of them unless the habitat can be restored, which usually is not possible yet; the situation may change in the future. But as it happens, a good many of those kinds of species which zoos tend to keep (Stuart 1991: 33–5) are under threat for reasons indepen-dent of the state of their habitats, so there is habitat worth returning them to, provided of course the threat can be dealt with. It is now recognised by the International Union for the Conservation of Nature (IUCN), and so by many conservationists who are not zoo-based, that captive breeding with a possibility of reintroduction is a significant supplement to the direct protection of wild habitats and their occupants.

'Explosion' is hardly an over-dramatic term for the human population increase. There is a strong possibility of enormous threats to natural habitats, and to larger vertebrates in particular, in the next century, and not so far into it. One can sneer at this nightmare scenario as a fantasy dreamed up by zoos to give them a *raison d'être* (Johnson 1990: 15), but the possibility is too real for it to be responsible to ignore it. Zoos are taking it seriously. Working together, they could probably maintain most of the larger mammal species, and many of the birds and reptiles (Seal 1991: 40–1) for, if necessary, a century or centuries – until the human population increase ceases and goes into reverse. This is a highly responsible preparation for an all too likely emergency, one we all of course hope will not arise.

We need to think on two time-scales. One is the long-term time-scale, on which we need to plan the possibility of a global Noah's Ark operating in the ocean of a human population of plague proportions, with possible reintroductions long in the future. On the other, short-term time-scale we must survey the situation today, seeing what habitats and what species are under what particular threat, what we should be looking after, and what we should be planning, and/or proceeding, to reintroduce. This is happening with the Captive Breeding Specialist Group (CBSG), a subgroup of the Species Survival Commission, a commission of IUCN. Two kinds of analysis are done, of wild populations (for example a Population Viability Analysis (PVA) for the Golden Lion tamarin), and of captive populations (for example the Global Captive Action Plan for Primates). So the total world situation for any species really is being looked at, as far as possible, and appropriate action taken for the species, not for zoos' own interests. There is no question here of individuals of a species being brought to a zoo from the wild because the zoo wants to keep them. The wild population and the captive population are being studied together, and appropriate action worked out with reference to both.

It is very important that we be equally concerned about the immediate situation, however seriously we take the nightmare future threats. For some people object to zoos' captive breeding as a tool for conservation on the grounds that it may make people think there is no need to conserve habitats, because zoos are looking after the actual species. I take it for granted that zoos do not think this, but they must make clear they don't, by stressing that the special help they can offer the cause of conservation, that of captive breeding and possible reintroduction, is by no means a distraction from or in any way counter to the interests of habitat protection. Reintroduction operations themselves direct attention to maintaining, indeed restoring, the wild habitat, for reintroductions are pointless unless the habitat is there. They stimulate interest and essential support from local populations (Durrell and Mallinson 1987).

Suppose a habitat cannot be protected; why is it pointless to attempt to rescue any species which will otherwise be lost too, especially when there is a chance of reintroducing them to a protected habitat in the future (Midgley 1987: 63–5)? If the National Gallery is on fire, we don't immediately accept the sad loss of all its paintings. We try to rescue the best ones quickly. This seems the obvious course with outstanding species similarly, if we assume they can survive in zoos (as the Père David's deer, to take just one example, obviously has). That certain species strike us as outstanding, the cases of the oryx and the condor clearly illustrate. This in no way devalues any species we cannot rescue. If we cannot save all, this is no reason for not saving any.

Reputable zoos are not now damaging any wild populations by removing animals from them (whether or not this happened in the past) (Brambell 1985: 222–3). Any capture of animals in the wild and their ensuing transport is now subject to the Convention on International Trade in Endangered Species (CITES) regulations (Lyster 1985: 239–77), in the drawing up of which zoos' representatives (such as Dr Michael Brambell (1985: 224–30), Director of Chester Zoo) have themselves been involved. Of course rules can be broken, and nowhere more probably than in the case of those covering trade in animals. There is a need to strengthen the regulations preventing trade in endangered animals, and for more enforcement of them, but this is to do with private collectors, not reputable zoos (Brambell 1985: 221; Nichol 1987).

Animals should today not normally be taken from the wild at all, unless for some reason there is an 'excess' of them (as with baboons, for example, in some parts of Africa) or there is a serious conservational case for taking them, and if they are it should normally be by properly organised expeditions or proper authorities in the countries concerned, who can ensure that the 'right' individuals are being removed – i.e. individuals from a species whose collection can be justified, and individuals whom the population in question can stand the loss of – and also that the animals are caught and transported as humanely as possible (Brambell 1985: 223).

We have moved into a new era of captive breeding, where a whole captive population can be managed as a whole, a development spearheaded by the International Species Inventory System (ISIS) in America, now supplemented by the Animal Record

Keeping System (ARKS) in Britain (Foose 1977: 70; Flesness 1977: 77; Tudge 1991d: 108–9). Such developments are possible because of growing understanding of population genetics, as well of course as computer technology. Stud books, inter-zoo committees, and arrangements thus readily made for non-commercial moves between zoos, are all part of this integrated management of captive populations (Tudge 1991d: 106–9).

A population of fifty breeding animals in the very short term, or 500 in the very long term, if managed as a whole, should be enough to avoid inbreeding and to ensure the survival of a gene pool substantially the same as the wild gene pool of the species in question; to ensure the continuance of nearly as much variation between individuals as would occur in the wild population (Frankel and Soulé 1981: 74, 91). This means there is every chance that animals from such a captive population will in the future, if reintroduced to the wild, have the genetic capacity to respond to changes in the environment in the way that a naturally evolving population does. Thus we can regard such captive breeding, where we are talking about the careful genetic management of a large enough captive population, as in a real sense close to 'true' conservation. Although the population will of course not be in its actual wild habitat, it will be very close to being a natural population genetically, so it will be a 'living', developing thing, very different from something in a merely preserved state such as we think of as being preserved in a museum. And also its members will be ready, because of their genetic makeup, for reintroduction to the wild, able to adapt to the natural environment and become in the fullest sense members of a wild population again.

While the total captive population should be managed as a whole, it is at the same time desirable that that population should be split up among various collections. This is a safeguard against the spread of infection as well as being genetically advantageous (provided each separate population is of a certain minimum size) (Chesser et al. 1980: 148).

There are problems. One is the extent to which pairing of animals needs to be managed (Midgley 1987: 58). But this is hardly more in a new centrally organised system than is necessary anyway in any individual zoo. The animals are still free to respond or not as they choose to different partners, and a great deal more free than in many modern farming systems. Again, mating partners have to be arranged in all selective breeding. If we accept this

– and no one who keeps a pedigree dog is in a position to condemn it – then it cannot be overwhelmingly objectionable with animals in zoos, though it may be considerably more difficult to implement (Foose 1980: 154–5; Campbell 1979: 216–26). The other drawback is the need for transport of animals between zoos. Zoos need here to exercise the utmost care, and perhaps need careful regulation, but at least it is not a case here of large groups of animals being moved *en bloc*, and the very value of particular individual animals – that is, monetary as well as otherwise – as well as unavoidable recognition of their various special requirements, should encourage high standards.

While some zoos are much larger, and some much better, than others (not necessarily the same ones in both cases), the integrated management of captive populations means that smaller zoos have a useful role to play, provided they co-operate, and accept the need for computerised records accessible to other zoos, and to follow instructions which may sometimes be to cease breeding from favourite and trusty animals.

This is not easy, as Mary Midgley rightly emphasises, but as a partly computerised integrated management is altering the situation, and making it perfectly possible for small zoos to be part of a larger system, it is an overstatement to say 'Most zoos are quite unable to contribute effectively to [serious conservation]' (Midgley 1987: 58–9). Only time will tell, and it is up to 'most zoos' to prove her wrong.

BREEDING TECHNOLOGY

Other breeding technology, such as the development of sperm and egg storage, fertilisation in vitro, embryo transplantation and the like, can all be seen as part of a total armoury of weapons which it is good to have available if necessary (Hearn and Hodges 1985: 123–204). A certain parallel can be drawn with humans, in that such methods as artificial insemination, stimulation of ovulation by hormone injection and so on, are methods used (if at all) when natural methods have failed: similarly we would only use such methods in captive breeding when natural methods are ineffective or unavailable (e.g. an attempt to stimulate ovulation in a lone female Komodo dragon at San Diego and impregnate her with stored sperm from a now dead male ('Science' 1986). The two cases are not an exact parallel in that research into artificial breeding involves, in varying degrees, experimentation on animals which are not themselves needing assistance as humans seeking medical or other technological help would be. But such research can be justified by its serious purpose, provided of course that it does not involve serious discomfort or worse for the animals concerned. Its spirit can reasonably be seen as a wish to leave no stone unturned in having all possible knowledge and every possible technical aid available for any particular need, should it occur, in the sphere of captive breeding for conservation. The problems are manmade. It is responsible to arm ourselves in all ways possible to try to solve them.

Mary Midgley's (1987: 58 ff.) distrust of an overdose of faith in technology to solve all problems is understandable: no 'technical fix', she feels, is going to be without 'socially disturbing consequences'. But I wonder if even this is so. Foose and others can foresee a combined system of wild and captive populations, where the latter can be used to strengthen the former, perhaps with 'reproductive technology' being used to avoid disrupting natural populations (e.g. introducing sperm or embryos 'into animals already resident in the natural habitat') (Foose *et al.* 1985: 21). Such interference with wild populations may seem distasteful – I can imagine the critic saying 'It's bad enough their messing about with their captive animals; can't they leave the wild ones alone?' – but already some degree of management is probably essential for almost any population of large animals. If an increased degree of technological manipulation is going to help to solve the problems which are likely to face us as pressure on the wild increases still further in coming years, then it is irresponsible of us not to develop it now if we can. It is irresponsible not to manage if managing is necessary and we think we are capable of it. Technological manipulation aimed at good management, aimed at conservation, is therefore acceptable and its development creditable.

CULLING

A newspaper report of the culling of deer ('Killing time at the zoo') at Whipsnade (*Scottish Daily Express*, 14 November 1984) treated the incident as if it were shocking that captive animals should be killed because of excess numbers. (Through an organisational mistake, the careful shooting, by a marksman in a landrover, had occurred while the zoo was open.) But unless zoos can effectively prevent successful breeding by some other method, which is not always practical, killing of certain animals is virtually essential. Jamieson (1985: 115) sensibly recognises this, but Richard North (1983a: 109) who, unlike the *Daily Express*, should know better, speaks of captive-bred animals being 'butchered'. If our objection to any culling whatever is such that we consider it makes the whole practice of captivity unacceptable, then we must, to be consistent, equally condemn the allowing of red deer to roam (comparatively) free in Scotland. For equally, in the absence of natural predators, it is impossible to avoid the need to cull (Stephen 1974: 11).

Besides, it is hardly open, at least to non-vegetarians, to regard the humane killing of captive-bred wild animals as morally wrong but the slaughter of cattle and pigs as acceptable. Many working animals, such as greyhounds, are killed at the end of their working lives, as was the practice in the fifteenth century, as Dame Juliana Berners tells us in her poem 'The Properties of a Good Greyhound':

> The ninth year cart saddle,
> And when he is comen to that year
> Have him to the tanner,
> For the best hound that ever bitch had
> At nine year he is full bad.
>
> (MacBeth 1965: 132)

I do not advocate such positively heartless treatment of greyhounds, but it is unreasonable to bring the accusation of occasional killing of their animals against zoos as a particularly heinous crime, instead of an occasional regrettable necessity, of course to be carried out humanely if at all. The killing of surplus animals is taken for granted by both farmers and 'fancy' breeders (Cherrington 1983: 130; Green 1983).

The introduction of centralised breeding management does not make a radical difference, but it provides a second reason why some killing is in practice necessary. All such killing I would regard as a necessary evil.

The use of the term 'culling', as also of course the practice of culling, could be challenged, because of its implication that such killing of the surplus or dispensable members of a population is as acceptable, as unobjectionable, as the destroying of plants. It ought not to be so acceptable because animals are aware and have lives to lead as we do, whereas presumably whatever we do to plants is of no concern to the plants. Because of this obvious difference between animals and plants, culling animals, but not culling plants, is (at best) a necessary evil. Culling in zoos is out of virtual necessity, given, certainly, that we have zoos, which is not a necessity (but still very important). If that is accepted, then it seems reasonable to use a particular term, 'cull', for a particular kind of killing, done out of virtual necessity and humanely.

Maureen Duffy (1984: 87–90) strongly opposes the use of culling, in general (not by zoos particularly), for the reason that we are making an unjustifiable distinction between humans and animals in adopting so readily the solution of culling for problems of over-expanding animal populations (which, as she says, are always a result of human interference). She notes how we would not contemplate the same solution for human population problems. I respect her argument because I agree that animal lives are of value for the same kinds of reason as human lives are of value. My defence of culling is to plead necessity. For Duffy, this is not good enough: she feels we do not try hard enough to find other solutions, and no doubt she is right. She advocates birth control, and research to implement this with different species. Zoos should indeed use birth control where possible instead of putting themselves in a situation where they have to cull.

INTERFERENCE AND RESPONSIBILITY

This whole need for animal management, even manipulation, may seem objectionable. Certainly we should interfere as little as possible both with free living populations and with animals in captivity, provided we are also fulfilling our conservational responsibilities. For we have a dual set of responsibilities. We have our concern for animals as sentient individuals, who in some cases, most obviously (but by no means only) the great apes, are virtually persons (Midgley 1985; Duffy 1984: 80 ff.). This is animal welfare, and it should be a positive as well as a negative business, i.e. enriching captive animals' lives, not merely protecting them from suffering. But we also have our responsibility (a responsibility to other humans but not exclusively so) to conserve animals. We should do this too, while almost certainly granting animal welfare considerations precedence in the case of clashes between the two responsibilities.

REINTRODUCTION

I am assuming that reintroduction is likely to be possible in any particular case, which may seem unwise in view of the way Midgley (1987: 59–60) correctly emphasises the problems with reintroducing primates. Primates present particular difficulties (Lemmon 1987: 172–5), as with reintroductions of Golden Lion tamarins in Brazil in 1983 and 1984 (Tudge 1991d: 152–3). These tamarins were actually not used to real trees, and clearly should have had a period of training, of getting used to the features of the real world they had to cope with, before their reintroduction. Or better still, they should have been kept in much more naturalistic conditions all along. But these particular, and most unfortunate, mistakes are unlikely to be made again with a reintroduction operation. The lesson of the essential need for training has been well learnt (Tudge 1991d: 153).

But many reintroductions have already met with a good deal of success, such as those of the Hawaiian goose, European otter, Eagle owl, Arabian oryx, Scimitar-horned oryx, Père David's deer, and at least one tiger as described by Singh (1984: 11, 12, 87–8). (Durrell and Mallinson (1987) give many more examples of successful reintroductions.) Failure or partial failure does not prove that the nature of the zoo-bred animal is at fault: it may be a fault in the reintroduction procedure, as most obviously with the Golden Lion tamarins. There can also be genetic problems, as with the Hawaiian goose (Willock 1991: 95–7). But the whole approach to reintroductions – recognition of the need for preliminary feasibility studies and so on – is becoming more and more sophisticated and realistic (Stanley Price 1991). The saving and reintroduction of the Arabian oryx has been quite spectacularly successful (Tudge 1991d: 125–7, 141–50).

Arjan Singh (1984) has provided strong evidence of how a cat's basic hunting tendency and ability are innate, even though an opportunity for the 'fine-tuning' provided by practice or maternal training may be needed too. Singh (1984: 164, 173–5) shows how this can be provided by a human who knows what he is doing. But it is hardly surprising that a zoo-bred tiger could be reintroduced successfully. Many domestic cats could survive on their own if necessary (as many other feral animals such as goats do) (Tabor 1983: 59). True, domestic cats have more freedom than cats in a zoo. But consider mink bred on mink farms. Here are captive-bred carnivores, kept in pens either outside or in sheds, even selectively bred for special colour varieties (Aleutian, Palomino, Pastel, etc.) and yet they have escaped (of course only occasionally) and gone feral so successfully as to become a major pest (Lever 1977: 133–41). (Their coat colour reverts to the wild form in a few generations, as with other selectively bred colour variants of probably almost any animal.) If mink could read, one wonders what they would make of the dreadful problems of readjustment to the wild (such as 'inevitable deep addiction to a captive life-style' (Midgley 1987: 58–9)) that seem to have passed them by: mink refute any generalised claims of the overwhelming difficulties of reintroductions.

Singh (1984: 203–11), in the appendix to his book, notes the official unwillingness to accept it was possible to release successfully a captive-bred tiger, on the grounds that it couldn't support itself (which he shows not to be so). If it was in fact possible, it was regarded as undesirable because of the likelihood of the animal's becoming a man-eater (which again Singh seems to show convincingly to be fallacious), or because of the tiger's not being pure-bred. Singh argues that the latter point too is an imaginary worry, at least with a single animal whose genes will be 'swallowed up' in the gene pool (the tigress he released does breed successfully).

Obviously reintroductions must be approached responsibly (Jungius 1985: 47–55); a transition period is necessary. But with no species is it necessarily impossible.

Clearly the more we are able to provide a captive environment which stimulates the occupant and encourages a wide range of its natural behaviour, the more that individual is likely to be a potentially successful subject for reintroduction. Even though the environment of any particular zoo animal is not in itself going to make any difference to the genetic makeup of its descendants, it makes a great difference to the suitability of that particular animal for reintroduction.

So far as the genetic makeup is concerned, we should remember that periods of captivity by man are minute in length compared with evolutionary time. Even though selection of course operates in captivity, and this is so whatever we do to minimise it, it is still a very short time.

SPECIES SELECTION, VALUING AND FINANCE

The extent to which zoos can help by captive breeding to save endangered species is of course limited, and most obviously so by the minute selection of species from the animal kingdom as a whole that they are able to keep. But why should this invalidate the contribution that they *can* make to the immensely important cause of animal conservation, especially as it is likely to be possible for them, if necessary, to keep a very large portion of the larger – and threatened – vertebrates, mammals especially? We could, true, make the real situation clearer by calling zoos 'selected charismatic mega-vertebrate conservation centres' to emphasise their limited role, and perhaps then, just as bird gardens, presumably, need not feel morally inadequate for not even trying to breed endangered mammals, SCMCCs (or zoos) would not be condemned, as Kieran Mulvaney (1987: 152) seeks to condemn them, for having saved at the most a dozen species from extinction; 'a mere 0.00012 per cent of all the life-forms on earth', perhaps 'less species within the last 150 years than have become extinct within the last few days'. What Mulvaney leaves out is that we don't value all species equally, although he clearly differentiates between them as much as the rest of us. The evidence is there in his photograph, in the presence of his English setter (Mulvaney 1987: 145). Dogs are special – to humans. We would regret their extinction more than we would regret the extinction of any of the vast number of invertebrate species, mostly beetles, that allow Mulvaney to shrink, as he does, the zoo achievement. I accept that every species – protozoan, alga, bacterium – is of immense scientific interest and sometimes (e.g. many protozoans) of exquisite beauty too. Every one is the product of thousands of millions of years of evolution. Still more do I accept that to save the rainforest from the appalling way in which it is being destroyed for the shortest of short-term advantages is of the utmost importance, and much more important even than saving any charismatic mega-vertebrate (Mulvaney 87: 149–52). But what I do not accept is that the need to save natural habitats such as rainforests, and the millions of species contained in them, can in any way mean that it is not right to try to save such exceptional species – in terms of

151

their appeal to humans – as the Arabian oryx or the Californian condor. To save either of these is comparable, as an achievement, to saving the Taj Mahal.

My emphasis on the animals zoos keep as being invariably ones that appeal to humans may seem unduly anthropocentric, and it also fails to recognise the responsibility a zoo like Jersey feels to save species in need of help (such as many threatened island populations of boas, for example, or the Volcano rabbit, or peccaries) irrespective of their human appeal. The scientific importance of such work should not be underrated, or indeed the way in which Jersey emphasises the importance of conservation in the field and *ex situ* as two sides of one coin. But it is still the case that the saving of a species like the Arabian oryx can be quite properly compared to the saving of some great work of art and given proper credit as something immensely worth doing – even though it isn't as important as saving the South American rainforest.

Zoos are accused of swallowing up large sums of money which would be better spent protecting actual natural habitats, and it is noted that both Operation Oryx and the attempt to save the Californian condor by captive breeding have been immensely expensive (Mulvaney 1987: 153). Both the oryx and the condor are charismatic mega-vertebrates, and their appeal to us is and should be perfectly comparable to that of some great human work of art (like the Taj Mahal). We would spend millions to save that; it is creditable, not profligate, to spend millions trying to save the two species. The second point is that in these two cases captive breeding happens or happened to be the only way to do it, or at least seems the best way. Of course, if we could have saved either of these for the same or less money by protecting their habitats, that would have been the way to do it. But we are right to try to save them, and by the best method available in the particular circumstances.

To say that zoos' money would be better spent on the protection of natural habitats may be correct, but not necessarily more so than the fact that (as Mulvaney reminds us) the claims of disappearing forest are so desperately serious as to dwarf the claims to public money of the Royal Shakespeare Company or the Royal Opera House or any other such inessential institution. But in any case it is true of any zoo that much of its money comes from the gate, and, if the zoo did not exist, would in no way be available instead for conservation of wild habitats – just as, indeed, government grants for London Zoo (in as much as they exist) would, if withdrawn, be highly unlikely to be diverted to conservation in the wild instead (Rawlins 1985: 69; Wheater 1985: 116). On the other hand, if zoos directly or indirectly raise money for conservation in the wild, that is as it were a bonus for the wild: money that would not otherwise have been available.

SUPPLEMENTARY CONSERVATIONAL ROLES

Zoos' raising of money for wild habitats is an example of a supplementary conservational role.(Their scientific and educational roles are both in the end most obviously justified by the assistance they can give, and do give, to conservation.) Zoos can act as a powerhouse of motivation for concern about conservation; namely, enlisting the interest and concern of the public as well as actually raising money for conservation in the field. People are more likely to be concerned about the survival of animals of which they have experience and, while they can see them in their natural habitats on film and television, they can also be powerfully influenced by the more direct experience available in a zoo. This kind of conservational role for a zoo overlaps with its educational role.

Another interesting supplementary aid to conservation they may provide is that of diverting some of the pressure that would be felt if the zoos' millions of visitors really wanted and could afford to experience wildlife 'directly' in, say, East African national parks. It is sometimes remarked that people should not expect animals to be brought to them to look at, when they know that, if they want to see the Taj Mahal, they have no choice but to go and see it *in situ* (McKenna 1987: 34). There must be a very definite limit to the number of people who can see the Taj Majal *in situ* without damaging it! I am interested by the option now under discussion of constructing a model of Stonehenge because of tourist wear and tear, and a most marvellous and effective model was actually opened eight years ago of the Lascaux Caves in France, with their 15,000-year-old cave paintings. It is a problem well-known to the National Trust, who have a phrase 'honey pots' for public areas designed to do just what zoos can do – help to divert a large proportion of visitors from visiting and thus damaging the actual wild or near-wild areas. The Countryside Commission's advice to those interpreting sites to the public includes directions for protecting areas from over-use by visitors (Aldridge 1975: 13, 17).

Pressure from the public in national parks can affect cheetahs (Lever 1986) and leopards (Miles 1986), and turtle egg-laying (Hobley 1986) on a Greek island. Cherfas (1984: 199–201) discusses tourist pressure on coral reefs, as well as marvellous tourist opportunities for meeting turtles, Fairy penguins and Grey whales in the wild, but also the essential need for very careful management of such meetings (1984: 211–24). Probably nothing a zoo can provide can rival seeing wildlife in the wild. Neither do zoos necessarily dissuade many people from visiting African national parks, and they must sometimes do the opposite: encourage people who would not have thought of it otherwise to go and see the 'real thing'. But zoos may already, and certainly could in the future, provide, as it were, living models to help to protect the 'real thing'. The better the zoo can provide seemingly real habitats, the better it can fulfil this role.

One could take my model suggestion further and propose real models, for example laser sculptures replacing animals altogether, like the suggestion in a newspaper article that Zoo Check's 'suggested alternative [to zoos] is the creation of wildlife study centres displaying lifesize replicas of wild animals that would be such faithful imitations they would even feel and smell real' (Fitzgerald 1986). This might be a good idea if there were not other strong reasons for keeping actual animals, if we had good reason to suppose that the animals we wanted to replace were not in a state of well-being in the zoo, and if there were any likelihood of being able to construct models of a more than Disneyish nature.

So we see that zoos' conservational captive breeding role is not their sole proper justification for existing, though it is their most important one. But in any case a zoo cannot breed endangered species efficiently without the necessary experience, which means in practice that it cannot possibly keep only endangered animals. It would be highly irresponsible for a zoo to keep any endangered species – say, the Arabian oryx – if its staff had had no previous experience of keeping related, but less endangered species, of oryx or other antelope. (There are other minor roles for zoos in connection with habitat management, such as providing a place to send man-eating tigers to (WWF 1986: 439).)

10

SCIENCE IN ZOOS

How far can zoos' contribution to science be regarded as one of their major justifications? Dale Jamieson (1985: 112) divides the science done in zoos into two categories. Five or six categories, at least, seem necessary to me to reflect the range of zoos' scientific activities. Here are eight ways in which zoos help science:

TAXONOMY

Zoos can provide living examples for the study of taxonomy or classification, and this was a major role of zoos in the nineteenth century. It is now performed mainly by museums, whose study collections of items such as vertebrate skins, and dead invertebrates such as insects and crustaceans with their non-decaying exoskeletons, are likely to be far larger than any zoo's animal collection because of their permanence and ease of storage (compared to living animals). And in some ways museum specimens are no doubt more convenient to study. But it is actually much better, where possible, to have living specimens available, most obviously so that their behaviour patterns, themselves often significant taxonomic factors, can be studied. The Wildfowl Trust collection at Slimbridge is a much better place than a museum for studying the classification of swans, because one can for example observe variations in plumage care behaviour patterns – which are important in the swans' classification – and one can also weigh and measure the birds very accurately, which obviously requires live swans (Scott and the Wildfowl Trust 1972: 24, 277). Study of behaviour patterns is also useful in working out the relationships of mammals – for example, in confirming the close relationship of the so-called Celebes black ape to macaques – and it is convenient

155

to study such patterns in a captive group, even though one has to be aware of the likelihood that the animals' behaviour will not be identical to that in the wild state (Dixson 1977: 81).

And to acquire the dead specimens studied in museums, we have of course to start with living specimens, which may very well be animals in a zoo.

GENERAL OBSERVATION AND INVESTIGATION

Zoos provide opportunities for the recording of various data, such as the periods between births, lengths of gestation, details of courtship behaviour, notes on what particular animals eat, or details of their manner of eating. An example of the last would be just how particular Geoffroy's cats are in their feeding, and how they 'exhibit great dexterity in consuming certain parts of an animal according to their own special tastes', observed in the course of work at Glasgow Zoo (Law and Boyle 1984: 192).

Certain observations or discoveries may only be possible, and certainly only likely or practicable, when one has the animals at close quarters and, perhaps, in one's care (Ewer 1975: 1 ff.). Some observations will be part of more elaborate projects of a physiological or behavioural nature, or involve chemical analyses – say, of the constituents of gorilla milk, or of the saliva of different cats.

Zoos can provide important experimental opportunities for visiting scientists. Darwin, investigating in 1856 how seeds could be transported over oceans, fed seeds to fish (which unfortunately spat them out too soon), and dead sparrows, 'their crops stuffed with oats', to a bateleur eagle and a snowy owl, all at the Zoological Gardens. 'The Hawks,' wrote Darwin in a letter to Hooker, 'have behaved like gentlemen & have cast up pellets with lots of seeds in them' (Darwin 1990: 239–40, 248; Desmond and Moore 1991: 444–5). Here, if only in a minor way, London Zoo was assisting Darwin's study of natural selection, which included a need to explain how, if the world's plant and animal inhabitants had not been placed there by the Creator, islands (in particular) could be colonised by organisms from other areas.

Zoos can still play an essential part in investigations of, for example, behavioural ecology. One example is a recent investigation by David Houston (1988), a zoologist at Glasgow University, of why vultures often feed on lion droppings but never apparently on the dung of wild dogs or hyaenas – Dr Houston, a vulture specialist, had observed this during field studies in East Africa. His investigation included feeding lions, a leopard and a hyaena at Edinburgh Zoo, and a vulture at London Zoo, with food carrying a chemical marker (chromium oxide). The animals were not of course affected in any way, but it was possible to show that the hyaena digested about ten per cent more of its food than the lions and leopard, while the vulture digested a little more even than the hyaena. Houston correlates these differences in feeding efficiency with differences in gut weights and in feeding strategies. Cats have to accelerate very quickly when pursuing prey so cannot afford extra gut weight – such as would increase their digestive efficiency – but dogs, because they pursue prey over long distances, can. Vultures, because of their dependence in flight on rising air currents, can afford the extra weight of (proportionally) large guts allowing them to extract food even from lion droppings. This is only a rough summary of Houston's careful account, but the point is that he could not have carried out his investigation without making use of captive animals. He studies animals in the wild, but he can't find out everything about them that he needs to without – in this case, anyway – the support of study on animals in a zoo.

BREEDING TECHNOLOGY

Then there is still more elaborate and sophisticated physiological work, especially in the physiology of reproduction, such as was mentioned in Chapter 9. So far as Britain is concerned, such work occurs mostly in the Institute of Zoology of the Zoological Society of London. It is becoming more and more geared to the requirements of practical conservation, both with captive breeding and in the field (Tudge 1991c; Tudge 1991d: 169–92). Hearn has stressed the non-invasive nature of much of this work: that is, it does not involve drastic treatment of the animal (Hearn 1987: 29).

VETERINARY STUDY

Vast possibilities for the increase of veterinary knowledge arise from the care and treatment of animals in zoos: finding out what different species are susceptible to, and what is effective in treatment. It may seem that this knowledge is only needed because of the fact that various wild animals are kept in zoos. Thus, given we have such and such animals in zoos, it is of course creditable we should not only treat them but engage in research in order to treat them better; but such research can hardly be a justification for zoos, because we would not need it if we did not have zoos in the first place (Jamieson 1985: 113).

There is some truth in this. After all, veterinary science is essentially the applied science (and art) of caring for animals which man happens to keep and also, to a great extent, which he needs (or at least exploits). The very word 'veterinary' comes from the Latin for cattle (*veterinae*). But veterinary knowledge arising from study and treatment of zoo animals can be counted to some extent as desirable knowledge independently of its zoo applications in as much as:

1 Wild animals are related to domesticated animals, and can suffer from similar diseases. Understanding of the one inter-relates with and assists understanding of the other.

2 Understanding of diseases in wild animals can be of great theoretical interest, for example because of the part played by disease in evolution, and its genetic connections; and of practical importance quite apart from humans' keeping of animals, for example because of the fact that parasites of man or domestic animals – such as trypanosomes (the protozoans which cause sleeping sickness) – can be endemic in wild populations.

3 Knowledge concerning the efficient use of such techniques as the administering of drugs to anaesthetise animals and to revive them, and the application of such drugs by gun or blowpipe, is often needed in the management of wild animals, quite apart from any question of taking them for captivity, for example in operations to rescue wild animals from flooded areas, or areas scheduled for development.

So, while veterinary research in zoos is partly a matter of studying what different species suffer from in captive conditions, it is much more than this: much of what is learnt is likely to be applicable to animals in the wild state. Zoo post-mortem cases are often of particular veterinary interest because of the comparative rarity of the animals in normal veterinary practice.

GENETICS

One can hardly do genetic studies on animals in the wild state because one has no control over which individuals are mated. Zoo animals are not the obvious material either because, for example in the study of the genetics of mammalian coat colour, the mutations which geneticists need to study are most conveniently 'nurtured' among various small domestic animals. So rabbits, rats, mice and so on are great sources of genetic knowledge (Searle 1968: ix, 29). But zoos provide a useful supplement, making possible at least some study on the genes as they occur in (relatively) wild animals.

Zoos could play a greater role here were it not an essential aspect of their conservational responsibilities to avoid selective breeding, at least with animals rare in the wild; with animals common in captivity zoos may reasonably feel they have some licence to breed unusual variants. But note, in any case, that breeding as a leisure pursuit of the members of the various 'fancies' has, since before the days of Darwin, produced a vastly important amount of material for the scientific geneticist to investigate. Indeed, Darwin's own investigations of the work of selective breeders played a major part in the long mental gestation of his theory of evolution (Darwin 1968: 71–100) (and it is probable, incidentally, that the nature of heredity would have been understood far sooner and light thrown on an aspect of evolution which baffled Darwin if other contemporary biologists had been prepared, like him, to learn from the practical breeders (Dempster 1983: 82–6)). Anyhow, the study of domesticated, if not necessarily captive, animals was actually essential to what was perhaps the greatest scientific discovery since Newton. There is no question that keeping animals in captivity in a wide sense, although not normally as this occurs in zoos, is essential to much genetic study. With the development of the integrated management of conspecifics in different zoos as one population, as discussed in Chapter 9 above, there are considerable spin-offs from captive population studies for the understanding of the genetics of wild populations (Mace 1986: 63; Tudge 1991d: 70–113).

In at least two famous cases it was shown to be possible for zoos to go beyond saving endangered species and actually, by selective breeding, recreate extinct species. The German zoo directors Lutz Heck and Heinz Heck managed to breed back the aurochs, the wild ancestor of domestic cattle (Heck 1951; Zeuner 1963: 204–6). They also attempted similarly to breed back the tarpan, the European wild horse. How far either case is conservationally important, or indeed genetically valid, is a matter of dispute; but clearly that such genetic reconstruction is at least in some degree possible is of enormous scientific interest.

BEHAVIOUR

The kind of behavioural study usually done in zoos is observational, often with some experimental input, but with none such as to cause distress or injury to the animal. This would be, apart from moral considerations, inappropriate to zoos where the animals are there partly for exhibition and obviously not therefore available for scientific research such as would injure them, though Batten has claimed that this is not always so in America (1976: 32 ff.) (I am puzzled myself by a remark of Lord Zuckerman's about his predecessor Chalmers Mitchell's not seeking a Home Office licence for research (Zuckerman 1980; Bostock 1987: 429).) Behavioural observations in zoos are likely to be aimed at understanding the natural behaviour of the species concerned, rather than using it as a tool for understanding something else. This is ethology rather than psychological study, or rather than using the animal as a model for some human medical problem (as in a study of lead poisoning in zoo animals referred to by Jamieson (1985: 113)).

This kind of behavioural study, while presumably encouraged by London's Secretary in the late 1930s, Julian Huxley (himself an ethological pioneer), and while Zuckerman's famous study of baboon behaviour (Zuckerman 1932) is regarded as of seminal importance, seems not to have been in the ascendant at London in the post-war period. London's scientific status was then being re-established by the founding of the Institutes of Comparative Medicine and Reproductive Physiology (Matthews 1976: 283–4). The importance of ethology – that is, the study of animals' natural behaviour often in the field, and very much in its own right as a subject of interest – was by no means universally recognised among biologists forty years ago, but the situation is quite different today, as illustrated by remarkably contrasting comments on the usefulness of field studies expressed by a distinguished biologist, the late Peter Medawar (1951: 164; 1984: 82–3). The study of Celebes black macaques I mentioned above (Dixson 1977), and a remarkable study of chimpanzees at Arnhem, Holland (de Waal 1982), are just two examples of the recognised possibilities of zoo-based ethological study today (Goodall 1986: 13–14). Work of this kind is an elaboration of more isolated behavioural observations such as I referred to above. There is no sharp line between the two. Many kinds of 'captive' behavioural study are possible, for example, of the 'flight' of a flying lemur (Harrison 1959), of the grazing behaviour of wallabies (Clarke and Loudon 1985), or the swimming movements of a paper nautilus (Young 1960), or even gorilla social relations as experienced by temporarily becoming one of the group (Aspinall 1986).

One might reasonably question the value of captive behavioural study on the grounds of the possible abnormality of the behaviour observed. This has to be taken into account, and it clearly usually is (Dixson 1977: 81; de Waal 1982: 36). I have already commented in Chapter 3 on the Zuckerman (1932) study of baboons on Monkey Hill in the London Zoo, and how Rachels (1976: 210) makes too much of this as a demonstration of the unreliability of behaviour studies in zoos.

Much as the occurrence of abnormal behaviour in captivity is to be regretted, at least any which seems to indicate a condition of distress of some kind in the animal, it is not the case that study of such behaviour could have no general application other than to the study of animals' behaviour in artificial conditions (Morris 1966).

SOURCE FOR ANATOMICAL MATERIAL

Providing dead specimens (or part of them) for anatomical study is the most obvious way in which London Zoo assisted scientific research throughout its nineteenth-century existence (Matthews 1976: 282). And obviously other zoos can perform at least this function; the now defunct Belle Vue, for example (Cave 1985: 528). Of course, this is a function zoos perform less the better they become, but it is responsible of them to ensure that the best use is made of their animals after death.

Many animals are also a source of various 'biofacts' – for example, regularly moulted exoskeletons of arthropods like crabs, lobsters, tarantulas, scorpions; antlers, horns, hair, feathers; carapaces of turtles, sloughs of snakes, and shed scales of lizards. These, like dead specimens, can be studied. With regard both to dead specimens and 'biofacts', there is obviously no clear line between zoos and museums. A zoo could pass material on to a museum, or it could keep it, in which case there would be as it were a museum in the zoo. Museums can also keep live animals, such as fish or bees. A museum can own a zoo – or even two zoos and a botanic garden, like the Muséum d'Histoire Naturelle in Paris (Delacour 1966: 31).

MILIEU FOR SCIENTIFIC ACTIVITIES

One more way in which zoos can assist science is not itself a kind of research. A zoo can be a focal point for other scientific (and conservational) activities such as meetings or the publication of scientific journals, or scientific studies not depending directly or even indirectly on actual animals in the zoo. This is really the respect in which the Zoological Society of London was scientific from the start. (It produces for example no less than six series of publications, three of them dating from 1830, 1833 and 1864 respectively.) London is still a scientific society with its 'menagerie' a part but by no means the whole of its *raison d'être* (Zuckerman 1980: 11). One could compare the way in which a museum like the Natural History Museum is a centre of research not necessarily much connected, if at all, with the museum's public displays, perhaps even less so now than formerly. (I referred in Chapter 7 to the Natural History Museum's tendency in recent years to banish actual animal specimens to the basement and replace them by manufactured working models illustrating newer biological understanding.)

Zoos such as London and New York sponsor and fund field research, in Africa and elsewhere, research which it is argued (Jamieson 1985: 112) could easily be separated from its zoo 'base'. This may be so, but it is possible that the odd and intricate ways in which institutions themselves evolve and function mean that losing the one – the zoo – would mean losing the other too – the field research. In any case, studies in the wild and in captivity very often complement each other (Hearn 1987: 29).

ON ZOOS NOT BEING SCIENTIFIC

Perhaps this impressive list of the ways in which zoos can assist science should be followed by an admission that many zoos are not scientific. Most of those in Britain were not founded as scientific institutions, and are not directed or staffed by people trained in science or with, necessarily, any interest in making scientific observations. On the other hand, to take a few examples of British exceptions to this, London, Edinburgh, Chester, Paignton, Jersey, Marwell and Glasgow zoos, and the Woolly Monkey Sanctuary, are in many respects scientific institutions, in most cases with scientifically qualified directors or other senior staff, and certainly encouraging scientific studies.

In addition, as we saw in Chapter 2, the Federation of Zoological Gardens of Great Britain was founded in 1966 with the intention of raising zoo standards. From the start applicant zoos had to pass an inspection (with special attention to quality of animal care), followed by regular reinspections. The Federation, with support from the RSPCA, initiated a countrywide keepers' training scheme. All the Federation's member zoos, at least, encourage their keepers to take this course; many require it of them. All keepers taking the course have to submit a research project as part of it. The Federation also requires all its members to maintain basic animal records. Jamieson's (1985: 114–15) doubting of the genuineness of many zoos' conservational claims in view of their lack of records is reasonable enough; but it would not apply to those British zoos who belong to the Federation. And all Federation zoos, at least, encourage student and school scientific projects, some of which are serious studies recording results of great interest and use to zoo staff (for example, recent behavioural projects on Asiatic black bears and on tigers carried out at Glasgow Zoo by Paisley College students).

That many zoos' records are inadequate, though, is spelt out clearly by Durrell (1977: 149–52); he makes many other deserved criticisms of British zoos. The Jersey Wildlife Preservation Trust, which he founded, has long set an example with its scientifically-motivated staff, several of them academically qualified. They are encouraged to study their animals to the utmost, as well as maintaining them (with a concentration on breeding programmes). Jersey's developments have included the founding of their own International Training Centre for Conservation and Captive Breeding of Endangered Species (Durrell 1990: 154).

The Centre is now affiliated with the University of Kent, which in 1989 set up the Durrell Institute of Conservation and Ecology (Durrell 1990: 154–5).

THE USEFULNESS OF SCIENCE IN ZOOS

The scientific work in zoos could be divided into seven kinds, corresponding with my numbering above:

1 Taxonomic
2 'Basic observational'
3 Reproductive–physiological
4 Veterinary
5 Genetic
6 Behavioural
7 'Productional'.

Research in zoos could be classified in another way, as having one or more of three or possibly four aims:

1 To add to biological knowledge.
2 To assist care and breeding of animals in zoos.
3 To assist management and conservation of animals in the wild.
4 To assist the solution of human medical problems.

Which kinds of zoo science serve which aims? All the five main kinds of scientific study, 2–6, can probably contribute substantially to biological knowledge in its own right, to the applied science of keeping and breeding wild animals, and to the management of wild populations.

The obtaining of knowledge useful to man's medical care, while unusual, can occur, as in some work concerning marmoset breeding, which could assist understanding of some human stress conditions (Wiseman 1986). The particular example given by Jamieson (1985: 113), concerning lead poisoning in zoo animals as a model for study of the same condition in humans, deserves his comment of 'at best unimportant and at worst deplorable'. But it is hardly typical. Other knowledge too obtained in zoo studies could no doubt occasionally be relevant to the biological study of humans. A striking example would be de Waal's chimpanzee study (1982: 210–13).

Some knowledge can only be obtained from the study of animals in captivity rather than in the wild. Here are three clear examples of where certain significant information could not have been gained without keeping the animals concerned in captivity:

1   The fact that females in heat in Mongolian gerbil communities visit neighbouring communities to mate, returning to their own burrows where their young grow up under the care of their mother and uncles (Macdonald 1984: 677).

2   Details about the territory and behaviour of slow-worms, about which 'little can be concluded . . . without keeping them in captivity' because of their being 'so inconspicuous' (Frazer 1983: 179).

3   The extent to which chimpanzees' jockeying for power and position in their social relations amounts to 'politics'. A great deal was learnt about this (and could not have been learnt in the wild, because of the extremely close observations needed on fully identified individuals through an extensive period) in a study of the Chimpanzee Colony at Arnhem Zoo in Holland, referred to above (de Waal 1982: 18–19; Goodall 1986: 13).

Animal studies like (1) and (2) would probably not usually be done in a zoo. Gerbils and slow-worms are both rather small: this is a reason for the convenience of captive observations (Ewer 1975). Zoos tend, for obvious reasons, to keep large animals (though gerbils and slow-worms are both, incidentally, highly convenient for and effective in zoo education). Many of the interesting and important recent discoveries about some of the kinds of animal kept in zoos – lions, tigers, gorillas, orangutans – have been made in the wild. But much useful supplementary work, or comparable work such as that at Arnhem, has been done in zoos. There are several other zoo environments for particular primates which allow study of importance: for example gorillas at Antwerp, and at Howletts; chimpanzees at Taronga Zoo, Sydney, Edinburgh Zoo and Chester Zoo; and the Woolly Monkey Sanctuary. And much veterinary information and many 'general observations', particularly of course on reproduction, have been obtained from or made in captive situations.

So it can be, in principle, useful to study animals in a captive or artificial situation as contrasted with study in the wild. And often captive study is essential for eliciting certain information or solving some particular problem. Studying animals 'in captivity' is

not synonymous with studying them in zoos, and zoos are sometimes unsuitable for various reasons. But they can be very
suitable.

This doesn't in itself morally justify any captive study, still less
morally justify all zoos because some of them assist the obtaining
of new knowledge. It might still be the case that we shouldn't have
zoos; but we must recognise that their disappearance would be a
loss, and not only a minor loss, for scientific study. We have to be
satisfied on other grounds that the keeping of particular animals
in particular conditions is acceptable; but if we are, then the above
considerations must help to persuade us that such keeping has a
serious justification.

Most zoo-keepers probably, and very reasonably, identify zoos'
scientific work with their conservation work, accepting that zoos
have a particular conservation role in the captive breeding of
endangered species, and seeing their scientific role as helping
towards that. In practice, in the process of keeping the animal and
trying their hardest to get it to breed they learn and discover a
good deal.

The conservational justification for zoos is only really convincing if their staff are tackling their work scientifically – that is,
adopting a systematic and experimental approach, and being
aware of and responsive to relevant scientific information. True,
breeding is an art as well as a science, and human factors are
involved, such as the relationship between the animal and its
keeper. Formal scientific qualifications are no substitute for and
no guarantee of keepering ability or success. But the fact remains
that the keeper and the zoo itself must be scientific in some degree
if they are to be conservationally credible, for example in the
keeping of adequate records, and they should be as scientific in
their approach as they can manage.

Different degrees of scientific approach may be required with
different kinds of animal. For example, the breeding of certain
reptiles probably needs a very scientific approach, with an awareness of the importance of the various stimuli affecting the animal,
and scientific sophistication in adjusting them satisfactorily.

Some of the skills needed to keep and breed reptiles and
amphibians successfully are very important for science, and
extremely difficult to attain. This is graphically illustrated by the
work of the remarkable Austrian biologist, Paul Kammerer
(Koestler 1974). Earlier this century, Kammerer claimed remark-

able results from his work on the midwife toad, and how it adapted to damp conditions. This work, if confirmed, could have enormous evolutionary significance. But the testing of his results is probably out of the question, simply because no one seems to share Kammerer's own ability to keep and breed the animals through many generations (Koestler 1974: 12–13).

Obviously such skills as Kammerer's are exceptional. But in view of the scientific as well as other abilities needed in some animal keeping, there is a strong case for keeping such types of expertise available, even if not needed at the moment, in case of future need – for conserving them, in fact.

In some degree I am making a case for the scientific potential of zoos, rather than their present reality (though the reality is a good deal better than Jamieson makes out). Zoos need to work hard at captive breeding, at recording, etc., and not least because animals demand (to use my terms from Chapter 8) both conservation respect and rights respect.

We should regard it as irresponsible, even arrogant, to keep animals unless we are both doing our utmost to keep them as well as possible (the animals are in our hands; we, as humans, have taken on the responsibility of looking after them), and learning everything possible from keeping them.

11

EDUCATION IN ZOOS

By education I mean worthwhile instruction, or learning, or almost any situation which produces some desirable extension of our mental faculties. Education, to count as such, should not be trivial; still less can it be the inculcation of immoral attitudes or beliefs. Education is something we normally approve of, something valuable (Peters 1973: 15–16).

Animals should not be confined in zoos for any reasons, including education, if by 'confined' we understand 'kept in a way which does not ensure their well-being'. I have discussed in Chapters 5, 6 and 7 how they should be kept. If we have good reason to think any particular animals in a zoo are not in a state of well-being, any instruction or learning resulting from having them will be morally unjustified, because of its dependence on something unjustified – the confining of the animals concerned. And perhaps the instruction given will be invalidated by the additional message that it is acceptable to confine animals in poor conditions for our convenience. The most important thing on educational grounds, as well as on the grounds of our responsibility towards any animals we keep, is that their conditions should be, and should be seen to be, satisfactory. And if the animal should not, on conservation grounds, be there at all, or if acquiring it involved immoral behaviour (such as killing several other chimpanzees in order to capture one), then the educational use couldn't possibly compensate for such occurrences.

It is perfectly possible for a situation to be valuable to us in terms of our experience, but unjustifiable because of the ill-treatment to some animal (or human) which is involved. To vivisect animals, as Harvey (1964: 176 ff.) did in the seventeenth century to study the workings of their hearts, would in certain respects be very instructive; as an educational exercise (as well as for research purposes indeed, at least in the absence of anaesthesia), such actions would be grossly immoral. But with zoos, we must justify keeping animals by showing the degree to which our keeping of them is in their interests.

In some cases, in addition to an animal's being kept well, its being kept is justified on conservational grounds, or other strong grounds (for example, where an animal has been rescued following injury, and its return to the wild is inadvisable on humane grounds).

The point about the invalidation of the instruction is an important one, but it can be 'reversed'. That is, where any animals concerned are clearly and obviously being well-kept, we are giving positive moral instruction (demonstrating they need to be looked after properly, and showing how) in addition to whatever other study may be occurring.

If the moral challenge to the actual keeping of the animals can't be satisfactorily answered, then education considerations are just one additional reason why the zoo in question must set right what is wrong, or close. If the moral challenge can be satisfactorily answered, the opportunity to see and study animals in zoos is educationally valuable.

And it is valuable in several ways. To have animals – whether few or many, individuals or species – there in front of you is clearly a great advantage in learning about them. You can directly observe their structure, proportions, colour and pattern, details of the hair or whatever the body covering is, details of the sense organs, shape and size of their limbs, and so on. Most of this we might be able to see as well in mounted museum specimens, but the colours of such specimens fade, and living animals are not the same even throughout the year, still less throughout their lives. Observations of one characteristic of animals, their changeability, can be made much more obviously in a zoo than a museum. Other observations too are not possible at all in a museum. In a zoo we can observe how an animal moves its limbs, moves about, feeds, grooms itself, and in general how it behaves, including how it relates to its fellows.

Sometimes the zoo as a 'learning situation' is objected to as just not very useful, because the animals are not in their natural habitats, or else misleading, because of the animals' artificial conditions and abnormal behaviour. It's worth considering the comments the authors, Grove and Newell (1957: vii), of a well-known 'A' level biology textbook, make: 'We cannot too strongly urge that for true appreciation, a living animal is preferable to a dead one, and a dead one is better than any drawing or written description.' A zoo at least has real animals, live animals. And in some cases it would be in practice impossible to see those animals in their natural habitat (tigers are a striking example, as we'll see in Chapter 12). Besides, many zoo enclosures do in some respect simulate the animals' natural habitats. In any case, information about or discussion of the animals' natural habitats is often provided by zoo education staff, or school staff, or by guide books, information sheets or labels. Confrontation with the animal itself is a splendid starting point for appreciating its adaptations to its natural habitat. The abnormality of zoo animals' behaviour can easily be exaggerated, and, as we have seen, it is a fundamental requirement of keeping animals well to provide conditions which allow and encourage natural behaviour.

What Grove and Newell are emphasising in their comment is also part of the answer to the suggestion that zoo education could with advantage be fully replaced by the use of film and video (Jamieson 1985: 112). No doubt for many of us, the marvellous developments in natural history film-making in recent years have provided a whole new dimension to our understanding of the natural world. The opportunity for us all to watch on television cheetahs or elephants or lemurs, in their natural habitats, in some ways makes zoos educationally less important than in the last century. Films, indeed widely available illustrated books, have removed the urge or need that people had a century ago to flock to zoos (as we saw in Chapter 2).

But so far as actual study of animals is concerned, Grove and Newell's comment still holds. A live animal is better than a dead one, and a dead one than a book. And, we could add, an animal in its natural habitat is better than one in a zoo, and one in a zoo is better than one on film. Obviously film is a magnificent educational aid. But then Grove and Newell, as textbook authors, were hardly intending to imply that books too were not a magnificent educational aid. They were stressing the importance of actual animals for students of zoology – animals in the end, not books, being what zoologists study.

Zoos provide actual animals on which student zoologists (and qualified researchers) can make real observations. In a zoo one is not having suitable observations selected for one by a film director. Films are not in all respects more accurate, because their directors have to select shots of animals in action, whereas in real life some animals, such as lions, spend a 'great proportion of the day . . . sleeping and lolling around' in the wild as in zoos (Markowitz 1982: 196; Kiley-Worthington 1990: 130–1). One may say how dull the zoo is compared to a film. Sometimes it may be; but it's also in some respects more accurate in the scientific instruction it offers.

Behavioural study of animals in captivity is sometimes dismissed as too easy to be worth doing, but only someone who had never tried it would think this. Of course it is still more difficult in the field, even seemingly impossible, as Jane Goodall (van Lawick-Goodall 1973: 34) tells us she felt as she started upon the most extended and most famous field study of all time. But that is what makes the zoo so good as a halfway house. It is still extremely difficult to identify individuals (in a large group), to record behaviour systematically and interpret one's observations (de Waal 1982: 31–2). This is why a zoo can provide such good learning exercises, if nothing more. One is coming up against the problems of realities in a way which somebody who merely watched films could never appreciate. Of course the films and videos available today are enormous aids to scientific study and understanding. But watching them is not the same as making one's own observations.

Besides, many of the sequences in natural history series like *Life on Earth* have to be rigged, and a surprising number of television wildlife scenes apparently shot in deepest rainforest are actually shot in zoos. According to Marthe Kiley-Worthington (1990: 130–1) many kills in wildlife films are also arranged.

To the occasional comment that zoos are boring, or of little educational importance, I would respond with my own zoo experiences. The animals in zoos aren't all continually exciting, as they tend to be on films. But when I read how even young children are rather bored by zoos, I recall taking my 6-year-old niece years ago to Edinburgh Zoo. She may not have learnt much, but she was enormously excited at the prospect of seeing again her favourite 'elephant seal', and maintained this level of excitement for hours while rushing from animal to animal. She kept many animals as she grew older, later graduating in ecology, so perhaps her early enthusiasm for the zoo wasn't unconnected with her continuing adult interest in the natural world. (The interests of many biologists and naturalists seem to have been sparked off originally or encouraged by zoo encounters.)

When critics emphasise the ice-cream and sweets, as demonstrating the frivolity and non-educational value of zoo visits by young schoolchildren (Paterson 1979: 2–3; Scott 1973: 97), I recall guided tours with, say, 10-year-olds, who have observed all kinds of behaviour (Barbary rams challenging each other, peacocks displaying, lemurs engaging in 'stink-fights') and have clearly had a zoo visit which in no way deserved to be scorned as sub-educational. And when I read how zoos just don't offer any experience worth having, I have only to recall experiences of my own to know the inaccuracy of such a comment, experiences like observing dogfish and skates at London Zoo, and appreciating the grace of their swimming, and the precise way their gill openings operated, the grace too of turtles at London and in the Edinburgh Zoo aquarium, the beauty of enormous fanworms at the Schönbrunn Zoo in Vienna, and of ring-tailed lemurs in the Charles Clore Pavilion at London, and the careful, slow climbing of the pottos and lorises in the Nocturnal House below. These are odd examples of experiences I found valuable, for me indisputable evidence that some zoos offer some valuable experiences. I only mention them because, according to some people, zoos are so insufferably boring as not to be worth going to in any case.

It is claimed too that we should not be raising children's expectations unduly, for they have no right to see tigers for example – I agree; but if the tigers are in a state of well-being in a zoo, then seeing them can be a valuable experience for children and others.

It may be added that it's much more important for children to learn about and appreciate their own wildlife (McKenna 1987: 36). To see a weasel or a badger is a marvellous experience, and to appreciate such animals, our own wildlife, is probably more important than appreciating exotic but not more interesting animals from far countries. But the two are not exclusive alternatives. If our own wildlife is the more important to us, that is no reason for depriving children and others of the chance to experience something else that is also good, if less important – and of similar biological interest. It also of course happens to be the case that several British mammals are difficult to see. Thus those who manage to see them are likely to be having, partly because of the efforts they have to make, a richer experience. Of course we should encourage such real natural history. However the former director of Palacerigg Country Park near Glasgow, the late David Stephen, himself a distinguished field naturalist, chose to have at Palacerigg some enclosures (containing fine habitat reconstructions) to give visitors a fair chance of seeing such animals as wildcats and badgers. He knew a great deal about the wild lives of such animals, including just how unlikely most of us are to see them without such assistance. Thus the comment that our children should learn about our own wildlife, even though it is a sentiment we should all agree with, doesn't rule out zoos as also having a useful educational role to play. Of course in Africa our exotic animals are their (relatively) local wildlife. Jordan and Ormrod (1978: 66–7) have illustrated how much, in West Africa for example, a zoo gives people, who would never be able to otherwise, a chance to see and appreciate their own wildlife.

Sometimes it is brought as an objection to zoo education that most people don't go to zoos to be educated, 'and in any case the facilities offered by most zoos are lamentable' (Lever 1987), or that many zoos 'make no real effort at education' (Jamieson 1985: 111). These comments imply that zoo education as a whole can be criticised or even condemned on the grounds that some zoos' educational provision is poor. But the fact that some schools are very good is not affected by the fact that some other schools are very poor. Even if it is true that a great many zoos' educational provision is not very good, or even very genuine, the fact remains that certain zoos are clearly doing good educational work.

It may well be true that most people don't go to zoos to be educated, but that is not to say that the education – the rich experiences – are not available there for the taking. One reason for including some examples of what I have found myself to be worthwhile experiences in zoos was to indicate that such experiences are possible. It is also rather likely that a great many people besides me find some parts of some zoos equally rewarding. If most zoo visitors are not taking full advantage of their opportunities for learning and for rich experiences, this is probably just as true of museums – especially free ones. It also doesn't matter to the animals, as neither do the ice-cream and the sweets, provided they don't find their way into animals' enclosures. Still, although zoos receive a very wide range of visitors, including many without special interests or qualifications, it is disappointing that a study of

ZOOS AND ANIMAL RIGHTS

what visitors to zoos learn, or of how well-informed they are about animals, should reveal a level of animal knowledge only a little above that of the general public, and much less than many with a special interest or involvement in the countryside (Turner 1987: 29–32). This is something to which zoo educators need to pay attention. But it is important that the same researcher, Kellert, has also found in zoo visitors 'a great concern for issues of animal welfare and rights as shown by a high score on the moralistic scale and a low score on dominionistic', and a 'very high [score] on the humanistic scale', where 'humanistic' means 'primary interest and strong affection for individual animals, principally pets' (Turner 1987: 29–32). It may be that zoo visitors as a whole are not well informed about animals, that they have false ideas about them, but they apparently care about them and about their interests very highly, and appreciate them as individual living beings.

Just how much the simple chance to see animals and get close to them means to a great many people is demonstrated by a finding in a recent visitor study at Calderglen Country Park in East Kilbride. It turned out that a far larger proportion of the Park's total visitors than anyone had suspected, about 80 per cent in fact, visited the children's zoo in the course of visiting the Park – far more than visited the Park Interpretation Centre, which had been assumed to be a greater attraction. One old age pensioner visited the children's zoo every day to feed a particular donkey (Calderglen Country Park 1987). Such findings, and some of those of Kellert, show how another comment of Jamieson's (1985: 112), that most of the 'educational benefits of zoos [could] be obtained by presenting films, slides, lectures [or even] by exhibiting empty cages with explanations of why they were empty', is missing the point; biologically, films, for example, could in some ways replace zoos, though by no means in all ways, as we saw above in regard to behavioural studies. But so far as the value of meeting animals is concerned, films are quite irrelevant; they offer something fine, but little to do with what for many zoo visitors – whether general public or schoolchildren – is the most valuable element of their visit.

For David Cooper (1991), the phrase 'real-life encounters' may be a 'dramatic, loaded way to describe standing . . . staring at a creature which stares dully back', and some animal enclosures may deserve such censure; but that old age pensioner at Calderglen was presumably getting a 'real-life encounter' if it was worth returning for every day; it was a meeting with an animal, something more than just seeing it, as they could have done on television. This aspect of zoos I shall look at further in the next chapter.

There is a great wealth of approaches being tried in zoo education today, and a growing awareness of zoo education's importance, especially in some underdeveloped parts of the world. London and Paignton Zoos are the pioneers in this field.

All sorts of method are used, from very successful animal contact sessions at Edinburgh (often using invertebrates or the less popular vertebrates, like toads or garter snakes), to the use of different kinds of drama at Bristol and Marwell, and methods which stress the advantage of direct experience and hands on contact at the Wildfowl and Wetlands Trust and many other places. The Edinburgh 'zoo lab' provides all kinds of art materials and activities to try – like seeing what it feels like to have webbed feet, or flippers. Edinburgh Zoo also pioneered in the 1970s their 'interlink' approach, of providing programmes in partnership with various other organisations, from the Royal Botanic Garden or the Forestry Commission to the SPCA Animals' Home, so as to provide schools with a very worthwhile educational 'package'. A school might visit the Botanic Garden to study the plants of the rainforest, and then the zoo for a session looking at the animals which depend on those plants. The 'interlink' approach has received great interest in America and elsewhere.

Twycross has a particularly lively education department (Whitehead 1984); its staff have constructed a fine walk-through rainforest display, as well as many lively and interactive instruction labels around the zoo. In many zoo education departments, modelling, painting, mask-making, mobile-making and all sorts of other artistic activities, often with interesting biological connections, are available.

Paignton has a fine 'education lab', with many kinds of gadgets and devices all geared to wildlife instruction. Some zoos in America have developed sophisticated technological aids to 'experiencing' what it's like to see through a hawk's eyes, or to echo-locate like a bat. Interactive video, in addition to 'ordinary' video and tape-slides, is now being used.

Some educational services, such as that at Camperdown Park in Dundee, prefer a specifically non-technological approach which concentrates on contact with animals, sometimes tame hawks or eagles. There is clearly an interesting diversity of approaches in zoo education departments, though also today closely related, in England, to the requirements of the National Curriculum.

For twenty years or so there has been a growing International Association of Zoo Educators, which today holds biennial meetings successively in America, Europe or Africa, and Asia or Australasia. The Association is affiliated to IUCN, and its members very aware of their important role worldwide in stimulating concern among the young for disappearing wildlife. There is a growing involvement in the International Association by members from underdeveloped countries, where there is an urgent need to interest children in their own wildlife. In India, or central America (or many parts of Africa, as we saw above), most children will never see their own wild animals without the aid of zoos.

So there is a great deal going on in zoo education, and lively contributions being made to environmental education generally (Hatley n.d.), and to art, geography, history and English as well as biology, often at a wide range of academic levels.

In the end, the most important part of zoos' educational provision is their making available to children and adults real animals to observe, but there is a great deal that zoo educators can do either in person, or by means of educational aids produced by them for teachers to use, to concentrate that contact with animals into an educationally constructive experience, and one which helps to stimulate concern for the conservation of animals' wild habitats.

12

WHY KEEP REAL ANIMALS?

One further role, or multi-role, of zoos that should be recognised is that of a place for viewing, meeting, having contact with and being close to animals. Zoos, alongside parks in cities and trees in city streets, and flowers and aquariums in homes, are ways in which man enriches his own environment.

INVOLVEMENT WITH ANIMALS

Contact or involvement with animals seems important to many people, though not all. The traditional fondness of kings for horses and lions is only partly to be explained as a fondness (shared with many other people) for status symbols (Cherfas 1984: 17; Serpell 1986: 120 ff.). They also simply like having animals around, as obviously applies to the British royal family, and must have applied to Kubilai Khan too. (If it didn't, he must have found it, you would think, a trifle unnerving having lions and tigers strolling around the palace, as apparently reported by Marco Polo (Loisel 1912: I, 38).) Otherwise, why should they choose animals as status symbols rather than something else? The situation is rather that almost any activity or hobby which includes having or collecting items lends itself to having items which are, or are regarded as, of better quality than others of the same kind. So within any society of interested humans, status symbols emerge. Animal keepers of any kind tend in this direction. Any of the royal and the wealthy who go in for animals tend to select those regarded as more expensive or exclusive – though not always, as in the case of the British royal family's enthusiasm for corgis. Even allowing for the part played by tradition, the vast numbers of royal beasts down the millennia are striking evidence of a widespread

177

human fondness for animal involvement. Cherfas (1984: 22) is no doubt right to see a main attraction of hunting as the animal involvement it provides. For example, fox-hunting as a method of controlling foxes costs about £500 per fox. Whether or not fox-hunting is unnecessary or cruel, its mere expense indicates that it must have some extraordinarily strong appeal, and the involvement with horses and dogs is the most likely part of that appeal (Carroll 1984: 169–76). Involvement with animals must also be a large part of the appeal of horse-racing, of the keeping and breeding of (for example) budgerigars, mice, fish and all the other creatures with their own 'fancy' devoted to them, and of course the enormous degree of dog, cat and other pet or companion animal keeping (Serpell 1986).

ON ZOOLOGICAL AND OTHER GARDENS

It is worth considering the term 'zoological garden(s)', from which of course 'zoo' is derived. Gardens seem to have been a Persian invention, and although the Greek *paradaisos* was first used in Xenophon's *Anabasis* (1900: 5) in the early fourth century BC of Cyrus's hunting park, the concept of garden as it then developed in Europe seems essentially to be a cultivated bit of nature that you enjoy being in, that is peaceful, relaxing, and beautiful. (The term 'paradise' was used in the Septuagint, the Greek Old Testament, and in the New Testament came to be almost a synonym for heaven. 'Paradise' retained this sense in English, but was also a term used for a wild animal park.)

Although plants are the first essential of a garden, not only is it normal to find animals there, most obviously birds, but it has long been traditional to introduce animals, such as peacocks and 'ornamental waterfowl'. C.S. Lewis was reminded by Whipsnade of Eden or Paradise (1955b: 223; 1966: 154–5), and of course Eden traditionally contained animals. As Milton (with touches of Isaiah's vision of predator and prey at peace) portrayed it in *Paradise Lost*,

> About them frisking playd
> All Beasts of th'Earth, since wild, and of all chase
> In Wood or Wilderness, Forrest or Den;
> Sporting the Lion rampd, and in his paw
> Dandl'd the Kid; Bears, Tygers, Ounces, Pards
> Gambold before them; th'unwieldy Elephant

To make them mirth us'd all his might, and wreath'd
His lithe Proboscis.

(Milton 1958: 82 (IV, ll. 340–7))

Milton observes how the beasts of the chase were at peace like all the others in Eden, and it is fair at least to give credit to the selection of 'garden', essentially to us a symbol of humans and non-humans too at peace, as part of the designation of the Zoological Society's animal collection in 1826. At the very least this was a place where the animals were going to be safe from being hunted or baited. It was made clear to visiting equestrians that whips as well as horses were to be left outside, and it seems likely that the 'leafy, quiet surroundings and the happy way in which the animals responded was at . . . utter variance with the cracking whips, flares and "barkers" hitherto associated with creatures from distant lands' (Brightwell 1952: 15). Animals were not an attraction, even then, merely because of the absence of attractions like films. A kind of very popular 'proto-film' was already available in London: the 'Diorama', dissolving painted views of various great architectural sights, and the 'Colosseum', which showed a changing panoramic survey of London (Altick 1978: 128–72). Thus the success of the Zoological Gardens in the face of such rival attractions tells us something of the special attraction of animals.

ON REAL PLANTS AND ANIMALS

Gardens contain real plants; not, that is, plastic ones. Whatever it is that gardens do for us, presumably the plants we take into our houses, or the trees which line some city streets, also do for us, no doubt in a lesser degree. But do they – the trees, for example – have to be real to do this? This question became of practical importance in Los Angeles in 1972 when 900 plastic trees were erected, presumably because the atmospheric pollution threatened real ones (Tribe 1974). Would anything be lost? Real trees produce moisture and ease the effect of very hot weather, and they absorb dust and noise, so plastic trees clearly would not be a good physical substitute, even if they satisfied us mentally or spiritually. Perhaps in theory an artificial tree could be produced with all a tree's physical properties (so far as they were known) which could affect human beings. Would we still be losing out with the imitation? This could depend on whether we noticed the difference, though the possibility or likelihood of our knowing they were artificial just because we were told so cannot be left out of the issue. If we lost out just because of being told, though we would not have noticed otherwise, this could still be a real loss, if only in the way that gazing entranced on (as we thought) the 15,000-year-old Lascaux Cave paintings (see Chapter 9) and then being told they in fact were not the originals, though we would not have guessed, would make a difference (Elliot 1982: 81–93).

Many of us, anyway, strongly prefer real plants to plastic ones, and surely for sound reasons. What of plastic animals? These seem even worse, though Disney World 'audio-animatronic elephants' are a fine demonstration of technical wizardry if you like that kind of thing (Cherfas 1984: 225; Hediger 1974: 274). Iris Murdoch (1970) and Mary Midgley (1979: 359) have noted the merits (for us) of real kestrels over against plastic ones 'going up at carefully randomized intervals': suddenly seeing a kestrel could restore our mental well-being, but if we think of the kestrel merely as a device of 'mental hygiene' or if it actually were a computerised model set up for the purpose, then the whole point would be lost, and it would not have the reviving effect on us. There is no question both of the special effect that animals can have on us, and of the fact that this is somehow connected with the animals' being independent of us, that they are living their own lives, and are not existing merely in order to have such an effect on us.

There is something particularly admirable about animals living a free existence in what is (to varying degrees in different cases) their natural environment, and it is a sight of such an animal (Iris Murdoch's kestrel, say) which can most obviously and perhaps most powerfully uplift or refresh us. However, our companion or pet animals, and any animals that we keep or have contact with, can in some degree have this special kind of effect on us too. It is probably not the sort of thing which the people concerned put into words very much. They are likely to take it for granted in many cases. And there is evidence that keeping dogs or cats, for example, can lower blood pressure, and be beneficial particularly to depressed humans, something which we may be aware of but be very far from fully understanding, or even not be aware of but still benefit from (Serpell 1986: 76–86, 98–9).

Animals in zoos can have this effect on us too. There is the problem (as with some of the examples mentioned of animals that people keep), that animals in zoos are not living their natural lives.

Or if in some degree they are (and the desirability of working towards such ways of animal keeping were issues we looked at in Chapters 6 and 7), they are clearly not living (by definition) in their natural environment. And even if their conditions simulate or substitute for their natural environment very effectively, this is only because of our human management: the animals are living, as it were, by our favour and in the state we have arranged for them. However, this doesn't make very much difference. A horse is a different kind of being from ourselves, in a way something 'other', something that is closer than us to the natural world, even though we are visiting him in a stable. I don't say that a wild horse would not be still better, even a great deal better; but we couldn't get close to the wild horse, and most certainly we normally couldn't get close to a tiger in the wild. A journalist recently visiting Corbett Park, for example, had still not seen a tiger after spending eight hours on elephant-back for that purpose, and Prince Philip, visiting another park, probably would have been no luckier had not his royal status ensured scouts out all night in land rovers seeking tigers (Hamlyn 1987). A Japanese film crew arrived by arrangement at Chitwal National Park to film tigers but had still not set eyes – still less a camera – on one a fortnight later. With some animals, meeting them in the zoo and in the wild aren't alternatives. Most of us will meet them (and sometimes be refreshed or enriched by the experience) in the zoo or not at all.

And even though zoo animals are being looked after to a great extent, rather than looking after themselves, they are still in some ways living their own lives, even if it is just getting their respective kinds of food, being washed, or having their toenails trimmed, etc.; and in particular, of course, breeding (in some cases); or (if I can put it this way, because I think it is of particular significance) being born, and eventually (or too soon, in some cases) dying. In other words, life in the zoo is going on; and more precisely, the individual lives of a great many creatures, some of them very different from each other as well as from us, are going on. This is part of the ordinary interest in new births at the zoo (which newspapers make good use of). It is also a kind of awareness of nature, especially the births and the deaths, something that those of us who live in towns are likely to be much less well aware of than those in the country, a dimension of experience which E.B. White gets across in his book *Charlotte's Web* (1952). This is a children's story about a farm pig's friendship with a spider called Charlotte, who finally dies; her friend's grief is eased a little by meeting briefly (before they 'parachute' away) the vast number of Charlotte's children, who emerge from the cocoon she left behind. Living and dying is part of life on the farm, and it is hardly fanciful to observe that this fact, obviously equally true of a zoo, is part of its educational value, its potential richness for everybody, but especially those in cities.

Of course you are going to get this experience perhaps still more in the country, or better still in the wild, in wilderness areas, where you may be aware of a myriad organisms living their lives; you may even perhaps feel, like Wordsworth in *The Prelude*:

> the sentiment of Being spread
> O'er all that moves and all that seemeth still
> . . . the joy . . .
> Communing in this sort through earth and heaven
> With every form of creature.
> (Wordsworth 1909: 648 (Book 2, ll. 401–2, 410–12))

But you may meet nature too, if in a lesser way, feeding the hens or looking after the pigs (I am not thinking of intensive systems), or cleaning out the camels, hosing the elephant or feeding the cheetahs. People work in zoos because (in many cases) they, too, like contact with animals. And merely seeing the animals, or perhaps meeting them (which is not quite the same), offers some contact with nature too. Many naturalists have, like Konrad Lorenz, found it rewarding to keep animals. Even Peter Singer (1990: ii, 178), a self-confessed non-animal-lover, though a magnificent exponent of their claims to justice, mentions how becoming a vegetarian and growing his own vegetables 'brought me into closer contact with plants, the soil, and the seasons'. There are innumerable indications that looking after animals does something very similar. This is not in itself a justification for keeping animals, still less for eating meat. But it is a fact we should recognise.

COMMUNITIES OR PRISONS?

Is my picture of a zoo as an acceptable community of animals and humans more than a sentimental whitewashing of the true situation? It was fine for A.A. Milne to present his child's-eye view of the zoo as an exciting place for meeting animals. But weren't the animals themselves 'pathetic prisoners', to use a term Stephen Clark (1977: 37) applied to monkeys he noted in a 'provincial zoo', by contrast with the almost independently living monkeys at the Woolly Monkey Sanctuary? (Incidentally the Sanctuary is rather like a human and animal commune – and why not?) Recent criticisms emphasising how prison-like many zoo enclosures still are reiterate comments made by Galsworthy (1922: 189–91) of the London Zoo lion house and by Saki (Munro 1976: 479–82) of the Mappin Terraces. Of course there have been great improvements in this country – as the Mappin Terraces were a far-reaching development in their time – but not everywhere either in this country or abroad. The tiger cages at Rome Zoo were described in 1987 as bare prisons by two veterinary students. Cages in older menageries were no doubt even worse, and in some cases until quite recently.

But it is possible to keep animals, even powerful, dangerous ones, in very different enclosures, such as those of Howletts (for gorillas and tigers, for example), Marwell's (for ungulates, especially), Whipsnade's (for ungulates, elephants, and lions). There were, at least in some degree, redeeming features of many older zoos also. There was another side to the older London Zoo, and even to menageries like Bostock and Wombwell's. At London there were the animals' relationships with their keepers, not least the large cats (indeed, even at the Tower Zoo). This was not enough compensation, but was something. Elephants, camels, llamas gave rides and met the public, and led active lives. Elephants not only met the public at London, they even (I suggest) joked with them. At least one man provided enrichment for wolves. Where such activity is possible, work such as horses engage in is likely to be good for other animals too. C.S. Lewis not only appreciated the wallabies at Whipsnade; he also appreciated the bears, so much so that a tame bear appears in his *That Hideous Strength*, a 'great, snuffly, wheezy, beady-eyed, loose-skinned, gor-bellied brown bear' called Mr Bultitude (Lewis 1955: 97), ob-viously based on a bear he knew (and called Bultitude) at Whipsnade (Lewis 1966: 154–5).

There was another kind of contact, now outlawed in British zoos, that of feeding the animals. This is rightly objected to now because of what we know of the harm done to animals' health by uncontrolled public feeding. This is unavoidable, but a pity because offering an animal a present, such as food, is not only a way in which a human can indulge himself. It is a natural way of establishing a relationship with an animal, as well of course as producing some behaviour which is interesting to watch:

> If you try to talk to the bison he never quite
> understands;
> You can't shake hands with a mingo – he doesn't like
> shaking hands,
> And lions and roaring tigers hate saying, 'How do you
> do?' –
> But I give buns to the elephant when I go down to the
> Zoo!

> (Milne 1965: 46–7)

I say a 'natural' way, because members of various non-human species sometimes communicate among themselves in this way. It is also possibly innate in humans (Jones 1967). In its time, feeding was a valuable activity in the zoo (even though we now know how bad it was for animals' health). Roger Wheater, Director of Edinburgh Zoo, suggests that handling of stick insects, contact with tame boas and so on, are the acceptable modern substitute for the former animal contact through feeding.

At its best we have a situation in a zoo where with many of the animals we enjoy a relationship approaching the sort that we can have with a companion or pet animal. Of course this will never be possible with all, and it wouldn't necessarily be desirable with all if it were possible, because we need to balance the value of such a relationship with an obviously tame animal with the need to prevent animals in zoos becoming too dissimilar from their wild counterparts. There is a real problem here, but it is not an overwhelming one, not least because the differences between wild and domestic animals are less substantial than often supposed. Where it is possible, this is one way in which animals can be kept acceptably: where they are trained in varying degrees, have contact with members of the public as well as zoo staff, and have plenty of activity. Of course, their enclosures must also be of high standard.

But is the relationship with humans a valuable one? Isn't the only admirable state for an animal a wild one? Why should this be so if we grant that our relationship with a domestic animal can be a valuable one? It is difficult to dispute that our relationship with dogs is symbiotic (though Juliet Clutton-Brock (1992) does). If our relationship with dogs is mutually valuable, why shouldn't a relationship with some other species, a relationship a little like that of human and dog, be valuable also? Lewis (1957: 126 ff.) went so far as to regard the state of an animal living at close quarters and peace with man as the ideal one, as portrayed with Mr Bultitude. (It is interesting that Lewis was rebuked in a letter by Evelyn Underhill for apparently suggesting that the nature of domestic cows, turned by man into mere milk-producing machines – this before the dawn of intensive husbandry! – was for a moment comparable in splendour with that of the wild-living animal.) I don't agree with Lewis that even such an idyllic state as he portrays would be superior to the wild state, but he is right, even so, to emphasise the remarkable and special nature of the relationship possible with an animal such as a dog, a relationship possible, I believe, in some degree too with a relatively wild animal in a zoo.

Such a relationship can be valuable to the animal as well as to the human, as also a comparison sometimes made between the animal in good captivity and man in a civilised state is in some degree valid (Hediger 1964: 180; Hediger 1974: 73). Clearly zoo animals (and this will apply even where they have little relationship with their keepers or anyone else) at least have medical and other protection, which is a substantial advantage of their state, even though they require even more zoo conditions which fulfil their needs, especially that of meaningful occupation.

13

TAKING ANIMALS FROM THE WILD

Capturing an animal – from the wild state – is considerably more difficult to justify than keeping it in a zoo. With a zoo animal we should be able to demonstrate convincingly that it is in a state of well-being, that it is being kept well. But an animal cannot be kept well until it has adjusted to captivity (if it wasn't born into it) and has, as it were, accepted the situation. So we can't defend the process of capture in this way; capture, even carried out efficiently, is likely to be stressful for an animal; and it seems, in any case, an improper invasion of its right to be left alone to live its own kind of life. I have argued that the well-adjusted zoo animal is slightly domesticated; this of course by definition can't be so of the wild animal.

So the matter has been left until now to make clear the strength of the conservational, scientific, educational and 'environmental' cases for keeping animals. For only these, plus the likelihood of the captured animal's ending in good conditions in a zoo, and adjusted to its life there, can justify taking it from the wild.

Perhaps only a strong conservational need alone could justify capturing an animal, or for that matter even keeping it (Bostock 1981). This would be the only justification for capturing some endangered animal. But if we make it a necessary reason for capturing or keeping any animal, we are put in a situation where we must depend on chance capturing activities by other individuals in the past, and not even necessarily just in the past. There might be situations where we accept that we can keep animal A because someone else X (of whose activity we disapprove) has captured it and for some reason it has come into our hands. This could be ludicrous: it might well be much better that we, or someone we have arranged with, should responsibly collect the animal rather than that X should; and it seems unfortunate to have to depend on X's illicit doings.

Besides, if there is such a strong case for the scientific and educational roles of zoos, it seems unreasonable entirely to outlaw the necessary preliminary act of taking an animal from the wild except in those circumstances where it is endangered but able to be helped by captive breeding.

The essential provision for justified capturing is that it be responsible. This means that it must be done carefully and as humanely as possible by professional or trained people with some official permission or certification and whose motivation is not simply that of helping themselves to an easy source of money.

We saw earlier (in Chapter 3) how animals' rights should be recognised as similar to ours, and it is individuals who have rights, not species, because it is individuals who can suffer and also find satisfaction in living. So even where our motives are conservational alone – where we are clearly showing conservation respect for the species concerned – it can still seem an invasion of the individuals' rights rudely to capture them.

I argued in Chapter 3 that the animal's right to freedom was not invaded if it was kept in conditions (like a farmyard for hens) in which most of its natural behaviour could be expressed. Similarly here, if we can make the act of capture such that the animal is stressed as little as possible, and then transport it in conditions in which it is little upset, and if, as arranged by us, the animal is being taken to a zoo where it will be provided with the best conditions – then we have gone a long way towards respecting its right to freedom. For we have every reason to expect that the animal will, after a not very disturbing period, end up cared for in good conditions, and generally in a state of well-being.

If in addition the animal is being taken for genuine conservational reasons, then our action is clearly justified. This would obviously be so with the taking of the last surviving free male condors, though of course this is a very unusual case (Houston 1985), and with cases where we are following the instructions of the IUCN Captive Breeding Specialist Group – as we saw in Chapter 9.

It would also be so where the animal in question was so numerous in the wild, perhaps regarded as a pest species, that it was likely to be shot or otherwise killed. Baboons are sometimes locally regarded in Africa as a pest species. Sometimes elephants are. Despite the terrible question mark hanging over the very survival of African elephants today, they can easily become so numerous in particular areas as to require culling. Cockatoos in some areas of Australia are shot by farmers to protect their crops.

We cannot say that it is categorically wrong to take an animal from the wild; it isn't indeed categorically wrong to lie or even kill another human being (though of course the latter is absolutely wrong except in very exceptional circumstances).

But what of the reality of the capturing of wild animals? Domalain (1978) gives an appalling picture from his own experience of wild animal trafficking in south-east Asia. He tells of gibbons (Domalain 1978: 16–44) and leopards and crocodiles (Domalain 1978: 25–6) captured by cruel means (caught in spiked pits or females killed for the obtaining of the young), then held for long periods in grossly inadequate containers, of disease killing many, of transport to Europe by irresponsible airlines, of delays and refusals to accept responsibility by those who had ordered consignments, of sick animals got rid of by unscrupulous traders as quickly as possible, of many dying even after reaching their destinations. The situation such as he describes it is clearly morally indefensible.

Even if Domalain's book isn't fully accurate or is exaggerated (which looks unlikely, but books can be written out of a grudge against former colleagues or rivals), it shows clearly just how much suffering can be caused by the trade in wild-caught animals. We have seen the human potential for cruelty; we know what some people will do if there is no check on their activities: if there are no controlling regulations or they aren't enforced.

It is an extra complication that according to Domalain the operations are more clandestine than they otherwise would be, and therefore also more inhumane, because of the need to dodge the various conservation regulations.

And of course it is obvious that transporting an animal, as well as capturing it, is going to be a stressful process even where the operation is done responsibly and with friendly human contact and comfort; where it is done by semi-criminals or persons interested only in the money, the suffering caused intentionally or by ignorance and lack of concern will clearly be much greater (Jordan and Ormrod 1978: 103–34; Nichol 1987; Reisner 1991). (Not that we meet such occurrences only in south-east Asia: the stress caused to literally millions of broiler chickens in British intensive systems caught up roughly at the end of their six-week lives for transport to slaughter is very great.)

I am not concerned here about the conservational aspects, because the CITES regulations are intended to control the trade in wild and particularly endangered animals; if regulations are broken or are not strong enough, zoos are not substantially responsible (as we saw in Chapter 9). According to Domalain, zoos are involved, but if so they are behaving illegally, and also disobeying the policy of, for example, the Zoo Federation in Britain (and would face expulsion if found out).

I am objecting to trading in wild caught living animals on welfare grounds, whether or not there is in a specific case any conservational reason for not taking them. Animals, however common, should not be captured (and traded in and so on) if this causes them substantial or extended suffering. Michael Brambell would echo my sentiments, but would probably explain the need to be realistic: CITES is a trade convention, not a welfare one. He makes the point that it is useful to have trade in a species controlled even just to ensure that the authorities can learn what is going on, so as to take action in the future if necessary. But again this is a conservational matter rather than a welfare one, and it is the latter which Domalain's book brings to our attention.

There is a case for the responsible catching of animals for conservational and in some degree scientific and educational purposes, but only where it is done by responsible expeditions, or by staff of conservation or government agencies in the countries concerned – or by accredited catchers if there was some check on them. Some professional catchers of wild animals are remarkable and humane people – Raymond Hook for example (Pollard 1963). But effective checks are difficult: we are in a murky world reminiscent of the slave trade. The catching should be done by authorised persons for conservation reasons, indeed, but still more for welfare reasons. The whole set-up described by Domalain, which is a world away from the proper keeping of animals, should be outlawed. A proper expedition means that the animals are caught properly; that they are then looked after properly, and transported properly (as, for example, on Jersey's expeditions). Domalains (1978: 53) concedes that a properly organised expedition is a different matter from the sort of thing he describes. I am not arguing that only zoos should be able to collect, or that only they are capable of responsibly collecting, animals from the wild. An expedition organised by, say, the British Herpetological Association would doubtless be very responsible. But there should be firm checks, on welfare grounds, on the credentials of the collectors: they would need to be accredited with the BHS above, or some other reputable organisation.

There is another qualification, and that is that in some cases, for example with cockatoos in Australia, the birds are killed as pests, but their export for reputable collectors illegal. What happens as a result is not simply that all the birds are killed when some of them might have gone to be kept by genuine parrot enthusiasts, which would seem a happier fate for them, but that many are exported illegally by dealers prepared to transport them in appallingly inhumane ways. So in fact there is sometimes a good case on humane grounds for the relaxing of certain strict conservational regulations against animal export.

So I can hardly condemn all trading even in wild caught animals. But there should be requirements of licensing, on welfare grounds, of the persons involved. I don't have an unrealistic faith in the effectiveness of licensing regulations. I am merely stating the moral situation: that uncontrolled trading cannot be justified. The economic difficulties of putting this into practice, the need of poor countries for money from exports of wildlife and wildlife products, I appreciate. But I am not saying it should all be banned; I am saying it should be controlled, and on welfare grounds, not just conservational grounds.

The selling of an animal is not necessarily bad in itself. (After all, footballers are sold by their clubs: this doesn't mean they aren't respected or treated properly! The more distinguished they are, the higher the prices they fetch.) Breeding dogs or any other animal and selling them can be a highly reputable occupation – indeed it is more likely to be such if the animals are very valuable, as great care is accordingly more likely to be taken over them. But when animals are just caught and treated as expendable, and managed by people who do not know how to do it, the consequences for the individual animals can clearly be quite appalling. (The job would be very difficult for anyone, even well-qualified and well-intentioned, to do adequately because of the number of different species likely to be involved.)

So dealers should only normally be dealing in captive-born animals. If animals are to be taken from the wild they should be collected by zoo personnel themselves, or by members of reputable organisations like the BHS (above), or by persons known to them, or by responsible officials of the governments of the countries concerned. Zoos probably in many cases choose in any case to purchase captive-bred animals for various reasons, such as the likelihood of their being free of injuries likely to be incurred in capture, and because they are more likely to know which animals they are buying, and know their history. (Many animals are now exchanged or lent between zoos without money being involved.) But zoos should make their policy very clearly to refrain entirely from any purchase of wild-caught animals, quite apart from any conservation considerations, unless they know and can vouch for the person in charge of the actual catching and transport of the animal.

14

CONCLUSION

We have seen that various relatively wild animals can be kept in zoos in what may reasonably be regarded as a state of well-being, and I have discussed various criteria by which to judge the suitability of their conditions. No doubt much zoo-keeping today is still, by those criteria, falling short of what our responsibility to the animals concerned requires. And humans are fallible, sometimes even cruel, so the continuing of some sub-standard zoo-keeping is hardly surprising. It may be even virtually certain so long as zoos continue at all. So ought we just to abolish them? Is this the right moral solution, whether or not it is practical?

I don't think so, for such reasons as these:

1   Certain zoos are of a very high standard, in the way their animals' needs are catered for, and in their conservational aims and achievements.

2   New ethological research is showing us, and is likely to do so more and more, how we can keep various relatively wild animals fully satisfactorily.

3   Only the coming years may reveal how short-sighted zoos' abolition could be. They may have an enormously important role to play in safeguarding many large vertebrate species in a world overrun by one dominant primate species.

4   One conservational role arises from a very important educational role, that of encouraging empathy with and appreciation of other living beings in zoo visitors, adults and children. Even if this is a clearer achievement of zoos than their instructional role, it is a very important one (indeed more so than academic instruction, though the two should go hand in hand). It is a conservational role because such

empathy and appreciation are a source of concern for the conservation of animals in their natural habitats.

So the abolishing of zoos would mean losing much of great value. Roy Hattersley (1991) finds London Zoo still essentially a menagerie compared to the elephants he can see charging across the screen of his television set. Well, elephant keeping at London has been strongly criticised (Travers 1987), and Casson's great Elephant House is very far from ideal, as I have made clear. But I have myself very much enjoyed watching elephants at Whipsnade, partly because they were clearly enjoying themselves. London has recently made considerable changes to its own approach to elephant keeping, reintroducing close handling, with elephants walking among the public and so on, as was a traditional part of London Zoo in the 1930s and before. But it is true that zoos aren't very good with elephants; several (like Edinburgh and Glasgow) have decided not to keep them. Chester, on the other hand, has long had a deserved reputation for its success in keeping (and breeding) elephants.

But what Mr Hattersley fails to appreciate is that London, as an extremely important part of the British zoo network, which is already linked up – for example by ARKS – to the American zoo network, may very well help to save, whether or not elephants, a great many other vertebrate species from extinction. Without zoos, it is quite possible that all sorts of animals will in the future be charging across our television screens merely in historical film of the days before the great twenty-first century extinction. If Hattersley would still prefer that zoos didn't bother, if the animals can't be saved in the wild, this would be, in my view, an act of vandalism; we would be showing a great lack of what I called (in Chapter 8) conservation respect.

Hattersley is, though, expressing a view many others share, for example with regard to chimpanzees or gorillas: if we can't save them in the wild, isn't it better to let them go extinct gracefully rather than keep them in 'prisons'? Zoo enclosures for great apes or any other animals do not need to be, and of course should not be, anything like prisons. The gorillas at Howletts (for example) are in a sort of gorilla holiday camp, but one from which, when the time is right, they are very likely to be able to make a successful transition back to the wild state.

I have not examined poor zoo-keeping at any length in this book because others, whom I have referred to, have done that

193

very adequately, and because I wanted to present some aspects of zoos which are not always appreciated. The abuses involved in animal catching and transport are very real, and there is a strong need for the strictest controls on such catching and transport – and for investigation by such admirable groups as the Environmental Investigation Agency – because of the cruelty involved as well as the conservational damage. It is unlikely that such abuse has anything to do with reputable zoos – but of course there should be no zoos except reputable ones. I have stressed the part played by the Federation of Zoos in raising zoo standards in Britain. But the strictest of controls on the wildlife trade are needed – indeed, with the trade in wild birds for example, there is a good case for its abolition – and controls are desirable too for zoos themselves. In most cases people's own decency and responsibility will make such controls superfluous, and this applies to many both professional and amateur, who keep animals. But the outrageous cruelty of some humans – whether through intention or just neglect – deprives us of any guarantee that it is safe just to trust to people's own good natures.

Critics of zoos (they include many of course who work in them!) should be listened to, and their criticisms complied with where they cannot be shown to be mistaken. But some opponents of zoos let their respect for truth be blunted by their reforming zeal. They use any effective weapon, even dishonesty, in the fight against – as they see them – remorseless exploiters of animals. An example would be the kind of article which implies that zoos regard their conservational captive breeding as the only significant kind of conservation. Of course zoos see their role as no more than a supplement – but still a very important supplement – to the protection of animals' natural habitats.

Sometimes those running zoos can be hypocritical, not least in their readiness to claim all zoo-keeping as genuinely conservational in aim or achievement. But some opponents of zoos can also be hypocritical or muddled, not least in their espousal of the probable need for conservational breeding centres essentially distinct from existing zoos. Sir Christopher Lever (1987: 16), summarising Roland Boyes's views, defines such a centre as necessarily specialist, scientific and conservational, and explicitly denies that any zoo fulfils those expectations. But it should stare him in the face that, to take one obvious example, the Jersey Wildlife Preservation Trust is specialist, scientific and conservational – and Lever (1987: 12) has himself praised its management! What is the point of criticising (say) British zoos, perhaps justifiably in many respects, while determinedly refusing to pay credit to the work of zoos like Jersey?

There is in some critics a reluctance, also, to recognise that some zoos, despite their failings, are capable of evolving, and likely to evolve, into the right kind of zoo or conservational breeding centre. Institutions, which of course include zoos, themselves tend to evolve, and we are much more likely to arrive at a fully satisfactory zoo by improving a less satisfactory one than by trying to start a fully satisfactory zoo from scratch. In any case, even if this were the best course in some ways, it is unlikely to be the best course with institutions that keep animals. For if we close zoos down, and then set about starting 'proper' conservational breeding centres, where on earth are the animals to come from? Surely not (in most cases) from the wild, for even today's imperfect zoos recognise the moral objections (apart from the legal ones) to taking endangered animals from there.

We started with the French Revolution, and the attempt to free the animals in the Versailles menagerie. I have made clear my own view that we should recognise animals' rights, as well of course as human rights. But revolutions, even though they are usually attempts to put right, once and for all, very real oppressions, have grave drawbacks – they tend to get out of hand. Even Thomas Paine found himself, while in Paris a year or two after his book *Rights of Man* (1969; first published 1791), in great danger of being sent to the guillotine, despite all the magnificent support he had given to the French Revolution. And Edmund Burke (1986; first published 1790), whose book Paine's was a reply to, seemed extraordinarily perceptive a year or two after *his* book, when the reign of terror seemed to demonstrate all too horribly the sort of dangers in revolutionary upheavals that his book had drawn attention to. Burke was a reformer, but he believed in evolution – that institutions should be improved, but gradually, not torn down and built again (Burke 1986: 106). This way we build on all the human experience, much of it perhaps unconscious, that has built those institutions through the centuries. Obviously some institutions are so bad they should be got rid of. But we have all seen in the late 1980s how glad many Europeans and Russians have been (despite their problems) at the dismantling, after seventy years, of the effects of that great revolution of 1917.

Zoos may seem inconsequent, mere children's playthings, by comparison with the great world of politics. But if there is even a chance that zoos can help with the threats facing wildlife from the human population explosion, then zoos are anything but insignificant. It may be that we shouldn't have had them; through history many animals have been kept in poor conditions, or died in the course of being taken from their natural habitats. But zoos are still here, and ironically they could now be great saviours – of wildlife. And they do embody considerable experience and knowledge about how to keep animals; and there have been substantial improvements in many zoos, as we have seen. So much the wisest course now is the Burkeian approach of evolution, not revolution – to encourage zoos to develop as they should, because they are useful now (whatever the situation in the past) and because they may become quite enormously important in the future.

I haven't defined zoos at any point, and perhaps there isn't much need – after all, the term only came into general use thanks to a music-hall artist! – but perhaps I ought to have done in view of some zoo opponents' tendency to define 'zoo' in such a way that 'zoos are bad' becomes a necessary truth. That is, they immediately exclude any example one offers of a good zoo, if they admire it also, from being a zoo. This of course is partly playing with terms.

The diversity of zoos' origins should assist us in directing (so far as we can) the ways in which they develop in the future. As we saw in Chapter 2, in some respects deerparks should be regarded as the best zoos of past centuries. After all, why shouldn't the extremely large enclosures of a zoo such as Whipsnade be regarded as being evolved from deerparks as much as from menageries? One pioneer of conservational captive breeding was, of course, the 11th Duke of Bedford, whose deerpark can have had few rivals throughout history. Modern 'deerparks', or large animal parks, may be in many cases the best zoos (or whatever we choose to call them) for captive breeding of ungulates and perhaps some carnivores. But there is a role, too, for zoos of smaller area near cities, provided they can keep their animals, and select which animals they keep, by the kind of criteria I have outlined. Where it can be shown that the animals in such zoos are thriving – which in many cases will involve the kind of zoo environmental enrichment which we have looked at – then those zoos are desirable because of the enormous possibilities they provide for human enrichment, not just recreation or entertainment, but biological, emotional, moral, even spiritual enrichment.

There are those who favour (were it possible) a complete separation of animals and humans. They would like our species to have no contact with other species, not even domestic animals, still less wild ones. Marthe Kiley-Worthington (1990: 195) has labelled this approach or policy 'animal apartheid'. The long history of zoos and animal keeping has shown us how deep in humans must lie the desire for contact with other species. However misguided much of past (and even recent) zoo-keeping has been, it testifies to a great desire for close involvement with other animals.

Perhaps I can leave the last word on the value of being close to animals to C. S. Lewis, whose appreciation of Whipsnade we have already seen. In April 1962, George Sayer was driving Lewis back to Cambridge from a period in hospital. They stopped briefly by the Duke of Bedford's great estates at Woburn, wandered along a little path (marked Private!), and were suddenly 'in a glade surrounded by a number of miniature deer. Jack [C. S. Lewis] was entranced. "You know, while I was writing the Narnia books I never imagined anything as lovely as this," he said.' They tried on another occasion to find the deer again, but failed. '"Well," said Jack, "as I found once before, you can't expect the same miracle twice"' (Sayer 1988: 246).

BIBLIOGRAPHY

Adams, R. (1987) letter, *The Independent*, 20 August.

Adamson, J. (1962) *Born Free: A Lioness of Two Worlds*, London: Collins/Fontana.

Aitken, T. (1990) 'Penguin protest and an architectural joke', letter, *The Times*, 30 October.

Aldridge, D. (1975) *Principles of Countryside Interpretation and Interpretive Planning: Guide to Countryside Interpretation Part One*, Edinburgh: HMSO for Countryside Commission for Scotland.

Alldis, J. (1973) *Animals as Friends*, Newton Abbott: David & Charles.

Allison, L. (1987) 'A feudal feud', *The Countryman* 92, 3: 98–103.

Altick, R. D. (1978) *The Shows of London*, London: Harvard University Press.

Ammann, K. and K. (1984) *Cheetah*, London: The Bodley Head.

Aristotle (1968) *Parts of Animals, Movement of Animals, Progression of Animals*, trans. A. L. Peck and E. S. Forster, London: Heinemann.

Aspinall, J. (1976) *The Best of Friends*, London: Macmillan.

—— (1979) 'Man's place in nature', in D. Paterson and R. D. Ryder (eds) *Animals' Rights – a Symposium*, London: Centaur.

—— (1986) 'The Howletts gorilla bands', *International Zoo News* 195, 33/1: 11–19.

—— (1991) 'Guest editorial', *International Zoo News*, 228: 2–4.

'Astragal' (1991) 'Animal crackers', *The Architects' Journal*, 5 February: 14–15.

Bacon, F. (1949) *Essays*, London: Oxford University Press.

Barber, R. (1964) *Henry Plantagenet*, London: Barrie & Rockliff/Pall Mall Press.

Bareham, J. R. (1973) 'General behaviour patterns of wild animals in captivity', in UFAW Symposium, *The Welfare and Management of Wild Animals in Captivity*, Potters Bar, Herts: Universities' Federation for Animal Welfare.

Barnett, S. A. (1970) *'Instinct' and 'Intelligence': the Behaviour of Animals and Men*, Harmondsworth: Penguin.

Bartlett, A. D. (1899) *Wild Animals in Captivity*, (ed.) E. Bartlett, London: Chapman & Hall.

BIBLIOGRAPHY

Bateson, G. (1980) *Mind and Nature: A Necessary Unity*, London: Collins/Fontana.

Batten, P. (1976) *Living Trophies*, New York: Cowell.

Bedford, Hastings Duke of (1949) *The Years of Transition*, London: Andrew Dakers.

Bennett, E. T. (1829) *The Tower Menagerie*, London: Robert Jennings.

Benson, J. (1978) 'Duty and the beast', *Philosophy* 53, 206: 529–49.

Bertram, B. (1980) letter, *The Times*, 6 September.

Bleibtreu, J. (1968) *The Parable of the Beast*, London: Gollancz.

Blunt, W. (1976) *The Ark in the Park*, London: Hamish Hamilton.

Bompas, G. C. (1885) *Life of Frank Buckland*, London: Smith, Elder.

Boorer, M. (1969) *Wild Cats*, London: Hamlyn.

Bostock, S. St C. (1981) 'Zoo education and the ethics of keeping animals in captivity', *International Association of Zoo Educators Newsletter* 6.

—— (1987) 'The moral justification for keeping animals in captivity', Ph.D. thesis, University of Glasgow.

Bowman, J. C. (1977) *Animals for Man*, London: Arnold.

Brambell, M. (1973) 'The requirements of carnivores and ungulates in captivity', in UFAW Symposium, *The Welfare and Management of Wild Animals in Captivity*, Potters Bar, Herts: Universities' Federation for Animal Welfare.

—— (1985) 'Trade in and exploitation of endangered exotic species of animals', in J. P. Hearn and J. K. Hodges (eds) *Advances in Animal Conservation, Symposia of the Zoological Society of London* 54: 222–3.

Brennan, A. (1984) 'The moral standing of natural objects', *Environmental Ethics* 6: 35–56.

Brightwell, L. R. (n.d.) *Zoo Calendar*, London: Hutchinson.

—— (1952) *The Zoo Story*, London: Museum Press.

Brockington, F. (1958) *World Health*, Harmondsworth: Penguin.

Brodie, F. M. (1971) *The Devil Drives: A Life of Sir Richard Burton*, Harmondsworth: Penguin.

Burgess, K. (1968) 'The behaviour and training of a Killer whale at San Diego Sea World', *International Zoo Yearbook* 8: 202–5.

Burke, E. (1986) *Reflections on the Revolution in France*, Harmondsworth: Penguin.

Calderglen Country Park (1987) *Visitor Survey 1986–1987*, East Kilbride District Council with Centre for Land Management Systems, Strathclyde University.

Callicott, J. B. (1983) 'Animal Liberation: A Triangular Affair', in D. Scherer and T. Attig (eds) *Ethics and the Environment*, Englewood Cliffs, NJ: Prentice-Hall.

Campbell, S. (1979) *Lifeboats to Ararat*, London: Weidenfeld & Nicolson.

Carrington, R. (1962) *Elephants*, Harmondsworth: Penguin.

Carroll, T. (1984) *Diary of a Fox-hunting Man*, London: Hamilton.

Cary, M. and Warmington, E. H. (1963) *The Ancient Explorers*, Harmondsworth: Penguin.

Castillo, B. Diaz del (1928) *The Discovery and Conquest of Mexico 1517–1521*, trans. A. P. Maudslay, London: Routledge.

Cave. A. J. E. (1985) 'An unrecorded specimen of the Javan rhinoceros (*Rhinoceros sondaicus*)', *Journal of Zoology* (A) 207: 528.

Ceram, C. W. (1952) *Gods, Graves, and Scholars*, London: Gollancz.

Chamove, A. S., Anderson, J. R., Morgan-Jones, S. C. and Jones, S. (1982) 'Deep woodchip litter: hygiene, feeding, and behavioural enhancement in eight primate species', *International Journal for the Study of Animal Problems* 3, 4: 308–17.

Chaucer, Geoffrey (1960) 'The manciple's tale', in *Canterbury Tales*, London: Dent.

Cherfas, J. (1984) *Zoo 2000: A Look beyond the Bars*, London: BBC.

—— (1986) 'What price whales?', *New Scientist* 114, 1511: 36–9.

—— (1987) 'The nature of the beast', *New Scientist* 115, 1578: 80.

Cherrington, J. (1983) *A Farming Year*, London: Hodder & Stoughton.

Chesser, R. K., Smith, M. H. and Brisbin, I. L. (1980) 'Management and maintenance of genetic variability in endangered species', *International Zoo Yearbook* 20: 148.

Cicero (1982) *Selected Letters*, trans. D. R. Shackleton Bailey, Harmondsworth: Penguin.

Clark, S. R. L. (1977a) *The Moral Status of Animals*, Oxford: Oxford University Press.

—— (1977b) 'Animal rights', letter, *Theology* 80: 288–9.

—— (1979) 'The rights of wild things', *Inquiry* 22, 1–2: 171–88.

—— (1982) *The Nature of the Beast*, Oxford: Oxford University Press.

—— (1988) 'Is humanity a natural kind?', in T. Ingold (ed.) *What is an Animal?*, London: Unwin Hyman.

—— (1989) 'Animals', in J. O. Urmson and J. Rée (eds) *The Concise Encyclopaedia of Western Philosophy and Philosophers*, London: Unwin Hyman.

Clarke, J. and Loudon, A. S. I. (1985) 'The effect of differences in herbage height on the grazing behaviour of lactating Bennett's wallabies (*Macropus rufogriseus rufogriseus*)', *Journal of Zoology* (A) 205: 537.

Clutton-Brock, J. (1981) *Domesticated Animals*, London: Heinemann/British Museum (Natural History).

—— (1992) 'How the wild beasts were tamed', *New Scientist* 133, 1808, 15 February: 41–3.

Coleridge, S. T. (1959) *Selected Poems*, (ed.) J. Reeve, London: Heinemann.

Cooper, D. E. (1991) 'How we burden our beasts', letter, *Guardian*, 11 April.

Cooper, M. E. (1987) *An Introduction to Animal Law*, London: Academic Press.

Corbett, J. (1955) *Man-eaters of Kumaon*, Harmondsworth: Penguin.

Cornish, C. J. (1895) *Life at the Zoo: Notes and Traditions of the Regent's Park Gardens*, London: Seeley & Co.

Cortes, Hernando (1972) *Letters from Mexico*, trans. A. R. Pagden, London: Oxford University Press.

Cottingham, J. (1978) 'A brute to the brutes?: Descartes' treatment of animals', *Philosophy* 53, 206: 551–9.

Darwin, C. (1901) *The Descent of Man*, London: Murray.

—— (1929) *Autobiography of Charles Darwin*, (ed.) F. Darwin, London: Watts.

—— (1968) *The Origin of Species*, Harmondsworth: Penguin.

—— (1988) *The Correspondence of Charles Darwin, Volume 4, 1847–1850*, (eds.) F. Burkhardt and S. Smith, Cambridge: Cambridge University Press.

—— (1990) *The Correspondence of Charles Darwin, Volume 6, 1856–1857*, (eds.) F. Burkhardt and S. Smith, Cambridge: Cambridge University Press.

Davies, P. (1981) *Roots: Family Histories of Familiar Words*, New York: McGraw-Hill.

Dawkins, M. S. (1980) *Animal Suffering, the Science of Animal Welfare*, London: Chapman & Hall.

De Beer, G. (1971) *Homology: An Unsolved Problem*, Oxford: Oxford University Press.

—— (1972) *Adaptation*, London: Oxford University Press.

Delacour, J. (1966) *The Living Air*, London: Country Life.

Dembeck, H. (1966) *Animals and Men*, London: Nelson.

Dempster, W. J. (1983) *Patrick Matthew and Natural Selection*, Edinburgh: Paul Harris.

Desmond, A. and Moore, J. (1991) *Darwin*, London: Michael Joseph.

De Waal, F. (1982) *Chimpanzee Politics*, London: Cape.

Diamond, J. (1991) *The Rise and Fall of the Third Chimpanzee*, London: Radius.

Dixson, A. F. (1977) 'Observations on the displays, menstrual cycles and sexual behaviour of the "Black Ape" of Celebes (*Macaca nigra*)', *Journal of Zoology* 182: 63–84.

Domalain, J. -Y. (1978) *The Animal Connection*, London: Heinemann.

Domesday (1986) *Domesday 1086–1986: Exhibition Guide*, London: Millbank Publications.

Downie, R. S. and Telfer, E. (1980) *Caring and Curing*, London: Methuen.

Dubos, R. (1980) *The Wooing of Earth*, London: The Athlone Press.

Duffy, M. (1984) *Men and Beasts*, London: Paladin/Granada.

Duncan, I. J. H. and Poole, T. B. (1990) 'Promoting the welfare of farm and captive animals', in P. Monaghan and D. G. M. Wood-Gush (eds) *Managing the Behaviour of Animals*, London: Chapman and Hall.

Dunn, A. M. (1968) 'The wild ruminant as reservoir host of helminth infection', *Symposia of the Zoological Society of London* 24: 221–48.

Durrell, G. (1959) *My Family and Other Animals*, Harmondsworth: Penguin.

—— (1977) *The Stationary Ark*, Glasgow: Fontana/Collins.

—— (1990) *The Ark's Anniversary*, London: Collins.

Durrell, L. and Mallinson, J. (1987) 'Reintroduction as a political and educational tool for conservation', *Dodo: Journal of Jersey Wildlife Preservation Trust* 24: 6–19.

Dworkin, R. (1978) *Taking Rights Seriously*, London: Duckworth.

Ehrlich, P. R (1971) *The Population Bomb*, London: Ballantyne/Friends of the Earth and Pan Books.

Elliot, R. (1980) 'Why preserve species?', *Environmental Philosophy*: 8–29.

—— (1982) 'Faking nature', *Inquiry* 25: 81–93.

Eltringham, K. (1984) 'Elephants in zoos', *Biologist* 31, 2: 108–11.

Erlande-Brandenburg, A. (1978) *La Dame à la Licorne*, Paris: Les Editions de la Réunion des Musées Nationaux.

Ewer, R. F. (1953) 'Adaptation', *New Biology*, London: Penguin 13: 117–19.
—— (1975) 'Why study small mammals?', *International Zoo Yearbook* 15: 1–4.
Fiedler, W. (1976) *Tiergarten Schönbrunn: Geschichte und Aufgabe*, Vienna: Verband der wissenschaftlichen Gesellschaften Österreichs.
Fiennes, R. N. T. -W. (1960) 'Tuberculosis of a puma cub (*Felis concolor*) accompanied by skeletal deformities resembling rickets', *Proceedings of the Zoological Society of London* 133: 595.
—— (1965) *Man, Nature and Disease*, London: New English/Signet.
Finsterbusch, C. A. (1980) *Cockfighting all over the World*, Hindhead, Surrey: Saiga.
Fisher, J. (1966) *Zoos of the World*, London: Aldus.
Fitzgerald, M. A. (1986) 'Born Free star leads campaign to ban zoos', *The Independent*, 31 December.
Flesness, N. R. (1977) 'Gene pool conservation and computer analysis', *International Zoo Yearbook* 17: 77.
Foose, T. J. (1977) 'Demographic models for management of captive populations', *International Zoo Yearbook* 17: 70.
—— (1980) 'Demographic management of endangered species in captivity', *International Zoo Yearbook* 20: 154–5.
Foose, T. J., Seal, U. S. and Flesness, N. R. (1985) 'Conserving animal genetic resources', *IUCN Bulletin* 16, 1–3: 20–21.
Fox, M. W. (1971) *Behaviour of Wolves, Dogs and related Canids*, London: Cape.
—— (1986) *Returning to Eden: Animal Rights and Human Responsibility*, Malabar, Florida: Krieger.
Frankel, O. H. and Soulé, M. E. (1981) *Conservation and Evolution*, Cambridge: Cambridge University Press.
Frazer, D. (1983) *Reptiles and Amphibians in Britain*, London: Collins.
Frey, R. G. (1980) *Interests and Rights: The Case Against Animals*, Oxford: Clarendon Press.
— (1983) *Rights, Killing, and Suffering*, Oxford: Blackwell.
Galsworthy, J. (1922) *The Forsyte Saga*, London: Heinemann.
Gardiner, S. (1987) 'Pick up a penguin, Lubetkin's Penguin Pool at London Zoo', *Observer*, 15 March.
Garnett, D. (1985) *Lady into Fox and A Man in the Zoo*, London: Hogarth Press.
Gilbert, J. M. (1979) *Hunting and Hunting Reserves in Medieval Scotland*, Edinburgh: John Donald.
Glancey, J. (1989) 'Nicholas Freeman', *The Independent*, 21 November.
Glickman, S. E. and Sroges, R. W. (1966) 'Curiosity in zoo animals', *Behaviour* 26: 151–88.
Godlovitch, S. and R. and Harris, J. (1971) *Animals, Men and Morals*, London: Gollancz.
Goodall, J. (1986) *The Chimpanzees of Gombe, Patterns of Behavior*, Cambridge, Massachusetts: Harvard University Press.
Grayson, A. K. (1976) *Assyrian Royal Inscriptions* vol. 2, Wiesbaden: Otto Harrassowitz.
Green, M. (1983) 'Such mice people', *Observer*, 21 August.

Griffin, D. R. (1976) *The Question of Animal Awareness*, New York: Rockefeller Press.

Grove, A. J. and Newell, G. E. (1957) *Animal Biology*, London: University Tutorial Press.

Grzimek, B. (1966) *Wild Animal White Man*, London: Andre Deutsch and Thames & Hudson.

Gunn, A. S. (1980) 'Why should we care about rare species?', *Environmental Ethics* 2: 17–37.

Hagenbeck, C. (1909) *Beasts and Men*, London: Longmans & Green.

Hagenbeck, L. (1956) *Animals are my Life*, London: The Bodley Head.

Hamlyn, M. (1987) 'On the trail of a tiger hunter', *The Times*, 7 February: 7.

Hancocks, D. (1971) *Animals and Architecture*, London: Hugh Evelyn.

—— (1980) 'Naturalistic solutions to zoo design problems', *Zoo Design* (Herbert Whitley Trust, Paignton Zoological Gardens) 3: 166–73.

—— (1989a) 'Seeking to create illusions of wild places: Master Planning Guidelines for the Melbourne Zoo Part I', *Landscape Australia* 3/1989: 258–67.

—— (1989b) 'Seeking to create illusions of wild places Part II', *Landscape Australia* 4/1989: 421–8.

—— (1990) 'Seeking to create illusions of wild places Part III', *Landscape Australia* 1/1990: 62–9.

—— (1991a) 'So long, old zoo', *BBC Wildlife*, June 1991: 424.

—— (1991b) 'View from the zoo, David Hancocks replies', *BBC Wildlife*, August 1991: 582.

—— (1991c) 'Guest Editorial', *International Zoo News* 230: 2–3.

Hardy, A. (1975) *The Biology of God*, London: Cape.

Harrison, J. L. (1959) 'Defaecation in the flying lemur *Cynocephalus variegatus*', *Proceedings of the Zoological Society of London* 133: 179–80.

Harrison, P. (1991) 'Do animals feel pain?', *Philosophy* 66: 25–40.

Harrison, R. (1979) 'Ethical questions concerning modern livestock farming', in D. Paterson and R. D. Ryder (eds) *Animals' Rights – a Symposium*, Fontwell: Centaur.

Hart-Davis, D. (1987) 'How zoos could keep wild animals in their place', *The Sunday Telegraph*, 12 July.

—— (1991) 'The day lions came to Wiltshire', *The Independent*, 2 March.

Harvey, W. (1964) 'Of the motions of the heart, as seen in the dissections of living animals', in A. Rook (ed.) *The Origins and Growth of Biology*, Harmondsworth: Penguin.

Hatley, J. (n.d.) 'The role of the zoo in environmental education today', *Review of Environmental Education Developments* (Journal of the Council for Environmental Education) 12, 1: 3–6.

Hattersley, R. (1991) 'Today's zoo as Victorian caricature', *Guardian*, 13 April.

Hearn, J. P. (1987) 'Research in the zoo. How does it help animals in captivity and in the wild?', in T. E. Gibson and D. A. Paterson (eds) *The Welfare of Animals in Captivity*, British Veterinary Association Animal Welfare Foundation Fourth Symposium.

Hearn, J. P. and Hodges, J. K. (eds) (1985) *Advances in Animal Conservation*, *Symposia of the Zoological Society of London* 54.

Hearne, V. (1987) *Adam's Task*, London: Heinemann.

Hebb, D. O. (1946) 'Emotion in man and animal: an analysis of the intuitive processes of recognition', *Psychological Review* 53: 88–106.

Heck, H. (1951) 'The breeding-back of the aurochs', *Oryx* 1, 3: 117–22.

Hediger, H. (1964) *Wild Animals in Captivity*, New York: Dover.

—— (1968) *The Psychology and Behaviour of Animals in Zoos and Circuses*, New York: Dover.

—— (1974) *Man and Animal in the Zoo, Zoo Biology*, London: Routledge & Kegan Paul.

Herodotus (1954) *The Histories*, trans. A. de Sélincourt, Harmondsworth: Penguin.

Hibbert, C. (1982) *The French Revolution*, Harmondsworth: Penguin.

Hindle, E. (1964) foreword to H. Hediger, *Wild Animals in Captivity*, New York: Dover.

Hobley, B. (1986) letter, *The Times*, 14 July.

Hollands, C. (1979) 'Animal Welfare year in retrospect', in D. Paterson and R. D. Ryder (eds) *Animals' Rights – a Symposium*, Fontwell: Centaur.

—— (1985) 'Animal rights in the political arena', in P. Singer (ed.) *In Defence of Animals*, Oxford: Blackwell.

Holmes, R. (1989) *Coleridge: Early Visions*, London: Hodder & Stoughton.

Hook, B. (ed.) (1982) *Cambridge Encyclopaedia of China*, Cambridge: Cambridge University Press.

House of Commons (1991) *House of Commons Environment Committee Fifth Report: London Zoo*, London: HMSO.

Housley, S. J. (1928) *Sailing Made Easy and Comfort in Small Craft*, London: Blake's.

Houston, D. (1985) 'Can the Californian condor survive?', *Oryx* 19, 3: 135–6.

—— (1988) 'Digestive efficiency and hunting behaviour in cats, dogs and vultures', *Journal of Zoology* 216: 603–5.

Hughes, D. G. and Bennett, P. M. (1991) 'Captive breeding and the conservation of invertebrates', *International Zoo Yearbook* 30: 45–51.

Hull, D. L. (1978) 'A matter of individuality', *Philosophy of Science* 45: 335–60.

Hume, C. W. (1982) *Man and Beast*, South Mimms: Universities' Federation for Animal Welfare.

Humphrey, N. (1977) Review of *The Question of Animal Awareness*, by D. R. Griffin, *Animal Behaviour* 25: 521–2.

—— (1984) *Consciousness Regained*, Oxford and New York: Oxford University Press.

—— (1986) *The Inner Eye*, London and Boston: Faber & Faber.

Huntingford, F. (1984) *The Study of Animal Behaviour*, London: Chapman & Hall.

Hutchins, M., Hancocks, D. and Crockett, C. (1984) 'Naturalistic solutions to the behavioral problems of captive animals', *Der Zoologischer Garten*, 1/2: 28–42.

Huxley, E. (1981) *Whipsnade: Captive Breeding for Survival*, London: Collins.

Huxley, J. (1970) *Memories*, London: George Allen & Unwin.

James, M. R. (1970) 'The haunted doll's house', in *Collected Ghost Stories*, London: Edward Arnold.

Jamieson, D. (1985) 'Against zoos', in P. Singer (ed.) *In Defence of Animals*, Oxford: Blackwell.

Jennison, G. (1937) *Animals for Show and Pleasure in Ancient Rome*, Manchester: Manchester University Press.

Johnson, A. (1991) *Factory Farming*, Oxford: Basil Blackwell.

Johnson, W. (1990) *The Rose-tinted Menagerie*, London: Heretic Books.

Jolly, A. (1972) *The Evolution of Primate Behaviour*, New York: Macmillan.

Jones, D. M. (1987) 'Welfare in the wild and in captivity: how do they compare?', in T. E. Gibson (ed.) *The Welfare of Animals in Captivity*, British Veterinary Association Animal Welfare Foundation Fourth Symposium.

Jones, M. L. and Manton, V. J. A. (1983) 'History in captivity', in B. B. Beck and C. M. Wemmer (eds) *The Biology and Management of an Extinct Species: Père David's Deer*, Park Ridge, N.J.: Noyes Publications.

Jones, N. G. B. (1967) 'An ethological study of some aspects of children in nursery school', in D. Morris (ed.) *Primate Ethology*, London: Weidenfeld & Nicolson.

Jordan, B. and Ormrod, S. (1978) *The Last Great Wild Beast Show*, London: Constable.

Jordan, W. J. (1979) 'Altruism and aggression in animals', in D. Paterson and R. D. Ryder (eds) *Animals' Rights – a Symposium*, Fontwell: Centaur.

Jungius, H. (1985) 'Prospects for re-introduction', in J. P. Hearn and J. K. Hodges (eds) *Advances in Animal Conservation, Symposia of the Zoological Society of London* 54: 47–55.

Jungius, H. and Loudon, A. (1985) 'Recommendations for the Re-introduction of the Père David's Deer to China', report, International Union for Conservation of Nature and Natural Resources/World Wildlife Fund.

Kamenka, E. (1978) 'The anatomy of an idea', in E. Kamenka and A. E. Tay (eds) *Human Rights*, London: Arnold.

Keeling, C. H. (1984) *Where the Lion Trod: A Study of Forgotten Zoological Gardens*, Guildford: Clam.

Kellert, S. (1979) 'Zoological parks in American society', paper delivered to American Association of Zoological Parks and Aquaria.

—— (1987) 'The educational potential of the zoo and its visitor', *Philadelphia Zoo Review* 3,1: 7–13.

Kiley-Worthington, M. (1990) *Animals in Circuses and Zoos: Chiron's World?*, Basildon: Little Eco-farms Publishing.

Koestler, A. (1974) *The Case of the Midwife Toad*, London: Pan.

Lack, D. (1970) *The Natural Regulation of Animal Numbers*, Oxford: Clarendon.

Lambourne, L. (1990) 'Penitentiary for penguins', letter, *The Times*, 27 October.

Lauer, J. -P. (1976) *Saqqara: The Royal Cemetery of Memphis*, London: Thames & Hudson.

Lausch, E. (1975) *Manipulation*, London: Fontana/Collins.

Law, G. (1991) 'Behavioural enrichment', in J. Partridge (ed.) *Management Guidelines for Exotic Cats*, Bristol: The Association of British Wild Animal Keepers.

Law, G. and Boyle, H. (1984) 'Breeding the Geoffroy's cat, *Felis geoffroyi*, at Glasgow Zoo', *International Zoo Yearbook* 23: 192.

Law, G., Boyle, H. and Johnston, J. (1986a) 'Notes on the management of the African Crested porcupine (*Hystrix cristata*) at Glasgow Zoo', *Ratel* (Journal of Association of British Wild Animal Keepers) 13, 1: 27–30.

—— (1986b) 'Notes on polar bear management at Glasgow Zoo', *Ratel* 13, 2: 56–8.

Law, G., Boyle, H., Johnston, J. and MacDonald, A. (1990a) 'Food Presentation, Part 1: Bears', *Ratel* 17, 2: 44–6.

—— (1990b) 'Food Presentation, Part 2: Cats', *Ratel* 17, 4: 103–5.

Leahy, M. P. T. (1991) *Against Liberation: Putting Animals into Perspective*, London and New York: Routledge.

Legge, J. (1871) *The Chinese Classics*, vol. 4, part 2: *The She King*, London: Trubner.

Lemmon, T. (1987) 'The long way back to nature', *BBC Wildlife* 5, 4: 172–5.

Leopold, A. (1987) *A Sand County Almanac*, New York and Oxford: Oxford University Press.

Lever, C. (1977) *The Naturalised Animals of the British Isles*, London: Hutchinson.

—— (1986) letter, *The Times*, 27 June.

—— (1987) 'Introduction', in V. McKenna, W. Travers and J. Wray (eds) *Beyond the Bars*, Wellingborough: Thorsons.

Levin, A. (1979) 'Learning the art of motorcycle maintenance and a lot more besides', *Observer*, 8 July.

Lewis, C. S. (1955a) *That Hideous Strength*, London: Pan.

—— (1955b) *Surprised by Joy*, London: Bles.

—— (1957) *The Problem of Pain*, London: Collins/Fontana.

—— (1966) *Letters of C. S. Lewis* (ed.) W. H. Lewis, London: Bles.

Lieberman, P. (1991) *Uniquely Human: The Evolution of Speech, Thought, and Selfless Behaviour*, Cambridge, Massachusetts and London: Harvard U.P.

Linzey, A. (1987) *Christianity and the Rights of Animals*, London: SPCK.

Livingstone, D. (1910) *Missionary Travels*, London: Ward, Lock.

Lockley, R. M. (1961) *The Pan Book of Cage Birds*, London: Pan.

Loisel, G. (1912) *Histoire des ménageries de l'antiquité à nos jours*. 3 vols, Paris: Octave Doin et Fils and Henri Laurens.

Loizos, C. (1967) 'Play behaviour in higher primates: a review', in D. Morris (ed.) *Primate Ethology*, London: Weidenfeld & Nicolson.

Lyster, S. (1985) *International Wildlife Law*, Cambridge: Grotius.

MacBeth, G. (ed.) (1965) *The Penguin Book of Animal Verse*, Harmondsworth: Penguin.

MacCulloch, J. A. (1920) 'Serpent-worship', in J. Hastings (ed.), *Encyclopaedia of Religion and Ethics*, Edinburgh: Clark.

Macdonald, D. (ed.) (1984) *The Encyclopaedia of Mammals: 2*, London: Allen & Unwin.

Mace, G. (1986) 'Captive breeding for conservation', *Ratel* 13, 2: 62–4.

McKenna, V. (1987) 'Past, present – future indicative' in V. McKenna, W. Travers and J. Wray (eds) *Beyond the Bars*, Wellingborough: Thorsons.

Mallinson, J. (1978) *The Shadow of Extinction*, London: Macmillan.

Margulis, L. and Sagan, D. (1987) *Microcosmos: Four Billion Years of Evolution from our Microbial Ancestors*, London: Allen & Unwin.

Markowitz, H. (1982) *Behavioral Enrichment in the Zoo*, New York: Van Nostrand Reinhold.

Matthews, L. H. (1976) 'The Zoo: 150 years of research', *Nature* 261, 5558: 281–4.

Mead, C. (1987) 'Do birds mourn?', *BBC Wildlife* 5, 7: 360–1.

Medawar, P. B. (1951) 'Zoology', in A. E. Heath (ed.) *Scientific Thought in the Twentieth Century*, London: Watts.

Medawar, P. B. and J. S. (1984) *Aristotle to Zoos: A Philosophical Dictionary of Biology*, London: Weidenfeld & Nicolson.

Mencius (1970) *Mencius*, trans. D. C. Lau, Harmondsworth: Penguin.

Meyer-Holzapfel, M. (1968) 'Abnormal behaviour in zoo animals', in M. W. Fox (ed.) *Abnormal Behaviour in Animals*, Philadelphia: W. B. Saunders.

Middlemiss, J. L. (1987) *A Zoo on Wheels: Bostock and Wombwell's Menagerie*, Burton-on-Trent: Dalebrook.

Midgley, M. (1976) 'The concept of beastliness', in T. Regan and P. Singer (eds) *Animal Rights and Human Obligations*, Englewood Cliffs, N.J.: Prentice-Hall.

—— (1979) *Beast and Man*, Hassocks, Sussex: Harvester.

—— (1983a) *Heart and Mind: the Varieties of Moral Experience*, London: Methuen.

—— (1983b) *Animals and Why They Matter*, Harmondsworth: Penguin.

—— (1985) 'Persons and non-persons', in P. Singer (ed.) *In Defence of Animals*, Oxford: Blackwell.

—— (1987) 'Keeping species on ice', in V. McKenna, W. Travers and J. Wray (eds) *Beyond the Bars*, Wellingborough: Thorsons.

Miles, H. (1986) 'The cat in the car-park', *BBC Wildlife* 4, 10: 462–6.

Miller, M. (1986) 'Gardens as works of art: the problem of uniqueness', *British Journal of Aesthetics* 26, 3: 252–6.

Miller, W. C. and West, G. P. (1972) *Black's Veterinary Dictionary*, London: Black.

Milne, A. A. (1965) *When We Were Very Young*, London: Methuen.

Milton, J. (1958) *The Poetical Works*, H. Darbishire (ed.), London: Oxford University Press.

Mitford, N. (1955) *Madame de Pompadour*, London: Reprint Society.

Montefiore, H. (1977) Review of A. Linzey, *Animal Rights*, *Theology* 80: 72–3.

Moore, H. (1968) 'Henry Moore, "The Sculptor Speaks," 1937', in H. B. Chipp, *Theories of Modern Art*, Berkeley and Los Angeles: University of California Press.

Moorehead, A. (1962) *No Room in the Ark*, Harmondsworth: Penguin.

Moran, W. L. (1987) *Les lettres d'El Amarna* (Littératures anciennes du Proche Orient, vol. 13), Paris: Les éditions du cerf.

Morley, D. W. (1953) *The Ant World*, Harmondsworth: Penguin.

Morris, D. (1964) 'The response of animals to a restricted environment', *Symposia of the Zoological Society of London* 13: 99–118.

—— (1966) 'The rigidification of behaviour', *Philosophical Transactions of the Royal Society, London*, B, 251: 327–30.

Morris, D. and R. (1968) *Men and Apes*, London: Sphere.

Morris, J. (1990) 'Andrew Grant', *The Independent Magazine*, 3 March: 54.

Mountfort, G. (1973) *Tigers*, Newton Abbott: David & Charles.

Mugford, R. A. (1981) 'The social skills of dogs as an indicator of animal-awareness', in D. G. M. Wood-Gush, M. Dawkins, and R. Ewbank (eds) *Self-awareness in Domesticated Animals*, Potters Bar, Herts: Universities' Federation for Animal Welfare.

Mullan, B. and Marvin, G. (1987) *Zoo Culture*, London: Weidenfeld & Nicolson.

Mulvaney, K. (1987) 'Conservation as a human problem', in V. McKenna, W. Travers and J. Wray (eds) *Beyond the Bars*, Wellingborough: Thorsons.

Munro, H. H. (1976) 'The Mappined Life', in *The Complete Works of Saki*, New York: Doubleday.

Murdoch, I. (1970) *The Sovereignty of Good*, London: Routledge & Kegan Paul.

Nagel, T. (1979) *Mortal Questions*, Cambridge: Cambridge University Press.

Nichol, J. (1987) *The Animal Smugglers*, London: Christopher Helm.

Nisbet, E. G. (1990) 'Jack of all trades', letter, *Nature* 347, 25 October: 704.

North, R. (1983a) *The Animals Report*, Harmondsworth: Penguin.

—— (1983b) *Wild Britain*, London: Century.

Oates, J. (1979) *Babylon*, London: Thames & Hudson.

O'Grady, R. J. P., Law, G., Boyle, H., MacDonald, A. and Johnston, J. (1990) 'Himalayan black bear *Selenarctos thibetanus* exhibit at Glasgow Zoo', *International Zoo Yearbook* 29: 233–40.

Olmstead, A. T. (1923) *History of Assyria*, New York and London: Charles Scribner's Sons.

Olney, P. (1990) 'In the penguin pool', letter, *The Times*, 31 October.

Oppenheim, A. L. (1977) *Ancient Mesopotamia: Portrait of a Dead Civilisation*, Chicago & London: University of Chicago Press.

Ormrod, S. A. (1987) 'Standards for modern captive animal management', in T. E. Gibson (ed.) *The Welfare of Animals in Captivity*, British Veterinary Association Animal Welfare Foundation Fourth Symposium.

Paine, T. (1969) *Rights of Man*, (ed.) H. Collins, Harmondsworth: Penguin.

Pascal, L. (1986) 'Judgement Day', in P. Singer (ed.) *Applied Ethics*, Oxford: Oxford University Press.

Paterson, D. A. (1979) 'Editorial', *Humane Education Journal* 2, 1: 2–3.

Paterson, D. A. and Ryder, R. D. (1979) *Animals' Rights – a Symposium*, London: Centaur.

Patrick, D. and Geddie, W. (eds) (1923) 'Deer-forests', in *Chambers's Encyclopaedia*, London and Edinburgh: W & R Chambers.

Pearson, H. (1950) *Gilbert and Sullivan*, Harmondsworth: Penguin.

Peters, R. S. (1973) 'Aims of education – a conceptual enquiry', in R. S. Peters (ed.) *The Philosophy of Education*, London: Oxford University Press.

Pirsig, R. M. (1976) *Zen and the Art of Motorcycle Maintenance*, London: Corgi.

Pitman, J. (1992) 'Taiwanese traders see gold in stocks of rhino horn', *The Times*, 7 March.

Pliny (1856) *The Natural History of Pliny*, trans. J. Bostock and H. T. Riley, London: Henry G. Bohn.

Pollard, J. (1963) *African Zoo Man*, London: Robert Hale.

Polo, M. (1958) *The Travels of Marco Polo*, trans. R. Latham, Harmondsworth: Penguin.

Prescott, W. H. (n.d.) *History of the Conquest of Mexico and History of the Conquest of Peru*, New York: The Modern Library [first pub. 1847].

Putnam, R. (1988) *The Natural History of Deer*, London: Christopher Helm.

Rachels, J. (1976) 'Do animals have a right to liberty?', in P. Singer and T. Regan (eds) *Animal Rights and Human Obligations*, New Jersey: Prentice-Hall.

—— (1987) 'Darwin, species, and morality', *The Monist* 70: 98–113.

Rawlins, C. G. C. (1985) 'Zoos and conservation: the last 20 years', in J. P. Hearn and J. K. Hodges (eds) *Advances in Animal Conservation, Symposia of the Zoological Society of London* 54: 56–69.

Reading, M. (1991) 'Animals and men', *The Architects' Journal*, 5 February: 28–37.

Redmond, I. (1986) 'The good relation', *BBC Wildlife* 4, 3: 103–7.

Regan, T. (1983) *The Case for Animal Rights*, London: Routledge & Kegan Paul.

Reisner, M. (1991) *Game Wars: The Undercover Pursuit of Wildlife Poachers*, London: Secker & Warburg.

Rickaby, J. (1976) 'Of the so-called rights of animals', in P. Singer and T. Regan (eds) *Animal Rights and Human Obligations*, New Jersey: Prentice-Hall.

Ritvo, H. (1990) *The Animal Estate: The English and Other Creatures in the Victorian Age*, Harmondsworth: Penguin.

Rodman, J. (1977) 'The liberation of nature?' *Inquiry* 20: 83–145.

Rogers, R. W. (1915) *A History of Babylonia and Assyria* Volume I, New York: Abingdon Press.

Rollin, B. E. (1981) *Animal Rights and Human Morality*, New York: Prometheus.

—— (1990) *The Unheeded Cry: Animal Consciousness, Animal Pain and Science*, Oxford: Oxford University Press.

Roots, C. (1971) *Exotic Birds for Cage and Aviary*, London: Cassell.

Rose, S. (1966) *The Chemistry of Life*, Harmondsworth: Penguin.

Rosenfield, L. C. (1968) *From Beast-machine to Man-machine*, New York: Octagon Books.

Rothschild, M. and Clay, T. (1961) *Fleas, Flukes and Cuckoos, a Study of Bird Parasites*, London: Arrow.

Rowell, T. (1972) *The Social Behaviour of Monkeys*, Harmondsworth: Penguin.

Russell, B. (1953) *Mysticism and Logic*, Harmondsworth: Penguin.

Ryder, R. (1975) *Victims of Science*, London: Davis-Poynter.

—— (1979) 'The struggle against speciesism', in D. Paterson and R. D. Ryder (eds) *Animals' Rights – a Symposium*, London: Centaur.

—— (1989) *Animal Revolution, Changing Attitudes towards Speciesism*, Oxford: Blackwell.

Saggs, H. W. F. (1984) *The Might that Was Assyria*, London: Sidgwick & Jackson.

Salt, H. S. (1980) *Animals' Rights*, London: Centaur.

Samstag, T. (1981) 'Zoo accused of waste in breeding pandas', *The Times*, 17 October.

Sayer, G. (1988) *Jack: C. S. Lewis and his Times*, London: Macmillan.

Schaller, G. B. (1972) *The Year of the Gorilla*, London: Collins.

Schomberg, G. (1957) *British Zoos: A Study of Animals in Captivity*, London: Allan Wingate.

—— (1970) *The Penguin Guide to British Zoos*, Harmondsworth: Penguin.

'Science' (1986) 'Zoo fights for Komodo dragons', Science Report, *The Times*, 27 June.

Scott, P. and the Wildfowl Trust (1972) *The Swans*, London: Michael Joseph.

Scott, W. N. (1973) 'UFAW's point of view', in UFAW Symposium, *The Welfare and Management of Wild Animals in Captivity*, Potters Bar, Herts: Universities' Federation for Animal Welfare.

Scullard, H. H. (1974) *The Elephant in the Greek and Roman World*, London: Thames & Hudson.

Seal, U. S. (1991) 'Life after extinction', *Symposia of the Zoological Society of London* 62: 39–55.

Searle, A. G. (1968) *Comparative Genetics of Coat Colour in Mammals*, London: Logos.

Serpell, J. (1986) *In the Company of Animals*, Oxford: Blackwell.

Shepherdson, D., Carman, M. and Bemment, N. (1988) 'Lar gibbon duets', Environmental Enrichment Report no. 1, South Mimms: Universities' Federation for Animal Welfare.

Singer, P. (1979a) *Practical Ethics*, Cambridge: Cambridge University Press.

—— (1979b) 'Not for humans only: the place of non-humans in environmental issues', in K. E. Goodpaster and K. M. Sayre (eds) *Ethics and Problems of the 21st Century*, Notre Dame: University of Notre Dame Press.

—— (1990) *Animal Liberation*, London: Cape.

Singh, A. (1984) *Tiger! Tiger!*, London: Cape.

Smart, J. J. C. (1984) *Ethics, Persuasion and Truth*, London: Routledge & Kegan Paul.

Smith, A. (1979) *Animals on View*, London: Mayflower.

Smith, H. S. (1969) 'Animal domestication and animal cult in dynastic Egypt', in P. J. Ucko and G. W. Dimbleby (eds) *The Domestication and Exploitation of Plants and Animals*, London: Duckworth.

Southey, R. (1985) 'The dancing bear', in J. Wynne-Tyson (ed.) *The Extended Circle: A Dictionary of Humane Thought*, Fontwell, Sussex: Centaur.

Spence, T. J. B. (ed.) (1980) *Hamlet*, Harmondsworth: Penguin.

Sprigge, T. L. S. (1979) 'Metaphysics, physicalism, and animal rights', *Inquiry* 22, 1–2: 101–43.

Spurway, H. (1952) 'Can wild animals be kept in captivity?', in M. L. Johnson and M. Abercrombie (eds) *New Biology 13*, London: Penguin.

Stanley Price, M. R. (1991) 'A review of mammal re-introductions, and the role of the Re-introduction Specialist Group of IUCN/SSC', *Symposia of the Zoological Society of London* 62: 9–25.

Steiner, G. (1985) *The Language of Silence*, London: Faber & Faber.

Stenton, M. S. (1952) *English Society in the Early Middle Ages (1066–1307)*, Harmondsworth: Penguin.

Stephen, D. (1974) *Highland Animals*, Inverness: Highlands and Islands Development Board.

Stevenson, M. F. (1983) 'The captive environment: its effect on exploratory and related behavioural responses in wild animals', in J. Archer and L. Birke (eds) *Exploration in Animals and Humans*, Wokingham: Van Nostrand Reinhold.

Stone, C. D. (1974) *Should Trees Have Standing?*, Los Altos, California: Kaufmann.

Street, P. (1965) *Animals in Captivity*, London: Faber & Faber.

Stresemann, E. (1975) *Ornithology from Aristotle to the Present*, Cambridge, Massachusetts and London: Harvard University Press.

Stuart, S. N. (1991) 'Re-introductions: to what extent are they needed?', *Symposia of the Zoological Society of London* 62: 27–37.

Suetonius (1957) *The Twelve Caesars*, trans. R. Graves, Harmondsworth: Penguin.

Tabor, R. (1983) *The Wildlife of the Domestic Cat*, London: Arrow.

Tavistock, Marquess of (1983) 'Foreword', in B. B. Beck and C. M. Wemmer (eds), *The Biology and Management of an Extinct Species: Père David's Deer*, Park Ridge, N.J.: Noyes Publications.

Taylor, B. (1971) *Stubbs*, London: Phaidon.

Taylor, G. R. (1981) *The Natural History of the Mind*, London: Granada.

Taylor, S. H. (1990) 'The Rainforest, Cleveland Metroparks Zoo', booklet, Cleveland, Ohio: Cleveland Metroparks Zoo.

Terrace, H. (1989) 'Thoughts without words', in C. Blakemore and S. Greenfield (eds) *Mindwaves*, Oxford: Blackwell.

Tester, K. (1991) *Animals and Society: The Humanity of Animal Rights*, London and New York: Routledge.

Thomas, K. (1984) *Man and the Natural World, Changing Attitudes in England 1500–1800*, Harmondsworth: Penguin.

Thouless, C. R. and Chongqi, L. (1987) 'Milu reintroduction project', Interim Report: WWF/Ministry of Forestry of the People's Republic of China.

Tong, E. H. (1973) 'The requirements of ungulates and carnivores in safari parks', UFAW Symposium, *The Welfare and Management of Wild Animals in Captivity*, Potters Bar, Herts: Universities' Federation for Animal Welfare.

Toovey, J. W. (1976) '150 years of building at London Zoo', *Symposia of the Zoological Society of London* 40: 179–202.

Travers, B. (1987) 'Inadmissible evidence', in V. McKenna, W. Travers and J. Wray (eds) *Beyond the Bars*, Wellingborough: Thorsons.

Tribe, L. H. (1974) 'Ways not to think about plastic trees, new foundations for environmental law', *Yale Law Journal* 83: 1315–48.

Tromborg, C., Markowitz, H. and Mitchell, G. (1991) 'Was Hediger wrong?', *American Association of Zoological Parks and Aquariums Annual Conference Proceedings*, 576–85.

Tudge, C. (1987a) 'Romance outruns reason', *New Scientist* 116, 1580: 72–3.

—— (1987b) 'Rembrandts in the sky', *New Scientist* 116, 1580: 74–5.

—— (1991a) 'A wild time at the zoo', *New Scientist* 5 January.

—— (1991b) *Global Ecology*, London: The Natural History Museum.

—— (1991c) *Science for Conservation: The Research of the Zoological Society of London*, London: Zoological Society of London.

—— (1991d) *Last Animals at the Zoo*, London: Hutchinson Radius.

Turner, W. R. (1987) 'Observations on conservation and the zoo visitor', *Journal of the International Association of Zoo Educators* 17: 29–32.

Van Lawick-Goodall, J. (1973) *In the Shadow of Man*, London: Fontana/Collins.

Victorian Society (1992) 'Creature comforts: the problems of London Zoo', joint report issued by the Victorian Society and the Thirties Society.

Vyvyan, J. (1969) *In Pity and in Anger*, London: Joseph.

Webster, J. (1991) 'Farm animal welfare, science and humanity', *Biologist* 38, 5: 160–2.

Wedgwood, J. C. and Nevins, A. (eds) (1942) *Forever Freedom*, Harmondsworth: Penguin.

Welland, D. (ed.) (1974) *The United States*, London: Methuen.

Wells, B. W. P. (1983) *Body and Personality*, London: Longman.

Wheater, R. J. (1985) 'Zoos of the Future', in J. P. Hearn and J. K. Hodges (eds) *Advances in Animal Conservation, Symposia of the Zoological Society of London 54: 112–14*.

White, E. B. (1952) *Charlotte's Web*, London: Hamish Hamilton.

Whitehead, M. (1984) 'Zoos are for learning too: education and interpretation', *Biologist* 31, 2: 115–18.

Whitehouse, D. and R. (1975) *Archaeological Atlas of the World*, London: Thames & Hudson.

Williams, L. (1969) *Man and Monkey*, London: Panther.

Willock, C. (1991) *Wildfight: A History of Conservation*, London: Cape.

Wiseman, A. (1986) 'Human fertility project helps zoos', *The Times*, 6 August.

Wollheim, R. (1969) *F. H. Bradley*, Harmondsworth, Penguin.

—— (1970) *Art and its Objects*, Harmondsworth: Penguin.

Wollstonecraft, M. (1975) *Vindication of the Rights of Women*, Harmondsworth: Penguin.

Wood-Gush, D. G. M. (1983) *Elements of Ethology*, London: Chapman and Hall.

Wood-Gush, D., Stolba, A. and Miller, C. (1983) 'Exploration in farm animals and animal husbandry', in J. Archer and L. Birke (eds)

Exploration in Animals and Humans, Wokingham: Van Nostrand Reinhold.

Woolf, L. (1980) *An Autobiography, Volume 2, 1911–1969*, Oxford: Oxford University Press.

Wordsworth, W. (1909) *The Poetical Works*, T. Hutchinson (ed.), London: Oxford University Press.

WSPA (1991) 'In Japan's parks of hell', *Animals International* (World Society for the Protection of Animals) 39, Winter: 3.

WWF (1986) *WWF Conservation Year book 1985/86*, Godalming: World Wildlife Fund.

Wylson, P. (1984) 'The London Zoo', *Biologist* 31, 2: 107.

Xenophon (1900) *Anabasis 1*, A. S. Walpole (ed.), London: Macmillan.

Young, E. H. (1949) *Chatterton Square*, London: Reprint Society.

Young, J. Z. (1960) 'Observations on *Argonauta* and especially its method of feeding', *Proceedings of the Zoological Society of London* 133: 471–9.

Yule, H. (trans. and ed.) (1871) *The Book of Ser Marco Polo, the Venetian*, vols 1 and 2, London: John Murray.

Zeuner, F. E. (1963) *A History of Domesticated Animals*, London: Hutchinson.

Zuckerman, S. (1932) *The Social Life of Monkeys and Apes*, London: Routledge & Kegan Paul.

—— (ed.) (1980) *Great Zoos of the World: Their Origins and Significance*, London: Weidenfeld & Nicolson.

NAME INDEX

SUBJECT INDEX

abolition of zoos 1, 192, 195
acclimatisation 8–9, 28, 32, 61,
103
aesthetic aspects of animals
129–31; *see also* biological
aspects
Africa, educational importance of
zoos in 173
Alexandria 9
alligators 61
alpacas 81
American Declaration of
Independence 1–2, 43
American zoos 34–5, 175–6; *see
also* Arizona–Sonora Desert
Museum; Cleveland
Metroparks; New York; St
Louis; San Diego; Woodland
Park
Ammon, Garden of 8
amphibians 166
anaesthetising techniques 158
anatomy 16, 24–5, 27, 28, 72–3
animal apartheid 197
animal dealers 190–1
animal rights 1–6, 40–50, 135–8,
187; historical significance of
40; *see also* right
animal trafficking 188–9, 194
animal transport 5–6, 145, 188,
194
antelopes 7, 8, 10, 30, 32, 36, 53,
69
anthropomorphism 39–40, 91–2

Antwerp Zoo 34, 165
apes 88–9, 104, 148; *see also*
chimpanzees; gibbons;
gorillas; orangutans
architecture, zoo 109–13
Arizona–Sonora Desert Museum
34–5
ARKS (Animal Records Keeping
System) 143–4, 193
Arnhem Zoo 34, 104, 161, 165
art gallery 113, 126, 131; *see also*
Burrell Collection; National
Gallery
aurochs 19, 159–60
automata, animals regarded as
37, 40
awe 116, 139
Aztecs 21–4

baboon colony at London Zoo 33,
47; Zuckerman study of 47,
161
baboons 30–1, 39, 94, 143, 161,
187
badgers 15, 172, 173
bears 9, 10, 15, 24, 31, 52, 57, 67,
70, 93–4, 97, 104, 105, 109,
139, 163, 183; *see also* polar
bears
beaver 25
bees 162
beetles 7, 102, 131–2, 138, 151
behavioural ecology 156
behavioural engineering 105–6

220

science in zoos 24–5, 28, 34,
    155–67
seal, elephant 171
security, sense of 70
semi-naturalistic 103–6
sentience 37, 135, 136
servals 105
sheep 9, 53–4, 71, 74, 172
skates 172
slave trade 43, 53, 57, 189
sleeping sickness 139, 158
Slimbridge 35, 121, 155
slow-worms 164–5
snakes 11, 12, 22, 26, 28, 98, 100,
    139
Snow leopard 21
Snowdon Aviary 110, 119
specialists 97, 103
squirrels 17, 32
staring 100
status symbols, animals as 60, 177
Stellingen Zoo 31
stereotyped behaviour 88; causes
    of 89; and psychosis or
    madness 90
Stonehenge 153
story-driven approach to display
    115–17
stress 58, 69, 71, 100
swallows 65
swans 11, 19, 121, 155
Sydney Zoo 34, 165
symphony 126–7, 133
symbiotic relationship 185

Tacoma Zoo 34, 90
tameness, taming 51–2, 54–5, 94,
    95–6
Taj Mahal 131, 152, 153
tarpan 160
television see films
theatre 113–14
Thirties Society 110, 118
thought 38
tigers 10, 11, 12, 17, 18, 25, 26,
    29, 51, 52, 54, 60, 96, 133,
    138, 139, 149–50, 154, 163,
    165, 170, 172, 177, 181, 183
toad, midwife 166

tourist pressure on sites and
    natural environments 153–4
Tower of London, menagerie at
    15, 24
trade in animals 5–6, 190–1
training 31, 96, 109
trees 14, 17, 101, 179–80
triumph, Roman 12, 60, 120
trust, holding in 124–5
trypanosomes 158
tsetse fly 139
turtles 14, 154, 172
Twycross Zoo 175

ungulates 8, 9, 10, 67, 70, 183; see
    also alpacas; antelopes;
    aurochs; bison; bulls; Cadzow,
    cattle at; camels; cattle;
    Chillingham wild cattle; deer;
    donkey; giraffes;
    hippopotamuses; horses;
    llamas; oryxes; Père David's
    deer; pigs; Przewalski's horse;
    reindeer; rhinoceroses; sheep;
    tarpan; wildebeest; zebras
utilitarianism 41–2; and law 41–2

value, intrinsic 125
vandalism 127–8, 137
Vatican menagerie 20–1
vegetarianism 41, 182
Versailles menagerie 1, 24–6, 45,
    195
veterinary work 158
Victorian Society 110, 112, 118
video 170–1, 176
vultures 16, 156–7

wallabies 103, 161, 183
waterfowl 16, 18, 22, 94, 102, 178
weasel 138, 172
'well of despair' 49, 123
whales 129, 136, 154
Whipsnade 34, 146–7, 183, 193,
    197
wild: different meanings of 51–3;
    how far applicable to zoo
    animals 53–6; simulating 105;
    taking animals from 5–6,